Creative Teaching for Crea Learning in Higher Music

C000139568

This edited volume explores how selected researchers, students and academics name and frame creative teaching and learning as constructed through the rationalities, practices, relationships, events, objects and systems that are brought to educational sites and developed by learning communities. The concept of creative learning questions the starting points and opens up the outcomes of curriculum, and this frames creative teaching not only as a process of learning but as an agent of change. Within the book, the various creativities that are valued by different stakeholders teaching and studying in the higher music sector are delineated, and processes and understandings of creative teaching are articulated, both generally in higher music education and specifically through their application within the design of individual modules. This focus makes the text relevant to scholars, researchers and practitioners across many fields of music, including those working in musicology, composition, performance, music education, and music psychology. The book contributes new perspectives on our understanding of the role of creative teaching and learning and processes in creative teaching across the domain of music learning in higher music education sectors.

Elizabeth Haddon is Research Fellow in the Music Department at the University of York, UK, where she leads the MA in Music Education: Instrumental and Vocal Teaching, and also teaches piano. Her research focuses on pedagogy, creativity and musical performance, particularly in the higher education sector, and includes the book *Making Music in Britain: Interviews with those behind the notes* (Ashgate, 2006) as well as articles in peer-reviewed journals, book chapters and presentations at international conferences.

Pamela Burnard is Professor of Arts, Creativities and Education at the Faculty of Education, University of Cambridge, UK. She holds degrees in Music Performance, Music Education, Education and Philosophy. Her primary interest is creativities research for which she is internationally recognised. She is the author/co-author/editor of twelve books and multiple refereed journals. She is convenor of the Creativities in Intercultural Arts Network (CIAN), co-convenor of the British Education Research Association Creativities in Education SIG, host and convenor of the Building Interdisciplinary Bridges Across Cultures (BIBAC) International Biennial Conference. She serves on numerous editorial boards and is a Fellow of the Royal Society of Arts.

SEMPRE Studies in The Psychology of Music

Series Editors
Graham Welch, *University of London, UK*
Adam Ockelford, *Roehampton University, UK*
Ian Cross, *University of Cambridge, UK*

The theme for the series is the psychology of music, broadly defined. Topics include (i) musical development at different ages, (ii) exceptional musical development in the context of special educational needs, (iii) musical cognition and context, (iv) culture, mind and music, (v) micro to macro perspectives on the impact of music on the individual (from neurological studies through to social psychology), (vi) the development of advanced performance skills and (vii) affective perspectives on musical learning. The series presents the implications of research findings for a wide readership, including user-groups (music teachers, policy makers, parents) as well as the international academic and research communities. This expansive embrace, in terms of both subject matter and intended audience (drawing on basic and applied research from across the globe), is the distinguishing feature of the series, and it serves SEMPRE's distinctive mission, which is to promote and ensure coherent and symbiotic links between education, music and psychology research.

Recent titles in the series:

The Tangible in Music
Marko Aho

Artistic Practice as Research in Music: Theory, Criticism, Practice
Edited by Mine Doğantan-Dack

Advanced Musical Performance: Investigations in Higher Education Learning
Edited by Ioulia Papageorgi and Graham Welch

Collaborative Creative Thought and Practice in Music
Edited by Margaret S. Barrett

Coughing and Clapping: Investigating Audience Experience
Edited by Karen Burland and Stephanie Pitts

Embodied Knowledge in Ensemble Performance
J. Murphy McCaleb

Developing the Musician
Edited by Mary Stakelum

Music and Familiarity
Edited by Elaine King and Helen M. Prior

Creative Teaching for Creative Learning in Higher Music Education

Edited by
Elizabeth Haddon and Pamela Burnard

Routledge
Taylor & Francis Group

LONDON AND NEW YORK

First published 2016
by Routledge
2 Park Square, Milton Park, Abingdon, Oxon OX14 4RN

and by Routledge
711 Third Avenue, New York, NY 10017

First issued in paperback 2017

Routledge is an imprint of the Taylor and Francis Group, an informa business

British Library Cataloguing in Publication Data
A catalogue record for this book is available from the British Library

Library of Congress Cataloging in Publication Data
Names: Haddon, Elizabeth, 1966–, editor. | Burnard, Pamela, editor.
Title: Creative teaching for creative learning in higher music education / edited by
Elizabeth Haddon and Pamela Burnard.
Description: [2016] | Series: SEMPRE studies in the psychology of music |
Includes bibliographical references and index.
Identifiers: LCCN 2015038070 | ISBN 9781472455918 (hardcover: alk. paper) |
ISBN 9781315574714 (ebook)
Subjects: LCSH: Music in universities and colleges—Great Britain. | Music—Instruction
and study—Great Britain. | Creative ability. Classification: LCC MT18 .C75 2016 |
DDC 780.71/1—dc23
LC record available at http://lccn.loc.gov/2015038070

ISBN 13: 978-1-138-50499-8 (pbk)
ISBN 13: 978-1-4724-5591-8 (hbk)

Bach musicological font developed by © Yo Tomita

Typeset in Times New Roman
by codeMantra

Contents

PART II
Developing the creative lecturer and teacher

PART III
Philosophies, practices and pedagogies: Teaching for creative learning

Figures

Tables

Music examples

Contributors

Peter Argondizza, BA in Music, Master of Music and Doctor of Musical Arts, is an external examiner and adjudicator at the San Francisco Conservatory of Music. Previous teaching experience includes Lecturer at the Royal Conservatoire of Scotland, University of Strathclyde and work at Yale University and Stonybrook University, USA. His research interests include the lute works of Vincenzo Galilei and interdisciplinary work with psychology and civil engineering as well as creative learning and teaching. He is also an active performer and teacher on classical, Baroque and electric guitar, and has recently performed Ginastera's Guitar Sonata, op. 47, and Berio's *Sequenza XI* for guitar. In addition to performing concertos and solo concerts, he also freelances on mandolin, guitar, banjo and lute with Scottish Opera, the Royal Scottish National Orchestra and the BBC. Peter has commissioned and premiered solo and chamber works from composers Sally Beamish, Edward McGuire and Stephen Davismoon in the USA and the UK. Born in Brooklyn, New York, Peter was inspired by popular music of the 1960s. He started learning guitar at the age of 12, and went on to study jazz guitar, and North Indian Classical music with Sri Vasant Rai. Peter was the first guitarist to receive the Doctor of Musical Arts degree from Yale University.

Steven Berryman studied at Cardiff University, Wales and Royal Holloway, University of London, and completed a PhD in composition with Arlene Sierra. His composition teachers included Anthony Powers, Simon Holt and Judith Weir. Notable performances of his work include his String Quartet by the Elysian Quartet (Dartington International Summer School, 2005) and a commission from the South West Music School, UK, *Wandered Mind* for nine players (October 2010). Steven's orchestral piece *Cypher* (2010) was selected by the BBC National Orchestra of Wales for performance in its Welsh Composers Showcase in 2011. Steven's output is diverse, and includes music for Jamie Zubairi's one-man show *Unbroken Line*, incidental music for *Corpo: Lixa da Alma* (premiered at Cena Brasil Internacional 2012 in Rio de Janeiro) and a musical for a female-only cast, *Juniper Dreams* (2011). Steven is currently Director of Music at City of London School for Girls, and has previously taught at the North London Collegiate School and the Junior Department of the Royal Academy of Music. He has also acted as an examiner and moderator for GCSE and A level Music. In 2014, Steven was Fellow for Teach Through Music (led by Trinity Laban), and mentored teachers enrolled on the year-long programme in addition to giving seminars. Steven has contributed to *Music Teacher* magazine and Music Education UK, and has given presentations at conferences and courses on various aspects of the music curriculum for audiences of teachers and students.

Martin Blain is Reader in Music Composition at Manchester Metropolitan University (MMU), UK. Martin's research interests in collaborative practice and cross-disciplinary work continue to grow within the Department of Contemporary Arts, where he develops practical projects with students and staff. Before joining MMU Cheshire, he was Composer in Residence at Newcastle Playhouse, UK, where he developed work with the Northern Stage Ensemble Company. As a composer, Martin's research interests are concerned with the development of new music. His work can be seen as developing three distinct strands of musical composition: concert music – this includes works for orchestra, various chamber groups and solo artists, interdisciplinary practice – working in collaboration with dancers, film makers, theatre companies and visual artists – and music and technology. He is particularly interested in the interaction between live performer and technology.

Pamela Burnard is Professor in Music Education at the University of Cambridge, UK. Following undergraduate and graduate study at the Universities of Melbourne, Australia and Indiana in music and music education, she completed a PhD at Reading University, UK. Her research interests include musical creativities, creativity in education, creative learning, teaching for creativity, creativity assessment and industry links. Her research has been supported by major grants from the UK, Australia and Hong Kong, and has been published in leading journals and edited collections in the discipline of creative learning. Recent publications include *Musical Creativities in Practice* (2012) and *Teaching Music Creatively* (with Regina Murphy; 2013), *Developing Creativities in Higher Music Education* (2013) and *Creative Learning 3–11 and How We Document It* (with Anna Craft and Teresa Cremin; 2008). Pamela is Co-convenor of the British Educational Research Association Creativity in Education special interest group and a former editor of the *British Journal of Music Education*.

Natalie Edwards grew up in Chesterfield, UK, and began piano, flute and percussion lessons while at school. She graduated from the University of York in 2012 with first class honours, having specialised in a wide variety of topics including music in the community, gender studies, gamelan, devised performance and a dissertation based on the music of the 1984–85 UK miners' strike. She continued at the University of York to study for an MA in community music, undertaking a placement at York Theatre Royal and enjoying the freedom to explore and develop new workshop ideas. Throughout university, she was involved in many extracurricular activities, performing with ensembles as diverse as gospel choirs and brass bands and volunteering extensively in local schools, in libraries and with the elderly. Natalie's work experience has included a graduate role in university widening participation, where she helped run visit day and residential events to promote higher education for schoolchildren aged 9–17. More recently, she has been a youth theatre and education intern at Riding Lights Theatre Company in York, assisting with a range of youth theatres, including an additional needs group and drama provision in the Minster School, York. In the future, she hopes to continue in some form of education and outreach work, preferably within the arts, but is open to many possibilities.

John Robert Ferguson is a post-digital/electronic musician based in Brisbane, Australia, where he is Senior Lecturer and Head of Music Technology at Queensland Conservatorium Griffith University, Australia. Before this, he was Visiting Assistant Professor in the Music Department at Brown University, USA, and previously Lecturer in Music and Creative Music Technologies at Kingston University, UK. John's PhD, *New Relations for the Live Musician?*, was funded by the Arts and Humanities Research Council and completed in 2009 under the supervision of Bennett Hogg and Sally Jane Norman at Newcastle University, UK. His thesis charts an idiosyncratic zone within the continuum of what it is to be a live musician at the dawn of the twenty-first century. His current research focuses on performing technologies, raising the question: 'Are we performing the technology, or is it performing us?' John's work is published by *Leonardo Music Journal*, *Leonardo Electronic Almanac*, *Contemporary Music Review*, Cambridge University Press, Creative Sources Recordings, Soundmuseum.fm and Clinical Archives. He regularly performs internationally, and notable events include: New Interfaces for Musical Expression in Louisiana (2015) and London (2014), New York City Electroacoustic Music Festival (2014), Society for Electroacoustic Music in the United States, Wesleyan University, USA (2014), *International Computer Music Conference*, Athens (2014) and Huddersfield (2011), Brunel Electronic Analogue Music Festival, London (2012), Sonic Arts Research Centre, Belfast (2011), Borealis Festival for Contemporary Music, Bergen (2009), the Sage, Gateshead, UK (2009), Club Transmediale, Berlin (2008), AV Festival, Newcastle, UK (2008) and Studio for Electro Instrumental Music, Amsterdam (2008).[1]

Ambrose Field is Head of Department and Professor of Music at the University of York. His music is recorded on ECM (Munich) and Sargasso (London) and broadcast by the BBC and other international networks (SVR, RTE, ORF). His works have been performed at the Vienna Konzerthaus, the Chicago Early Music Festival, Parco della Musica, Rome, the A Cappella Festival, Leipzig, Perth International Arts Festival, Australia, Konvergencie Bratislava, Kultursommer Rheinland-Pfalz Germany, Institute of Contemporary Arts, London, Ultima Oslo, Tampere Vocal Music Festival, Finland, Kryptonale, Berlin, City of Birmingham Symphony Orchestra Centre, Birmingham, Voce-Versa, Milan, Huset-KBH, Copenhagen and Warsaw Autumn, and he has received other international commissions. Field studied music education at the

University of Cambridge, UK (PGCE) and composition (PhD) at City University, London. He served as Music Education Director of the UK's Sonic Arts Network (the forerunner to today's Sound and Music Organisation) in the late 1990s. His music has received several international awards, including three Prix Ars Electronica Honorary Mentions in 2006, 1997 and 1996. Ambrose has been a resident artist at Asphodel/Recombinant Media Labs in San Francisco and HFG in Karlsruhe, Germany, and a composer at Hungarian National Radio in Budapest funded by UNESCO. His work *Pod Twoją Obronę*, set in Polish for 25 solo voices, was commissioned for a special international event marking Górecki's eightieth birthday anniversary.

Karin Greenhead trained initially as a pianist/harpsichordist and violinist at the Royal College of Music, London, subsequently trained as a singer and has performed professionally in all these capacities, and also has experience as a composer, arranger and conductor. In addition to her formal training in music and Dalcroze Eurhythmics, she has studied several types of dance and body-awareness techniques, and her teaching has focused on the training of professional musicians, dancers and music teachers. A member of the Collège de l'Institut Jaques-Dalcroze, Geneva, and Director of Studies for Dalcroze UK, Karin is responsible for the professional training and examination of Dalcroze practitioners. She teaches frequently in Europe, North America and Asia, and regularly for the Royal Northern College of Music, Manchester and other UK conservatoires. Practitioner-turned-researcher, Karin's doctoral research is a phenomenological investigation into Dynamic Rehearsal – an application of Dalcroze principles to the rehearsal and performance of repertoire, solo and ensemble that she developed experimentally. Karin presents regularly at conferences and is a member of the Scientific Committee of the *International Conference of Dalcroze Studies*. She was Chair of the committee responsible for *L'identité Dalcrozienne/The Dalcroze Identity* (2011), and recently published in the *Journal of Dance and Somatic Practices*.

Christina Guillaumier is a pianist, musicologist and educator. She is currently Head of Undergraduate Programmes at the Royal College of Music, London, and is also a member of the Centre for Russian Music at Goldsmiths, University of London, where she supervises PhD students. Previous research roles include a visiting research fellowship at Princeton University and a postdoctoral research associate position at the Serge Prokofiev Archive in London. She is a published author and the recipient of several research awards, including UK Arts and Humanities Research Council and European Union project funding. Christina has extensive experience of music education and curriculum reform in the UK and EU context, having worked in the conservatoire industry for a decade. Her work includes higher education curriculum innovation, design and implementation; quality assurance and enhancement as well as academic management, research project development and implementation. She has served on undergraduate, graduate and doctoral programme and exam boards both in the UK and overseas. Current research interests include Russian music, music education and creativity and performance studies. Previous collaborative projects include the reconstruction and world premiere of the original version of Prokofiev's opera *War and Peace*, a project that was completed in 2010 and performed in Russia and Scotland. She is currently working on a monograph on Prokofiev's operas (under contract with Boydell and Brewer) as well as a co-edited volume of essays on Prokofiev studies.

John Habron is Senior Lecturer at Coventry University, UK, and Senior Research Fellow in the Musical Arts in Southern Africa: Resources and Applications research group at North-West University, South Africa. Having trained initially as a composer, he has moved into transdisciplinary research and now works across the areas of music and well-being, music education and spirituality in music. John's work has recently been published in *Journal of Research in Music Education, Journal of Dance and Somatic Practices, International Journal of Music Education* and *British Journal of Occupational Therapy*, as well as in the book *Music and Transcendence* (edited by Stone-Davis; Ashgate, 2015). John convenes the *International Conference of Dalcroze Studies* (Coventry 2013, Vienna 2015, Quebec City 2017) and chairs its Scientific Committee. He serves on the editorial board for several academic journals, and during 2015–16 is guest editor of *Approaches: An Interdisciplinary Journal of Music Therapy*. Regularly invited to teach abroad, most recently in Austria, Colombia, Ireland and Poland, he was also guest speaker at the *Music and Well-being International Conference*, North-West University, South Africa (2013) and at the 67th *International Conference Médecine de la Personne: Creativity and Giving Care*, Woltersdorf, Germany (2015). In his work as a music therapist, John works mainly with people with dementia.

Elizabeth Haddon is Research Fellow in Music at the University of York, where she leads the new MA in Music Education: Instrumental and Vocal Teaching, and also teaches piano. She is the author of *Making Music in Britain: Interviews with Those Behind the Notes* (Ashgate, 2006) and co-editor with Pamela Burnard of *Activating Diverse Musical Creativities: Teaching and Learning in Higher Music Education* (2015). Her research is published in leading peer-reviewed journals and has been presented at international conferences on music education and performance psychology, and her interests include instrumental and vocal pedagogy, the student learning experience and professional development.

Clare Hall is Lecturer in Performing Arts in the Faculty of Education, Monash University, Australia. She works with pre-service teachers in primary and early childhood education degrees and brings together over twenty years of experience as a musician and music educator in her teaching and research. Her research in the sociology of music education and the performing arts focuses on youth identities, creativities and issues of power and social justice in arts participation. Her first book, *Masculinity, Class and Music Education*, will be published by Palgrave.

Louise Harris is an electronic and audiovisual composer and Lecturer in Sonic and Audiovisual Practices at the University of Glasgow. She specialises in fixed and live audiovisual works utilising electronic music and computer-generated visual environments. Louise completed her PhD in music composition at Sheffield University; she previously studied composition at the University of York with Nicola LeFanu, and before that at Oxford University with Robert Saxton. Her audiovisual work has been performed and exhibited nationally and internationally, including at the AV Festival, Musica Viva Festival, *International Computer Music Conference*, Naisa SOUNDplay festival, Strasbourg Museum of Modern Art, Zentrum für Kunst und Medientechnologie, Karlsruhe, Germany, Piksel Festival, Bergen and the International Motion Festival, Cyprus.[2]

Fay Hield is Lecturer in Music Management and Ethnomusicology at the University of Sheffield, and delivers co-produced research on the Transmitting Musical Heritage project for the UK Arts and Humanities Research Council. She is a professional performer with several album releases, including *The Full English* (Topic Records, 2014), *Orfeo* (Topic Records, 2012) and *Looking Glass* (Topic Records, 2010). At every level, Fay combines practical experience with her research and teaching practices, including the establishment of a university folk group, development of civic engagement-based modules and engaging students on external performance projects.

Tim Howell is Reader at the Music Department, University of York, and specialises in the analysis of new music, especially from Finland. An internationally recognised authority on the music of Sibelius, his research has now broadened to encompass contemporary Finnish music as reflected in two major publications, *After Sibelius: Studies in Finnish Music* (Ashgate, 2006), which combines elements of composer biography and detailed analysis within the broader context of cultural and national identity, and *Kaija Saariaho: Visions, Narratives, Dialogues* (Ashgate, 2011), for which he was the main editor and contributed a chapter on Saariaho's concertos. He has recently devised, compiled and edited a volume of *Contemporary Music Review*, 'Musical Narratives: Studies in Time and Motion' (December 2014), contributing an article on Magnus Lindberg's recent orchestral music.

Mark Hutchinson is Lecturer in Music at York St John University, UK, with special interests in the fields of contemporary musical aesthetics, analysis and performance. In 2012 he completed a PhD at the University of York with Tim Howell, funded by the Arts and Humanities Research Council; he was subsequently a postdoctoral research fellow at the Humanities Research Centre at the University of York. His first book, *Coherence in New Music: Experience, Aesthetics, Analysis*, is published by Routledge (2016). He also keeps himself busy teaching and playing piano and oboe, listening to music (new or old) and enjoying the natural world.

H. Elisha Jo is a PhD candidate in music education at Western University, Canada. She received a BMus and an MMus in organ performance from

McGill University and an MMus in music education from Western University. Elisha's research interests include cultural meanings of creativity, identity construction and diasporic perceptions as seen through the lens of music teaching and learning. Concerned with a complex interplay of culture and identity, she engages in identity discourse of immigrant groups who may be regarded as situated 'in-between' with double or multiple ties and relationships to places that encompass multi-layered social, economic, cultural and political attachments. In her research, musical practices serve as a venue for exploring ethnic groups' identities. As a teacher and volunteer, she is actively involved with the Korean Canadian community and wishes to contribute further through her study of community-living older adults.

Nicky Losseff was educated at the Yehudi Menuhin School, the Royal Academy of Music and King's College London. She has worked as a school music teacher in the UK, Iceland and India. She was a British Academy postdoctoral fellow at the Music Department, University of York, where she is now Senior Lecturer. As a medievalist, Nicky is involved with Trio Mediaeval, providing them with editions and programme notes, and she has also made editions for the Hilliard Ensemble. Nicky has authored *The Best Concords: Polyphonic Music in Thirteenth-century Britain* (1994) and co-edited two Ashgate volumes, *The Idea of Music in Victorian Fiction* (with Sophie Fuller; 2004) and *Silence, Music, Silent Music* (with Jenny Doctor; 2007). She has written articles and book chapters on medieval polyphony, music in literature, and Bartók. Her current research examines interfaces between music and psychoanalysis, particularly in performance. She continues to perform regularly as a pianist.

Louise Mathieu is Professor at the Faculty of Music of Université Laval, Canada. She teaches Dalcroze Eurhythmics as well as qualitative methodologies in music education research. Director of Studies of the Dalcroze Society of Canada, she also acts as Vice President of the Collège de l'Institut Jaques-Dalcroze, Geneva. She serves on the editorial board of the journal *Recherche en Éducation Musicale*, is a peer reviewer for various scientific committees and is a member of the Scientific Committee of the *International Conference of Dalcroze Studies*. Besides a musical background (Bachelor of Music Education and Bachelor of Dalcroze Eurhythmics, Université Laval, Canada; Dalcroze Diplôme supérieur, Institut Jaques-Dalcroze, Geneva; Doctor of Arts, New York University, New York), her experience includes studies in acting, Feldenkrais and Gerda Alexander body awareness. She has directed and choreographed staged works, conducted choirs and instrumental ensembles and composed children's songs. A frequent lecturer and workshop leader in Canada, Europe, Asia and the USA, Louise also supervises music education research projects.

Stephen J. Messenger is a public school educator who has taught a diverse student body at elementary, secondary, undergraduate and graduate levels (his training includes special education, the teaching of reading, and English as a second language). Stephen earned a BA in English composition from Knox

College, USA, an MEd in reading from Pan-American University and an EdD from the University of Houston in administration and supervision. Stephen has been a visiting instructor of English composition, English literature, reading, and Teachers of English to Speakers of Other Languages at St Mary's College of Maryland, the College of Notre Dame of Maryland, the College of Southern Maryland, and the University of Texas at Brownsville/Texas Southmost College. Messenger's interests include investigating and learning/playing North American roots and Celtic music, Dead studies, jamband culture, community music, and telling/singing stories and songs. He co-edited and co-wrote *Community Music Today* (with Kari Veblen, Marissa Silverman and David Elliott; 2013).

Tim Palmer is an orchestral percussionist and a music educator. He has played as guest principal percussionist with many of the UK's orchestras and ensembles, and regularly works with the BBC Symphony Orchestra and the London Sinfonietta, for which he has also appeared as a soloist. He has led education projects for a number of leading arts organisations and was Musician in Residence at the National Maritime Museum during 2008–2009. Tim is Senior Lecturer in Music Education at Trinity Laban Conservatoire of Music and Dance, UK, where he specialises in creative project leadership and the role of the visiting artist in education and community settings. He set up and leads both the Teaching Musician PGCert/PGDip and the MA in Music Education and Performance.

Stephanie Pitts is Professor of Music Education at the University of Sheffield, with research interests in musical participation and the lifelong impact of music education. She is the author of books including *Valuing Musical Participation* (Ashgate, 2005) and *Chances and Choices: Exploring the Impact of Music Education* (2012). She is Director of the Sheffield Performer and Audience Research Centre, and has worked with the audiences of Music in the Round, the City of Birmingham Symphony Orchestra and the Edinburgh Jazz and Blues Festival on studies of live musical experience.

Ruth Slater is Professor of Baroque Violin and Director of the Baroque Ensemble at the Royal Conservatoire of Scotland (RCS), where she is also Lecturer in the Creative and Contextual Department. In this role, she leads specialist seminars in the 'Teaching Musician' classes for bowed strings. Ruth jointly wrote the 'Baroque Music' module at the RCS, which she co-ordinates, and she lectures on historically informed performance practice as well as giving practical classes. She is also a teacher on the 'Music in Society 'and 'Music in History' modules. Ruth is active as a diploma examiner for the Associated Board of the Royal Schools of Music both in the UK and the Far East. As a performer, she freelances widely, regularly directing period instrument performances and playing and recording with orchestras, including the Gabrieli Consort and Players and the Scottish Chamber Orchestra. She has worked extensively with many other groups, including Amsterdam Baroque, Orchestra of the Age of

Enlightenment, the Academy of Ancient Music, the Early Opera Company, Brandenburg Consort, Dunedin Consort and the Hanover Band (where she was principal second), often playing guest principal. As a soloist, she has appeared with many leading period instrument orchestras and ensembles, both in the UK and abroad, including Florilegium, the Hanover Band, London Handel Orchestra and Ludus Baroque.

Neil Sorrell teaches in the Music Department at the University of York. He obtained a BA in music from the University of Cambridge, UK in 1967, an MA in area studies (specialising in North Indian music) from the School of Oriental and African Studies, University of London, in 1969, and a PhD in ethnomusicology from Wesleyan University, USA in 1980. His doctoral thesis was on Indian music, and he co-authored a book on the subject with his teacher, the great sarangi player Pandit Ram Narayan. In 1980 he co-founded the English Gamelan Orchestra, the first group of British musicians dedicated to the study, composition and performance of music for the Javanese gamelan, and in 1981 he organised the manufacture by Tentrem Sarwanto of York's Gamelan Sekar Petak, the first complete Javanese gamelan in a British teaching institution. He has written, broadcast and lectured on Indian and Javanese music internationally.

Kari Veblen, musician and educator, is Professor of Music Education at Western University, Canada, where she teaches undergraduate and graduate courses. Over the past thirty-five years she has worked with music and people of all ages in diverse settings worldwide. Before coming to the University of Western Ontario in 2001, she served as a visiting scholar (Center for Research in Music Education, University of Toronto), a research associate (Irish World Music Centre, University of Limerick), a curriculum consultant to orchestras and schools, and an elementary music teacher. She earned a BA in music with minor in art from Knox College, USA and an MA in music and PhD from the University of Wisconsin–Madison. Veblen researches at the crossroads of music, education, the arts and society, and is currently beguiled by community music networks and individuals, lifelong music learning and teaching/learning traditional Irish/Celtic musics. She has published widely, with over seventy peer-reviewed works, including her fourth book, *Community Music Today* (with Stephen Messenger, Marissa Silverman and David Elliott; 2013). An international representative to the National Association for Music Education Adult and Community Special Research Interest Group, Veblen has served on many professional boards, including that of the International Society for Music Education. She is co-founder with David J. Elliott and associate editor with Lee Higgins of the *International Journal of Community Music*.

James Whittle is a composer, conductor and cellist. After graduating from the University of York with a BA in music (first class honours with distinction), he received Arts and Humanities Research Council Professional Development funding for his Master's degree in music by research, 'Composing and

Devising Music Theatre'. He is currently completing a PhD in composition, 'Music is Theatre is …', supervised by Roger Marsh and funded by a Sir Jack Lyons Research Scholarship. Whittle specialises in devising music-theatre pieces collaboratively with performers. These pieces blend composition and improvisation of musical performance, theatre and movement. He has collaborated with soloists Ian Pace and Alex Wilson, the ensembles Dr K Sextet, the Assembled and Chimera, and students at the Northern School of Contemporary Dance. As joint recipients of the Terry Holmes Composer/Performer Award in 2013, he and Victoria Bernath created *Remains of Elmet*, a music-theatre concerto for viola-vocalist, voices and instruments. His recent collaborations have included spoken word and audience participation, the promenade performance *Carnivore* (2014) and the site-specific interactive auction *That's Yer Lot!* devised with dancers Gracefool Collective, which featured at Vantage Art Prize 2013 and Leeds Transform Festival 2014. Though self-taught, James has conducted world and UK premieres of music by Beat Furrer, Eve Harrison and Hans Werner Henze; he made his Huddersfield Contemporary Music Festival debut in 2014, conducting new pieces by Philip Cashian, Naomi Pinnock and Ji Sun Yang. As a cellist, he has considerable experience of solo and ensemble performance, particularly of contemporary, experimental and improvised music. He has also collaborated with Castaway Goole Music Theatre and led multiple educational projects in York.[3]

Alice Wright completed her BA Hons degree in music at the University of York in 2014. While at university, she became involved with and developed a passion for opera, both in her academic and extracurricular life. She co-directed Offenbach's *Orpheus in the Underworld* and subsequently directed a semi-staged production of Britten's *Albert Herring* in her final year. Outside her degree, Alice was a production intern and props mistress on Northern Ireland Opera's production of *Noyes Fludde*. Alice currently holds the position of Artistic Assistant for English Touring Opera as well as surtitle operator at the Royal Opera House, London. Recent projects have included assistant-directing Richard Rodney Bennett's community opera *All the King's Men* in Bedford, UK, and collaborating with an amateur theatre company, Sedos, to co-produce and co-direct a new piece of musical theatre written by composers from the University of York called *On the Night*.

Notes

1 For more information, see http://johnrobertferguson.com (accessed March 28, 2016).
2 For more information, see http://www.louiseharris.co.uk (accessed March 28, 2016).
3 For more information, see www.james-whittle.co.uk (accessed March 28, 2016).

Series editors' preface

The enormous growth of research that has been evidenced over the past three decades continues into the many different phenomena that are embraced under the psychology of music 'umbrella'. Growth is evidenced in new journals, books, media interest, an expansion of professional associations (regionally and nationally, such as in Southern Europe and Latin America), and with increasing and diverse opportunities for formal study, including in non-English-speaking countries. Such growth of interest is not only from psychologists and musicians, but also from colleagues working in the clinical sciences, neurosciences, therapies, in the lifelong health and well-being communities, philosophy, musicology, social psychology, ethnomusicology and education across the lifespan. As part of this global community, the Society for Education, Music and Psychology Research (SEMPRE) celebrated its 40th Anniversary in 2012 and continues to be one of the world's leading and longstanding professional associations in the field. SEMPRE is the only international society that embraces formally an interest in the psychology of music, research and education, seeking to promote knowledge at the interface between the twin social sciences of psychology and education with one of the world's most pervasive art forms, music. SEMPRE was founded in 1972 and has published the journals *Psychology of Music* since 1973 and *Research Studies in Music Education* since 2008, both now produced in partnership with SAGE,[1] and we continue to seek new ways to reach out globally, both in print and online. We recognise that there is an ongoing need to promote the latest research findings to the widest possible audience. Through more extended publication formats, especially books, we are more likely to fulfil a key component of our mission that is to have a distinctive and positive impact on understanding, as well as on policy and practice internationally, both within and across our disciplinary boundaries. Hence, we welcome the strong collaborative partnership between SEMPRE and Ashgate.

The Ashgate *SEMPRE Studies in The Psychology of Music* series has been designed to address this international need since its inception in 2007. The theme for the series is the psychology of music, broadly defined. Topics include (among others): musical development and learning at different ages; musical cognition and context; culture, mind and music; creativity, composition and collaboration; micro to macro perspectives on the impact of music on the individual (from neurological studies through to social psychology); the development of advanced performance skills; musical behaviour and development in the context of special educational needs, and affective perspectives on musical learning. The series seeks to present the implications of research findings for a wide readership, including user-groups (music teachers, policy-makers, parents and carers, music professionals working in a range of formal, non-formal and informal settings), as well as the international academic teaching and research communities. A key distinguishing feature of the series is its broad focus that draws on basic and applied research from across the globe under the umbrella of SEMPRE's distinctive mission, which is to promote and ensure coherent and symbiotic links between education, music and psychology research.

We are very pleased to welcome this new text edited by Elizabeth Haddon and Pamela Burnard on *Creative Teaching for Creative Learning in Higher Music Education* in the SEMPRE series. This excellent compendium complements earlier books in the series that are focused on creativity by adding a new focus on creativity in higher music education. Both the editors are experienced authors, teachers and researchers in their own right, and also very experienced in music learning in higher education. Their personal interest in the enduring topic of creativity has allowed them to fashion, with their international authors, an engaging, varied and multifaceted narrative. The constituent chapters combine to provide us with deep insights into the symbiotic relationship between creative teaching and creative learning. The book is structured in three parts. The first focuses on personal experiences of secondary and higher education music from undergraduate students and teachers. The second part investigates aspects of practice-based and research-led teaching and the links with creativity. The third and final part has a more theoretical focus related to how creative learning and teaching might be conceptualised. Overall, this is a very engaging and stimulating set of readings, carefully put together by the editors that constitute an excellent and valuable addition to our understanding of how to make sense of, and use, creativity in a more purposeful way.

Graham Welch, University of London, UK;
Adam Ockelford, Roehampton University, UK;
and Ian Cross, University of Cambridge, UK

Note

1 See www.sempre.org.uk.

Acknowledgements

We would like to thank all of our contributing authors for their work, their willingness to attend to detail and their generosity in sharing examples of practice. We would also like to thank the team at Ashgate, in particular Laura Macy and Michael Bourne, for their support and advice. Thanks are due to our friends, families and colleagues for their support and encouragement, and especially to Ambrose Field for our initial discussion of creative teaching which stimulated the idea for the book. We acknowledge support from the Music Department at the University of York and from the UK Higher Education Academy, which funded a seminar day, Creative Teaching for Creative Learning in Higher Academic Music Education (2013, University of York), which featured papers by some of the authors in this volume. We also thank Mick Lynch for the cover design and Ed Crooks for his significant contributions towards preparing the work for publication. We hope that this volume provides a useful resource for all those who work in higher music education and that it also stimulates wider discussion of creative teaching and learning.

Elizabeth Haddon and Pamela Burnard

Introduction

Elizabeth Haddon

This volume was inspired by conversations with colleagues at the University of York, UK, which provided the initial impetus for a seminar day funded by the Higher Education Academy, Creative Teaching for Creative Learning in Higher Academic Music Education (2013, University of York), featuring papers by some of the contributing authors. Both the seminar day and this volume illustrate and promote creative pedagogical practices within higher music education; these are central to student engagement, ownership of learning, and subsequent employment.

Creativity is increasingly recognised as a major contributor to every level of education, from early years through to higher education, and has gained currency as a powerful driver for global economic growth (Burnard, 2014: xxvi). It has also become a lever for politicised debate urging governments to enhance provision of the arts in school and higher education and to promote positive values of the benefits of engagement with the creative arts (Newbigin, 2015; Shaw, 2015), which relates to industry, graduate employment and holistic well-being.

However, as Smith-Bingham notes, creativity is often seen as 'unpredictable, unmanageable and unquantifiable' (2006: 14), and in education, 'initiatives designed to nurture creativity [can] have requirements that conflict or compete with norms of operation and "standards" of performance and behaviour' (ibid.). The 'transformational power' of creativity also 'poses a clear challenge to organisational systems and institutional frameworks that rely, often necessarily, on compliance and constraint' (Kleiman, 2008: 216). This problematises creativity within an 'audit culture' where 'the value of creativity cannot easily be demonstrated, and therefore justified as an end in itself' (Smith-Bingham, 2006: 14). While this concern is ongoing, this volume provides evidence that creative teaching for creative learning not only builds capabilities and knowledge, but also instils positive learner attitudes, and therefore the value of creative engagement is clearly demonstrated to students. In addition, as chapters in this volume illustrate, it is possible that curriculum reform and institutional culture are enhanced through the primary consideration of creativity, and that inherent expectations of creative engagement and output can result in an environment in which creativity is described as an operational norm. Finally, creativity is manifest in these chapters as a primary driver not just for teaching, but also for reinvigoration of lecturers' conceptualisations of higher music education teaching and for revitalisation of their pedagogical practice, contributing to dynamic and evolving learning cultures.

Organisation of parts and chapters

This volume presents a collection of chapters by diverse authors who are expert in teaching and researching in the higher music education sector. It also offers the views of recent music graduates, providing a range of perspectives on creative teaching and learning. Part I explores the perspectives of those involved in pre-higher education and the views of students and lecturers in higher music education. Part II details the considerations of lecturers developing practice-based, research-led teaching, and explores connections and responses to creativity in the teaching and learning of trainee teachers. Part III examines lecturers' conceptualisations of creativity and teaching philosophies, and examines how these are manifest within practice and pedagogies within higher education institutions. These include issues of curriculum design, historically informed performance practice, music analysis, performers' and composers' relationships with musical works, Dalcroze Eurhythmics, non-Western musics, enterprise creativity and group creativity.

Part I: Articulating experience in secondary and higher music education

In Chapter 1, Steven Berryman sets the scene by discussing the changing role of creativity through the different stages of secondary music education in the UK. Berryman explores factors which have an impact on creativity, including variation in how teachers interpret the National Curriculum and how they consider the development of creative individual and group work in contexts involving diverse pupil needs and teaching approaches. Berryman suggests that an understanding of the context, nature and challenges of secondary music education is essential for those working in higher music education in order to facilitate students' transition from one learning context to another.

In Chapter 2, Natalie Edwards, James Whittle and Alice Wright explore how a sample of undergraduate music students experience and perceive creativity within the degree course, discussing how learning creatively within both departmental opportunities and extracurricular involvement encourages contact with varied influences, develops a range of skills and has direct relevance to enhancing both work within the degree course and skills and aptitudes for employability.

In Chapter 3, Elizabeth Haddon examines the views of lecturers in a university music department, moving from definitions of creativity to exploring the formation of teaching practices, detailing lecturers' aspirations for the learner, thoughts on sustaining a creative culture, and ways in which lecturers construct and deliver teaching for creative learning, and how this plays a fundamental role in reinvigorating teaching practice and commitment to sustaining a creative career in higher music education.

In Chapter 4, Pamela Burnard discusses why higher music education institutions should advocate creative teaching for creative learning, exploring affordances of new priorities, narratives, forms of knowledge and modes of communication between creative teachers and musicians through the creation of an improvisatory space. This is illustrated through discussion of partnership programmes where creative learning communities jointly construct improvisational flow in the classroom, in the studio and in rehearsal and instrumental lessons.

Part II: Developing the creative lecturer and teacher

In Chapter 5, Louise Harris considers lecturer and student perspectives on the nature of practice-based, research-led teaching within higher music education, examining the implications and meaning of 'research-led teaching', discussing facilitation of creative practice and professional identities within communities of practice, and exploring the relationships between creative teaching and learning and practice-based, research-led teaching.

In Chapter 6, Martin Blain discusses the position of practitioner-researcher doctoral research students in higher music education, examining recent developments in the methodology and articulation of practice-as-research and its dissemination as well as its relationship to the wider community. Blain offers two case studies, one involving a performer the other involving a composer, which serve to illustrate how practitioners develop, implement and reflect on creative strategies that directly affect the development of practice.

In Chapter 7, John Robert Ferguson explores the contribution of practice-as-research to creative teaching for creative learning in higher music education. Ferguson details and justifies the use of practice-as-research as a viable and valid academic method, examining research-led teaching and addressing associated questions of inclusion, innovation and the relationship between practical and theoretical learning.

In Chapter 8, Kari Veblen, H. Elisha Jo and Stephen J. Messenger explore creativity through perceptions of pre-service music educators concerning their engagement with activities to develop metacognitive thinking and collaborative music-making, finding that these educators possessed diverse understandings of what constituted creative opportunities and how these could be structured within the classroom, and that these related to their early childhood musical experiences as well as to their interaction and engagement with peers and with the demands of the course.

In Chapter 9, Clare Hall discusses working with pre-service primary school generalist teachers, extending their concepts of capabilities and competencies through 'musical sociology', a creative teaching approach designed to encourage and empower pre-service teachers which draws on their personal life histories and utilises sociocultural and emotional capital, particularly through experiences of motherhood, to inform and develop their capacities as creative teachers.

In Chapter 10, Tim Palmer explores work undertaken with two cohorts of trainee teachers in secondary music education, focusing on the intersection of analysis, improvisation and composition and students' perceptions of the processes involved, its relationship to contextual creative teaching practices, and discussing related concepts of enterprise pedagogy, mis-listening and nomadism which all inform the notion of 'play' and creativity as important tools for flexible educators able to facilitate multimodal musical behaviours and positive engagement.

Part III: Philosophies, practices and pedagogies: Teaching for creative learning

In Chapter 11, Mark Hutchinson and Tim Howell define a philosophy of creative musical analysis, demonstrating the interacting processes of analysis, listening and performance through discussion of student expectations and epistemology, and illustrating creative approaches to the teaching of musical analysis through two case studies which position analysis as a fundamentally creative activity underpinning musical understanding.

In Chapter 12, Nicky Losseff draws on psychoanalytic object relations theory, hermeneutics and counselling literature to explore creativity in the context of response to a musical work, investigating how MA music students conceptualise creative relationships with a musical work as performers and composers through processes of projection and introjection, and facilitating this understanding through the use of specially constructed graphic models illustrating the subject–object relationship.

In Chapter 13, Christina Guillaumier, Ruth Slater and Peter Argondizza address their concerns to enable creativity within curriculum reform at a UK conservatoire, discussing the integration of creative practice relating to historically informed performance practice with contextual work, merging academic, practical and creative skills, and articulating the value of the ensuing knowledge and understanding to wider concerns of employability and creative potential.

In Chapter 14, Neil Sorrell explores teaching and learning in two contrasting non-Western cultures, discussing the use of didactic tools in pedagogies of Indian and Javanese music. He proposes that the study of non-Western music may enhance creativity and reinforce aspects of musicality that also promote learner autonomy and positive relationships in learning, encouraging adaptability, flexibility and imagination.

In Chapter 15, Karin Greenhead, John Habron and Louise Mathieu discuss how the active, rigorous and creative principles and techniques used in Dalcroze Eurhythmics can address the needs of higher education music students, bridging the gap between the academic curriculum and practical studies through the concept of the 'mindful body' and promoting the centrality of the body to musical understanding, communication and creative artistic engagement.

In Chapter 16, Fay Hield and Stephanie Pitts explore creative and educational challenges presented in a module focusing on enterprise learning involving undergraduate music students and community partners. They discuss individual and group creativity, communication and ownership as well as creative processes involved in module design and issues of assessment.

In Chapter 17, Ambrose Field discusses effective group creativity, exploring strategies which may be used to facilitate the development of a functional group, detailing approaches to devising processes, examining issues concerning assessment, and demonstrating the viability of group creativity and its relevance to professional contexts as well as its value within higher music education.

Collectively, these chapters present a range of approaches to creative teaching for creative learning in higher music education within diverse contexts. It is hoped that the volume will act as a stimulating and valuable resource not only for those working in higher music education, but also for music students to facilitate reflection on the role that creative teaching and learning plays in their educative experiences. It is also hoped that the accounts of creative practice will encourage further consideration and promotion of the value of creative approaches to teaching and learning not just within higher music education, but at all levels of education, and therefore, that this volume can make a contribution to influence policy-making and to developing positive future creative cultures of music education.

References

Burnard, P. (2014). 'Introduction'. In: P. Burnard (ed.), *Developing Creativities in Higher Music Education: International Perspectives and Practices* (pp. xxvi–xxviii). Abingdon: Routledge.

Kleiman, P. (2008). 'Towards Transformation: Conceptions of Creativity in Higher Education'. *Innovations in Education and Teaching International*, 45(3), 209–17.

Newbigin, J. (17 June 2015). 'Academic Subjects Alone Won't "Set Every Child Up for Life"'. *The Guardian*. Retrieved 18 June 2015 from http://www.theguardian.com/higher-education-network/2015/jun/17/academic-subjects-alone-wont-set-every-child-up-for-life.

Shaw, C. (8 May 2015). 'Don't Stifle Creativity with More Cuts to Arts Education, Say Experts'. *The Guardian*. Retrieved 18 June 2015 from http://www.theguardian.com/higher-education-network/2015/may/08/dont-stifle-creativity-with-more-cuts-to-arts-education-say-experts.

Smith-Bingham, R. (2006). 'Public Policy, Innovation and the Need for Creativity'. In: N. Jackson, M. Oliver, M. Shaw and J. Wisdom (eds), *Developing Creativity in Higher Education: An Imaginative Curriculum* (pp. 10–18). London: Routledge.

Part I

Articulating experience in secondary and higher music education

1 Pre-higher education creativity

Composition in the classroom

Steven Berryman

Introduction and rationale

Music education qualifications appear to predicate a progression from minimal musical competence to a pre-professional level of training. Graded practical music examinations perhaps extol this idea of progression most overtly. The various classroom-based qualifications (such as those awarded during secondary school education) have been designed to be progressive, building on the previous qualification, and each examine the three strands of performance, composing and listening. It is important to recognise, however, that these qualifications may never have been intended as a progressive training towards higher education. These secondary school examinations may be standardised on a national and international level; however, curricula and examinations at higher education can vary from institution to institution.

Secondary school music education could be perceived as transitive; students may be moving schools between different levels, and as such it will be the task of the classroom music teacher to manage the transition of students with a variety of abilities and differing musical experiences. Students may have an extensive musical life outside school (which may include a broader range of creative approaches not always accommodated in the music classroom, such as collaborative creativity, non-Western instruments and non-Western notation). The study of Western music may preference single authors and notated composing, and therefore students may struggle to reconcile out-of-school musical experiences with their classroom-based experiences.

The progression from earlier stages of secondary school education through to the final stages involves an increased use of Western notation; the length of creative work (performances and compositions, for example) extends, and perhaps compared with earlier stages a greater percentage of the qualification comes from a written-based examination. There is increasing scope (depending on the qualification) for students to engage with music technology, non-Western musics and non-notated performances. Composition-based creativity remains less open to the variety afforded performances. Composition is also a compulsory part for nearly all levels, yet the teaching of this can be driven by assessment rather than the genuine pursuit of a compositional voice. In addition, in an attempt to make the assessment of creative work manageable by a diverse and large workforce of music teachers, the creative tasks devised perhaps limit the potential creativity.

It would appear that secondary school sector music education does not naturally progress to higher education; its generic nature – to accommodate a vast number of students – might not appear to be congruent with the aspirations of higher education. A transition needs to occur that considers the teaching approaches adopted before higher education study; it should take into account the methods of assessment and limited creative tasks to ensure students' confidence and expectations can be managed successfully in the early stages of higher education.

This chapter will look at the changing role of creativity from the earlier stages to the later stages of secondary school music education and reflect on the expectations of these various stages. It will be revealed that perhaps there is not a progression towards higher education, but a progression towards an imagined necessary level of music competency that prefers the length of creative tasks as a measure of increased music fluency while relegating the use of the written word as a lesser component. If the transition and progression from pre-higher education music studies is to be managed effectively, it is important for those involved in curriculum design at higher education level to embrace the more rapidly changing secondary school curriculum as their starting point.

Creativity in the secondary school sector curriculum

Music remains a compulsory part of school education in England and Wales until the end of Key Stage 3 (aged 13/14), and with the publication of a new National Curriculum (NC) Programme of Study (DfE, 2013), music continues to be considered as essentially the three strands of performing, creating (composing) and listening. The Key Stage 3 Programme of Study states that:

> Music is a universal language that embodies one of the highest forms of creativity. A high-quality music education should engage and inspire pupils to develop a love of music and their talent as musicians, and so increase their self-confidence, creativity and sense of achievement. As pupils progress, they should develop a critical engagement with music, allowing them to compose, and to listen with discrimination to the best in the musical canon.
>
> (DfE, 2013)

Creativity is professed to be an essential part of music education in this Programme of Study, and it states a further aim that students should 'understand and explore how music is created, produced and communicated, including through the interrelated dimensions: pitch, duration, dynamics, tempo, timbre, texture, structure and appropriate musical notations' (ibid.). Creativity is defined only as the creation of 'original' music, be it improvised or notated composition. Performance is seen as re-creating, and students should expect to be taught how to 'play and perform confidently in a range of solo and ensemble contexts using their voice, playing instruments musically, fluently and with accuracy and expression'. There is the expectation that these three strands of music (performing, creating and listening) are not to be separated, but taught holistically:

> Good music lessons engage pupils musically straight away – that is, by getting them to listen to and think about musical sound, or by involving them in a music-making task. Learning intentions are shared musically – for example, by the teacher modelling a song performance in tune with good diction, articulation and phrasing to show the pupils the intended musical outcome.
>
> (Ofsted, 2012a)

The expectation is that music is taught well when it is taught holistically rather than an attempt to artificially separate into the three strands identified by the NC.

Before the publication of a new NC Programme of Study, classroom-based music education was receiving less favourable press: the Ofsted press release 'Not Enough Music in Music Lessons' (Ofsted, 2012b) highlighted the results of a three-year survey that showed the quality and quantity of music teaching varied considerably; one in five schools inspected were deemed poor in their music teaching:

> In too many music lessons there was insufficient emphasis placed on active music making, and too much focus on talking or written exercises. The scarcity of good vocal work in secondary schools, where nearly half of those inspected were judged inadequate for singing, and the underuse of music technology across all levels were found to be significant barriers to pupils' musical progress.
>
> (Ofsted, 2012b)

It would be naïve to assume such a press release was a true reflection of music teaching nationally, but it is nonetheless an interesting issue to consider. If the NC is professing creativity to be an essential component of a good musical education, how can this be achieved with so little actual music going on within the classroom?

The vagueness of the National Curriculum is to be celebrated, as teachers can curate a curriculum that not only acknowledges their own musical interests and expertise, but also the diverse interests of their pupils. Conversely, this presents a real challenge for teachers. The most recent NC highlights teaching pupils to 'listen with increasing discrimination to a wide range of music from great composers and musicians' (a far from subtle reference to Western art music as the most important repertoire choice) and mentions that 'as pupils progress, they should develop a critical engagement with music, allowing them to compose, and to listen with discrimination to the best in the musical canon' (DfE, 2013). Such a canon invariably refers to the Western art music canon, but again, the vagueness of this statement permits teachers to plan a curriculum that is bespoke to the needs of their pupils rather than planning for imagined pupils.

Richard McNicol's keynote address at the 2011 *National Association of Music Educators Conference* gave a succinct and balanced account of the major developments in British music education since the 1970s. McNicol highlighted the value of John Paynter and Peter Aston and their book *Sound and Silence* (1970), which emphasises a music curriculum that prioritises a practical approach that ironically seems to have faded according to the aforementioned Ofsted press release; McNicol acknowledged those teachers who crafted a 'curriculum that engages and excites innumerable youngsters'. He drew attention to attempts by Kenneth Clarke to formalise the music curriculum which included the study of set works from the Western classical tradition – a practice that continues to inform the curricula at GCSE examination level and above.[1] These developments were not met with unanimous acquiescence – eminent classical musicians led the way in preventing these revisions from denying pupils a practice-based music curriculum. McNicol mentioned his pride in announcing the practice-based music curriculum in the UK to teachers abroad, and he rightly shows that music education in the UK was something to be envied internationally.

Music education at Key Stage 3 favours a holistic approach to music teaching, and the UK National Curriculum encourages a practical approach with collaborative creativity at its core. What can be seen is that there is not much progression towards Key Stage 4, but that a transition is required to meet the needs of the broad range of students who can opt for this next level.

Music at Key Stage 4 and beyond

The situation of music education before Key Stage 4 is seemingly very diverse; pupils can come from schools that have a strong tradition of music-making, or perhaps have engaged with little music during their school years and have found considerable opportunity outside their educational establishment. Thus, opportunities to be creative, beyond performing, can vary considerably. A collaborative method of teaching creative work at Key Stage 3, perhaps led prominently by the teacher, may entail students with little experience of individual creativity – that found in the Western art music convention of the solitary composer – before Key Stage 4. How teachers approach the further development of such creative work can also vary considerably; students may not have much opportunity to refine their work beyond initial attempts, and (due to time and logistics of the lessons) may only get one attempt at producing a creative response. Musical Futures gives greater time and responsibility to student-led activity,[2] but the adoption of such a strategy predicates group rather than individual work too. Creativity therefore becomes a group activity, much akin to the creative strategies detailed by Green (2002) in her study of learning approaches adopted by popular musicians, and also something that is done quickly rather than developed over a considerable length of time. There is a big shift in modality at Key Stage 4; students are now expected to work individually as composers, and there is the expectation that they will work over longer periods to develop their work. Before Key Stage 4, teachers can create their own assessment criteria for the outcomes of creative tasks (perhaps additionally assessing the creative process), yet at Key Stage 4, only the product is assessed and the assessment criteria are set nationally, indeed internationally.

Creativity at Key Stage 4 and beyond

Performance is assessed primarily as a re-creating activity, and students are judged on the complexity of the piece they perform and the extent to which it is accurate in accordance to a notated score. Rockschool has permitted teachers to find notated versions of non-art music repertoire that allow students to be assessed more comfortably by teachers.[3] Regardless of a music's providence, accuracy and technical competence remain assessment priorities. Judgements on the expressive nature of the performance figure less highly, but their prominence increases as students progress to Key Stage 5. The merits of examination via recorded performances are worthy of discussion elsewhere, but the use of recording further enhances the description of performance as a re-creating act that is more about accuracy than about the body of a performer expressing something artistically. In fact, the recorded performance anaesthetises the performer's body.

Composition tasks vary across the examination boards on offer at Key Stage 4. Some require students to compose to a brief (perhaps programmatic, or encourage students to connect their compositions to music they have studied in another area of their course), or there is free choice of content. There are numerous books that attempt to formalise the composing process for those teachers and students with less confidence.[4] Teachers were able to decide the levels of compositional success at Key Stage 3 and could place considerable value in the process of creative work; at Key Stage 4, the finished creative product is prioritised over what could be a carefully graded and enriching development of compositional technique.

At Key Stage 4, teachers are often faced with a diverse range of abilities. Some of their students may be immersed in Western art music (often prioritised at Key Stage 4), while others may have relatively little experience of it; some will be fluent in Western notation, while others might be from a musical tradition where aural transmission of musical learning is paramount. Teachers face a challenge in navigating these diverse needs, and therefore creative work can easily become formulaic. Teachers may be keen to cultivate pedagogical strategies that make a process of creativity in music something that results in finished compositions that score highly on their chosen examination board criteria. Examination boards place considerable emphasis on coursework at Key Stage 4 (often ranging from 60 to 70 per cent of the examination, of which performance can be half). The advent of controlled conditions for creative tasks has meant that students are now producing compositions under supervised conditions and within in a time limit which can range from 10 to 20 hours.[5] Composition is reduced to something measurable and assessable in perhaps a more rigorous way than the performance coursework. It is not surprising that teachers may find the assessment of composition difficult when examination boards place differing constraints on the compositions produced.

AQA[6] (2012) specifies that:

> Candidates are required to compose one piece of music and must choose two or more of the five Areas of Study. There must be a link to one of the three strands, which will be announced annually by AQA. Candidates have

up to 20 hours of Supervised Time in which to complete the composition, under informal supervision. Candidates' work must be monitored during this period by the teacher so that he/she is able to authenticate it as the candidate's own. There is no time limit in terms of the duration of the composition but candidates should be aware of the need to demonstrate sufficient development of musical ideas in the music and, as a consequence, very short pieces may not allow for this.

The first movement from Stravinsky's Three Pieces for String Quartet would not satisfy the final point in the composition requirement from AQA, and neither would many works in the 'canon'. It becomes evident that creative composition at Key Stage 4 and 5 is not an artistic endeavour, but more a demonstration of an ability to manipulate musical sounds and constructs to satisfy the needs of a brief; it is about showing increasing fluency with musical elements. Many teachers may consider this incongruent with the way professional composers operate, but in actuality composers often operate to a brief and negotiate artistic obstructions that may be put in place by them or are proposed by others. Mythologising about the activities of professional musicians and composers is perhaps another concern for school-based music educators, as they may perceive that the Key Stage 4 and 5 examination boards do little to connect the music activities of professionals with what their students do in the classroom, although this is not always the case.

It can be seen that there is a difficult transition to manage after Key Stage 3 and into Key Stage 4 – that of individual creativity. Collaborative composition is not assessed by public examinations at Key Stage 4, and students are expected not only to show artistic flair, but also to demonstrate an increasing fluency at manipulating a range of musical elements. Students are expected to undertake creative tasks under supervised time-controlled conditions. This suggests that only creative tasks observable by a teacher are acceptable at Key Stage 4 level for assessment. This is important to consider for higher education, as freedom in creative work at that level may engender a lack of confidence among students if they have progressed through a music education system that controls creative work through timed supervision.

Assessment becomes teaching

Examination boards all produce criteria for compositions. The interpretation of these criteria becomes perhaps a process of a producing a 'shopping list' of what compositions should contain in order to achieve a high mark. Assessment in music education is a weighty area, and many, particularly Martin Fautley (2010), have attempted to eradicate increasingly complex assessment at Key Stage 3 level (and earlier). Key Stage 4 and 5 composition assessment can be complex as there is a need to make the assessment criteria fit a great deal of potentiality.

Pearson Edexcel (2013) described a composition in its highest marking category as 'Impressive and imaginative in style, ideas and development. Complete (or almost complete) control of compositional methods and techniques used. Sense of musical wholeness with no passage sub-standard.' However concrete this holistic description of a high-scoring composition might be, it is inherently a description that is difficult to pin down objectively. Those teachers who are not additionally examining or moderating may only see work from their own classes, and as the numbers opting for Key Stage 4 and 5 qualifications in music remain the lowest of all arts subjects (often around 8 or 9 per cent will opt for music after Key Stage 3), teachers will not have seen a vast quantity of creative work. Teachers' confidence in applying marking criteria may be low in creative work, particularly if their own experience of composition is limited.

Creative work may be assessed holistically at higher education: students may struggle to work within less constrained circumstances as they may feel it is difficult to satisfy a less precise marking approach, and the transition from an assessment-driven creative approach to one that may favour the development of an individual creative voice may need careful management. Students' definition of 'success' with regards to creative work may need rethinking.

Diversity in teachers' and students' prior experiences

Music teachers may have undertaken a formal teaching qualification, yet their own musical qualifications and route into teaching can be as variable as those of the students they will encounter in the classroom. Teachers' own approaches to creative work will govern their teaching of it. It makes the process of formalising creative approaches that much more difficult when teachers' own experiences of creative work are so varied. Some may have been involved considerably in creative work at higher education and may self-identify as 'composers'; some may have been trained in musical idioms that prioritise creativity (popular music and jazz, perhaps), while some may have taken Western art music routes (conservatoires) as performers, where the creative element in their studies may have been minimal. With creativity (often in the form of composition) usually accounting for 30 per cent of Key Stage 4 and 5 work, many of those who enter the classroom teaching music may have anxieties about the teaching of composition.

With Ofsted (2009) extolling the virtues of music lessons that are 'musical', it would suggest that composition should be made a performative act rather than an activity based on the use of scores in some form. At Key Stage 4 and 5, compositions need to be submitted as a recording along with notation (and examiners are open to a variety of notations rather than exclusively Western art notation), or in lieu of notation, an annotation that describes the composition. Creating the score may indeed pose the greatest challenge for those pupils who work in a musical idiom that does not prioritise notation. It is worth noting that some students who may further their musical studies at higher education may not have notated a score, though it would appear less likely depending on the music course they apply to pursue. With the importance of a score – and undoubtedly many teachers will encourage their students to produce scores as a way of further ensuring students can achieve well against the set marking criteria – and the work being completed under controlled conditions, students will no longer be working on compositions (or similar creative tasks) with musical sounds, but exclusively with symbols. This perhaps could not be any further from the extolled virtues of outstanding music lessons as defined by Ofsted (2009).

Matters of style are as varied as the students in the typical music classroom; there is no requirement (though occasionally 'Western art music' is requested[7]) for a particular style at Key Stage 4 and 5 composition, and students are free to explore their musical preferences. However, acknowledging the aforementioned typical examination criteria shows that even permitting a range of styles is still confined by attempts for a composition to meet the requirements on the 'shopping list' of successful composition characteristics, particularly the reliance on 'repetition and contrast' as a means of structuring musical ideas. With so many musical elements needing manipulation in a 'successful' composition at Key Stage 4 and 5, I could hypothesise again that the majority of the compositions must surely be eighteenth- to nineteenth-century in character, incorporating a structure favouring the return of musical material and a harmonic language that mirrors the pandiatonicism of the first half of the twentieth century. Minimalism is a popular choice for Key Stage 4 composition submissions, perhaps because it is a compositional process that has concrete obstructions defined and clear characteristics that can be taught and demonstrated; examiners' reports often highlight the formulaic nature of such minimalist compositions. Twelve-bar blues is also a popular choice at Key Stage 4, with its set structure helping to scaffold the creative work of those who find composition challenging. It is this desire to find musical styles that are structured repetitively that could be seen to limit the creativity of a vast number of those taking Key Stage 4 music qualifications.

At Key Stage 5, the composition briefs vary from very precise programmatic or film music scene treatments to more open-ended concerns with a particularly extended form (sonata, theme and variations) and to compositions for a particular application, such as for dance or a significant occasion. The numbers taking Key Stage 5 qualifications are considerably lower than Key Stage 4, and they are more likely to fall within the two broader realms of Western art music and popular music and jazz. Music technology is permissible at all levels, and Key Stage 5 qualifications in music technology will expect creative work to prioritise the use of technology as much as the exploitation of musical elements. Even within these briefs, there is greater creative freedom; however, students are still to create their compositions under controlled conditions.

Contemporary art music in the classroom

Recent Western art music does not figure formally on Key Stage 4 and 5 specifications; how composers write today features even less often unless a teacher has experience of such work that they are able to share with their classes. The *Spectrum* series (Associated Board of the Royal Schools of Music, 1996) comprises commissioned works of varying levels of difficulty by living (and recently living) composers. Such music may not score well on the examination board criteria, and there can seem to be a bias against such recent compositional styles – ironically, at higher education it is this recent work that can often take precedence in the creative output of those studying composition. Secondary school music teachers may be biased against more recent art music – not that the internal logic of such works deny analysis, but because it becomes difficult to comprehend how such works are manifestations of the set criteria for creative work. Recent work may not manipulate musical elements as readily as earlier musical works, and thus it is perhaps worth observing that Key Stage 4 and 5 examination boards favour the musical logic of the common practice period.

Opportunities for younger musicians to engage in contemporary music have increased over the past ten years; there are more instances of composers working on projects with school-based groups as well as school-based musicians being involved in performances of new music and attending courses run by those professional musicians who are immersed in new music. Nevertheless, the secondary school classroom often seems to prefer the music of composers from the past, as something about the museum of musical works (after Goehr, 1992) allows students (and teachers) to mythologise about the creative act. Creative processes no longer become something that can be worked at and developed, which is perhaps seen keenly in the music classroom for Key Stage 3 students, but at Key Stage 4 and 5 it becomes more evident that only a select group of younger musicians can 'compose'. Where this assumption that only certain people are 'musicians' comes from is uncertain, and Ofsted (2009) remarks on it being cited as the reason why some students do not opt for Key Stage 4 music courses. The diversity of the creative work that happens currently in the UK and beyond should be more than enough evidence that there is no one approach to the creative act and it need not be a solitary one (though for the benefit of assessment, it has to be a solitary one, it would seem). Burnard (2012) has written persuasively about the creativity myths, and her case studies are important reading for music teachers at secondary school level.

It is important to recognise that students may enter higher education having never met a living composer or worked with active professionals, and may never have met a diverse range of music practitioners. Opportunities to work with living composers show that the creative act is not something mythical, but something variable – though how much living composers attempt to add to the creative myth through writing about their work is a subject for another book. The benefits of working with living composers help students understand vividly the continuing trajectory of the providence of musics. Sound and Music, the national agency for the promotion of new contemporary music in the UK, runs an annual residential summer school for young composers (attracting over seventy participants) to bring them into contact with professional composers and musicians. A 2014 participant (Sound and Music, 2014: 2) remarked that 'they treated us like professional composers and always did whatever they could to perfect our compositions'. The summer school aims to stretch the musical experiences of the participants, providing opportunities to work with new instrumental combinations and encounter new musical rhetoric, supported through mentoring by an established composer. More importantly, it provides extended time to work on a project that otherwise would be difficult to realise within the typical constraints of a school timetable. Another participant remarked that the tutors 'were all so professional and treated us with so much respect. They were so inspirational! You are constantly learning from the tutors, as they work at such a high level' (ibid.). Perhaps there is a sense for these students that the creative work they do within school is not 'professional', and that further ways to increase the authenticity of the composing experience within the classroom might help improve the confidence of younger musicians when they undertake Key Stage 4 and 5 composition coursework.

The Sound and Music Summer School splits the cohort into different groups, each focusing on a different style of composition (which in 2014 included working with voices, writing for film, instrumental composition). Over seven days, students work on a composition that is performed at the end of the week:

> One of the highlights of the week is seeing the students' reactions to having their initial ideas played by professional ensembles of the highest quality and then being guided to develop these pieces. This is an incredibly rare chance for these talented young people to learn and create beyond technical constraints, surrounded by peers of similar ability and interests and mentored by top professionals.
>
> (Sound and Music, 2014: 4)

The evaluation of the 2014 summer school showed that 75 per cent rated the summer school at four out of five or higher, and the majority of students reported the main difference compared with school provision as being the opportunity to work with professional players and composers; '93% report pushing their creative boundaries' and '91% report learning about new or different styles of music during the week'. Interestingly, the vast majority of those attending identified themselves as British and white, and nearly two-thirds were male.

The summer school shows there is clearly a demand for opportunities to make composition for older secondary school pupils more authentic by working with professional composers and musicians. I imagine the bias towards more recent art music styles at the summer school would be seen as incongruent to the marking criteria for Key Stage 4 and 5, yet ironically these types of works (where the composition processes have been more sophisticated through immersion in a particular style and the instrumental writing has been pushed to be truly idiomatic) can perform very well against the marking criteria.

Teachers engaging with creativity

'Teach Through Music' was a year-long, fully subsidised professional development programme for Key Stage 3 music teachers in London schools (state and independent), supported by the London Schools Excellence Fund.[8] Trinity Laban Conservatoire of Music and Dance was the lead partner in the programme, which represented a partnership of music education organisations with cultural organisations such as the South Bank Centre, Barbican Centre and Wigmore Hall Learning. The aim was to create a 'centre of excellence' for Key Stage 3 music teaching in London by offering a range of professional development opportunities that would complement the normal working lives of music teachers through evening seminars, whole-day events, concerts and other cultural events. Music Mark offered a sister programme, and nearly three hundred music teachers in London boroughs enrolled.[9] At the time of writing, the programme evaluation had not been written, but it will be interesting to see what impact this significant investment in the professional development of a large cohort of teachers will have on the quality of the lessons and musical experiences for London students. The most important aspect of the 'Teach Through Music' programme is not only the relentless focus on making music the 'dominant language of the classroom' (continuing the Ofsted desire for music lessons to be 'musical'), but how the programme prioritises the confidence of the teachers as musicians in all the training opportunities. A singing session with Pete Churchill engaged teachers in the activities they might use with students, and a creative task in a previous session involved teachers devising music to a graphic stimulus. If we are to encourage our students to think as musicians (whatever that thinking might be, however much it is mythologised), then having teachers thinking as musicians is paramount, as perhaps too often teachers may be thinking like examiners when facilitating creative work. Developing the confidence of teachers to be musicians in the classroom should be high on an agenda for initial teacher training.

Final thoughts

Without surveying every student currently taking a Key Stage 5 Music course, it would be difficult to ascertain perceptions of their future musical studies, particularly when focusing on creative work. I would suggest they perceive their school music-making as something inauthentic, something that is not 'professional', and that there would be the aspiration that subsequent creative activities pursued at higher education level will be coupled with an authenticity, as they would assume their lecturers and tutors to be 'professional' musicians. I wonder, too, whether the intricacies of marking criteria make the creative act something perceived as uncreative; the artistry is removed at secondary school due to an over-pursuit of the shopping list of 'successful' composition (or other creative tasks such as improvisation and arranging). At higher education level, students may be less prepared for the fluidity of assessment of creative tasks, and thus their confidence might be diminished. Previous creative tasks at secondary level are predicated on precise briefs that – although it is not the intention – inherently place too much of a ceiling on creative possibilities. By the end of secondary schooling in music, students are likely to fall into two categories: one where students feel that they can create music, and one where they feel they cannot. Through conditioning by schoolteachers (who may be reticent towards national marking criteria for creative tasks), students will perceive their creative work as inauthentic and also something beyond assessment, and the examination criteria as something that could never acknowledge fully the creative intricacies offered by composition. It will entail higher education receiving students who are used to creative tasks that result in a mark achieved through the pursuit of carefully used musical markers of 'success'; destabilising this view of creative tasks will involve careful mitigation of students' confidence, as entering a world of increased creative freedom could be a challenge, however welcome, for many students.

There are increasing opportunities for younger musicians to work with professional musicians, not only composers, and it is pleasing to see students are increasingly involved in new commissions by living composers. If this trend continues, it will help bridge the gap between the authentic and the perceived inauthenticity of musical experiences in and out of school. Most importantly, it will legitimise students' creative work, but there is more to be done in considering how best to make the creative components (that are a significant part of Key Stage 4 and 5 qualifications) less of an academic exercise and more of a process of creative ownership by students. Increasing the contact with active composers, regardless of the style of music these musical authors work in, will help improve the confidence of teachers and students alike in creative work in the classroom.

Notes

1 General Certificate of Secondary Education (GCSE) – a qualification taken by pupils aged 14–16 in secondary education in England, Wales and Northern Ireland. Pupils take a number of GCSEs in different subjects.
2 More can be read about this movement in music education at https://www.musical futures.org (accessed March 28, 2016).
3 Further information about this examinations system can be found at http://www.rslawards.com/music/graded-music-exams (accessed March 28, 2016).
4 For example, see Cole (1996), Russell and Harris (2004) and Cornick and Rae (2009).
5 Such conditions mean a teacher is present and informally supervising while a student is composing; some examination boards see the controlled conditions as the writing time, while any preparation and research for a composition is not counted.
6 Formerly known as the Assessment and Qualifications Alliance, a charitable body awarding qualifications (for example, GCSEs) in England, Wales and Northern Ireland.
7 Cambridge International Examinations GCSE (IGCSE) requires its candidates to enter one composition in Western art music.
8 Further information about this programme can be found at http://www.sound-connections.org.uk/teach-through-music (accessed March 28, 2016).
9 Further information about this programme can be found at http://www.musicmark.org.uk (accessed March 28, 2016).

References

AQA (2012). *GCSE Specification: Music 4210*. Manchester: AQA.
Associated Board of the Royal Schools of Music (1996). *Spectrum: 20 Contemporary Works for Solo Piano*. London: ABRSM Publishing.
Burnard, P. (2012). *Musical Creativities in Practice*. Oxford: Oxford University Press.
Cole, B. (1996). *The Composer's Handbook*. London: Schott.
Cornick, M. and Rae, J. (2009). *Sound Foundations: A Source of Reference and a Guide for Aspiring Composers*. London: Universal Edition.

DfE (2013). *National Curriculum in England: Music Programmes of Study; Key Stage 3.* London: Department for Education, Qualifications and Curriculum Authority.

Fautley, M. (2010). *Assessment in Music Education.* Oxford: Oxford University Press.

Goehr, L. (1992). *The Imaginary Museum of Musical Works.* Oxford: Oxford University Press.

Green, L. (2002). *How Popular Musicians Learn: A Way Ahead for Music Education.* Aldershot: Ashgate.

Ofsted (2009). *Making More of Music: An Evaluation of Music in Schools 2005/08.* London: Ofsted.

——— (2012a). *Music in Schools: Promoting Good Practice. Guidance from HMI for Teachers, Headteachers, and Music Hub Leaders When Observing Musical Teaching and Learning.* London: Ofsted.

——— (2 March 2012b). Press release: 'Not Enough Music in Music Lessons'. Retrieved 11 January 2015 from http://www.gov.uk/government/news/not-enough-music-in-music-lessons.

Paynter, J. and Aston, P. (1970). *Sound and Silence.* Cambridge: Cambridge University Press.

Pearson Edexcel (2013). *Level 3 Advanced Subsidiary GCE in Music (8MU01), First Examination 2014; Level 3 Advanced GCE in Music (9MU01), First Examination 2014.* Issue 5. London: Pearson.

Russell, B. and Harris, T. (2004). *The GCSE Composition Course: Teachers' Book.* London: Edition Peters.

Sound and Music (2014). *2014 Summer School for Young Composers.* Retrieved 11 January 2015 from http://www.soundandmusic.org/sites/default/files/projects/files/2014%20Summer%20School%20Report%20Final%20-%20version%20for%20website.pdf.

2 A student perspective on creativity in higher music education

Natalie Edwards, James Whittle and Alice Wright

Introduction

This chapter is a development of a paper delivered at the 2013 UK Higher Education Academy conference *Creative Teaching for Creative Learning in Higher Academic Music Education*, which took place at the University of York, UK. After an informal meeting with the organiser, Dr Liz Haddon, we volunteered to present on the experience of creativity by students studying the BA (Hons) Music degree at the University of York.[1] Our brief was to provide feedback on how we and other students felt we were being taught creatively throughout our degrees. We conducted a student survey[2] to discover what the participants' personal experiences of the academic course were and what 'creativity' meant to them. Through the survey responses we also learnt how extracurricular activities contributed to the participants' taught creativity and the impact creativity had on their academic work. The paper drew on our personal reflections of the degree programme and the survey. This chapter is an extension of our original findings.

We are not attempting to speak for the experience of all music students at the University of York in this chapter, nor to advertise the particular programme and teaching style. We are, however, aiming to give primary accounts of our and other students' perceived experiences of creativity at York, in order to begin a discussion on how students perceive creativity in their higher education. Although we have not had first-hand experience of different music programmes, after consideration we decided not to include the thoughts of students at other institutions, as we would struggle to represent these adequately within our short study. Our own undergraduate music degree experiences contrast due to our varied specialisms: James as a composer, cellist and conductor, Natalie as a community musician and flautist, and Alice as a singer and opera director. These variations make us well placed to give complementary views on the music programme, as we all had very different experiences of the same degree and are following contrasting career paths.

Some popular opinions of the music degree and its value include that it equips students with many transferable skills that can increase employability, for example, teamwork and time management. These skills are invaluable professionally, but also aid individual growth as people become more independent at university. We will discuss further the skills the degree develops later in the chapter.

Our main aim is to show how both the taught and the learnt creativity that students experience throughout their undergraduate degrees can help them develop not only academically and professionally, but also individually. To give insight into the creative life of a music undergraduate, we will look at both personal reflections and the opinions of our peers.

Introducing the survey

The survey was designed to find out how students defined creativity, and whether they perceived it to be a part of their course and overall university experience. The anonymous survey was created using SurveyMonkey[3] and distributed by email invitation to all undergraduate and postgraduate music students at the University of York. For the presentation, we analysed the responses to each question individually and presented our findings question by question; for this chapter, we have grouped responses into common themes. Our sample of 11 collected responses is small, so cannot be representative of the whole student cohort. Further research would provide far greater analytical detail; nevertheless, the responses do provide a starting point for discussion.

'Creativity' in our terms

The survey responses demonstrated a similarity between the ways in which our student peers thought about and expressed their experiences of creativity. All responses to the first question, 'What does creativity mean to you?', emphasised either one or both of two aspects of creativity: 'thinking' and 'doing'. While some respondents defined creativity as 'thinking outside the box' (Respondents 6, 7, 9), others described 'new ways of doing things' (Respondent 1), to 'produce something for yourself' (Respondent 4), or make 'something new' (Respondents 7, 10). Creativity can thus be described as a process occurring as thought and action. A capacity for 'independent thought' (Respondent 5) allows us to shape our ideas by identifying, conceptualising and rationalising information, then to determine action, in order to manage tasks and solve problems.

Most respondents described creativity as being their 'own' or as something 'unique that only I could think of' (Respondent 8), recognising that creative thought and action can occur only within one's own experience. Creativity, therefore, is experiential and individual, its central traits being freedom, choice and autonomy.

As an independent, personal process, creativity can provide a sense of ownership in individual and collaborative activities. Group creative processes are a key feature of education, perhaps due to the increased likelihood of an individual obtaining knowledge and learning from shared exposure to others' conceptual spaces. In this context especially, creativity can be exploratory, experienced as the awareness of agency that the participant has over an activity, or rather, their control over a situation and relative activity or passivity within a group.[4]

Creativity is active: it necessitates an engagement with an object or idea on a deeper level than just recognising its existence. It is possible to experience any context as being in some way educational. Creative thinking may employ 'logic, intuition, knowledge and experimentation to bring together many things' (Respondent 10). This idea would suggest that creativity is multifaceted.

These 'many things' are products of a certain way of thinking in a given context. By 'combining various influences' (Respondent 1) and rationalising knowledge new to their experience, students can develop established knowledge to provide 'new answers to old questions' (Respondent 1). Other respondents expressed the idea of a product of creativity being something that would 'interest others', or be 'new' or 'original'. Since these responses suggest underlying aesthetic or cultural assumptions about the function and value of art, it is sufficient to say that the conception and product of a creative process are always new to the participant.

The students' perspective of newness corroborates Boden's definition of P-creativity: that students will have ideas they could not have had before, but which may already exist. However, the focus on originality indicates a perceived pressure to be H-creative: to produce something completely new (Boden, 1996b: 76).

These definitions of creativity are not specific to a degree in music. The impetus to produce a 'creative' object in music (such as a composition or performance) can be compared to that in other disciplines, which motivates the writing of an essay or analysis of quantitative data. The required skills and knowledge for specific thought and actions may differ vastly, yet, in all cases, one must think to create, to produce. The way that arts subjects may be generalised as more creative than other subjects perhaps presumes a greater amount of agency over the product. As we will discuss further below, one's ability to be receptive to *creative teaching*, to characterise what creative teaching looks like, to understand what it is to learn creatively and be creative oneself, is affected by a variety of stimuli.

Creativity in the degree programme

Within the structure of the timetable at York, our contact time as second- and third-year music students consisted of 30 hours of lectures over four weeks of a 10-week term. The rest of our academic time in the term consisted of tutorials, independent study, and time to pursue other interests and extracurricular activities. The flexible academic course comprises one module per term, which the student chooses from a list covering many different periods and musical styles. The downside to this flexibility, however, is that students can only undertake one module and practical assessment a term,[5] while some may prefer more structure and variety.

From the beginning of their degree, students can tailor the course to what inspires them. Within each module, they can also choose how they want to be assessed – for example, through submitting an essay, composition or performance, or a combination thereof. This choice can help make students feel more confident and able to express themselves freely and creatively in a way that they choose. The system of one module a term allows students to focus in detail on one subject with one lecturer. This way of structuring an academic year gives students the feeling of self-determination. Although guided by lecturers, they are ultimately in control of the progression of their own work, which encourages them to be more independent and think creatively.

There are frequent interdisciplinary links in many modules that were available to our respondents, such as history and politics ('Weimar Music Theatre'), literature ('Words and Music'), movement ('The Body in Musical Performance') and languages ('Eighteenth Century Vocal Music'). These links increase creativity through encouraging students to widen their field of knowledge and become more aware of other areas of study.

The assessments for each module are flexible, giving students an immediate sense of ownership of what they are creating, as well as the possibility for passionate connection with the assessment topic, as determined by each individual. During their third year, students undertake a Solo Project, which can take the form of a dissertation, large-scale composition or performance project. Students can choose any topic to study and any combination of assessment, giving them complete freedom of choice and promoting a very creative approach.

There can be challenges in a creative course structure. Respondent 10 observed that there can be 'no linear sequence or sense of progression from one project and its subject to another'. Tension can also occur if a 'certain performance style' (Respondent 2) is seen as restrictive in reducing the autonomy of the student performer, thereby producing a rift between academic and creative processes.

In their first year, all music students take a Foundation Studies module. This aims to improve confidence, bridging the gap between A level and undergraduate study and ensuring that students are at a similar theoretical standard. It helps develop students' academic skills, enabling them to work more freely and therefore be more creative. The first year of university is about finding one's feet and becoming more independent. The grade obtained from the end-of-year mark does not contribute to the final degree result, encouraging students to take more creative risks during their first year and develop awareness of their own abilities. Subsequently, their creative choices can be informed by this freedom.

The seminar style of small-group teaching, including multiple undergraduate year groups, encourages students to participate and promotes active rather than passive learning. As Respondent 9 commented, 'in having seminars rather than lectures, our input always feels valued'. These seminars use visual and aural aids (such as Power-Point, video and audio files, hard copy handouts) and, often, practical activities such as whole-class musical analysis. Off-campus work features in modules such as 'Music in the Community', in which students are encouraged to assist and run workshops around York. These teaching styles transform students' social relations by increasing engagement, encouraging self-learning by sharing information with each other, and exploring ways in which they learn best, both individually and collaboratively.

Creativity through lecturers

Academic staff not only teach and assess students, but also support, guide and enthuse them throughout their degree. Their influence can help students feel comfortable, inspired and confident enough to stretch themselves and approach assignments in increasingly innovative ways. As Respondent 9 felt, 'every lecturer I have ever had has only wanted to extend our creativity, with presentation and performance tasks, or simply by giving us their own interpretation'.

One of the most important ways in which this supportive atmosphere is created from the beginning of the undergraduate's journey is through developing 'a nicer, more relaxed attitude between "teacher" and student' (Respondent 9). The majority of students come straight to university from school or college, where the roles of pupil and teacher are more clearly defined and formal. Therefore, although changes, such as calling university lecturers by their first names, may initially seem strange or even uncomfortable for new undergraduates, these can help break down barriers. Although the roles are still delineated, the less formal environment helps the student feel less intimidated by the lecturer's status and therefore encourages confidence to contribute more openly in both seminar and tutorial discussions.

It could be argued that the flexible nature of the York music degree benefits lecturers as well as undergraduates. The modules offered, with one or two exceptions, change every academic year, with some courses repeating every few years and others only ever appearing once. Lecturers are therefore not required to teach the same topics annually, but can instead deliver teaching related to areas of study that they are currently (or have recently been) engaging with and can readily enthuse about. This in turn aids the student, who can sense this passion and feel inspired.

Within seminars, lecturers boost creative thinking by encouraging all class members to question every idea or concept that they are given, playing devil's advocate to help students challenge their own opinions and consider evidence from various angles. This is particularly important to develop within the first year of university, when many students will be used to what is often a very different style of teaching at A level. With written work at A level assessed predominantly through exams rather than coursework, classes generally focused on limited areas of study and used comparatively few resources, presenting students with limited opportunities to develop independent thought or gain recognition for original ideas.

At degree level, however, there is rarely a 'right' answer, and the ability to think in new ways and question the opinions of others is vital. Through stimulating discussion facilitated by lecturers, students learn the importance of considering alternative viewpoints and gain confidence in their own abilities through increased understanding.

The format of these taught seminars is generally flexible and spontaneous in nature, allowing lecturers the space to focus in on discussions and topics that particularly enthuse students or dedicate more time to ideas that would benefit from further exploration. Activities within seminars often aim to stimulate creativity through methods other than discussion; Respondent 7 comments that 'in some projects we do physical exercises and we workshop different things to find the best way that something works.[6] This is fantastic because it gets us using our bodies as well as "academic" brains in order to get the most out of what we are learning.'

In addition to seminar-based teaching, all students are offered one-to-one tutorials following the taught component of each module, which can provide even more opportunities for the lecturer creatively to inspire the student. The advice given is rarely prescriptive, students being provided with points to consider and suggestions for suitable resources, but still left free to pursue their assignment topic in whichever way they find most interesting. Tutorials also provide students with a safe environment in which they can ask questions away from the opinions of others, allowing them to discuss more adventurous ideas in confidence. These tutorials become particularly valuable during the Solo Project, where they are the only official contact that the student has with an academic. With more regular individual contact (every few weeks), the student is able to get to know their tutor better and feel comfortable discussing their ideas with them.

Fostering a creative environment

Educational environments are designed to enable students to learn and research their subjects. While elements of the university environment contribute towards creative teaching and learning, specific interventions can be made by departments to promote these further. The more comfortable the student is in an environment, the more likely they are to be motivated, work hard and enjoy their time there.

Creative learning can be fostered through a sound environment of mutual respect and equality. Students taking the same university course or module share a common interest in its subject with their peers. A student may recognise that their peers have all chosen to be present and that therefore each has an investment in the course or module.

At York, all undergraduate year groups are taught together through a flexible modular system. The shared investment that this system motivates can help remove a sense of hierarchy between year groups, thereby encouraging knowledge sharing and collaboration.[7] Although this environment can be daunting at first, students will often find instead that university study is not a competition. Professionalism, empathy and respect are encouraged by lecturers, whose example makes it clear that the opinions of every student are valued in class.

A creative environment is encouraged further by co-operative activities in class. Opportunities to collaborate in groups range from discussing a source or researching and giving a presentation to devising a performance. Students may be required to talk or work with people they do not know or may not have collaborated with before. Alongside making new friends, students learn from the experiences and opinions of their peers, whose ideas and perspectives may challenge their own. The working partnerships that can develop may continue in extracurricular work, in other modules, or professionally after graduation.

The first module that all first-year undergraduates take at York is the six-week Practical Project, which culminates in two or three evening performances. Typically, the show is a unique newly devised production combining music and theatre on a theme (*Goodnight Gertrude*, on the work of Gertrude Stein, 2011; *John Cage Festival-Conference*, 2012), though sometimes standard works are staged (Bach's *St John Passion*, 2008; Bernstein's *Wonderful Town*, 2010; Weill's *The Threepenny Opera*, 2014). The purpose of the project is to help all new students settle into the university environment by collaborating in a team comprising members of the whole department. First-year students can be involved in any aspect of the production, from vocal or instrumental performance to set design, lighting and choreography. Directed overall by one or sometimes two lecturers, the project always involves some second- and third-year undergraduates, who submit critical work on the project's topic for their degree. The Practical Project therefore enables first-year students to establish a multitude of contacts, become accustomed to the department, and gain a sense of ownership, achievement and confidence through participating in a unique production.

For many, the three-year undergraduate course comes at a transitional stage from adolescence into young adulthood, as the student develops a greater level of self-awareness gradually over this period. Throughout the course, the ongoing Practical Studies module requires students to engage in and detail study of their main instrument or voice, plus complete a series of reflective reports on their learning and experience of live concerts. The evaluation of individual creative practices here can be significant for personal development. Reflective tasks and skills can be vital in helping the student to realise their progress and to address any issues that arise at this key stage.

Outside the main degree, the university environment includes extracurricular activities and opportunities, such as a multitude of sports, societies[8] and volunteering projects.[9] The diversity of opportunities allows students to engage in many activities outside their degree if they wish. Music students often find that many of their extracurricular activities are still musical, as Respondent 9 observed:

> I often feel that if unassessed musical projects, such as ensembles, orchestras, choirs and musicals, WERE a part of my degree I'd probably do unfathomably well! It is so easy to get involved with established university ensembles, as well as finding like-minded people to set up one's own. Lunchtime concerts are a brilliant way of showcasing skills that aren't shown in lectures and essays.

The line between curricular music and extracurricular musical activities can be less distinct than in other subjects. Students are likely to engage in activities that they enjoy and in which they find people who share their interests. The increase in demands on a student's time that this can create teaches the student to prioritise and balance their assessed work with extracurricular activities. As Respondent 1 commented, the 'limitations' of time and of activities a student can manage are 'more often self-imposed' as a result.

This idea of 'self-imposed' limitations implies that students set their own boundaries for what they learn and how much extracurricular work they take on. A larger amount and wider range of activities will allow the student to learn more about working with people as well as more about themselves and how they work. Wherever performance is involved, self-reflection and evaluation are more prominent as the very nature of rehearsal and performance involves an attitude of striving constantly to improve.

Performance- and management-based activities require a level of professionalism through the commitment both require over an extended period. Students are proactive in organising their own projects, concerts and events. Being involved in another student's (or another society's) project gives students valuable experience of developing their own professionalism and empathy.

Curricular and extracurricular skill development

We have discussed many ways in which music students are able to develop their creativity through various aspects of the undergraduate course and the learning environment surrounding them. We will now reflect on the specific creative skills promoted by involvement in both academic and extracurricular activities, particularly those which would benefit the student even after graduation.

A great number of these skills are mentioned by Respondent 10, who felt that involvement in this degree programme resulted in being 'taught how to teach myself ... and focus myself in practical skills: self-reliance, self-motivation and discipline, concentration, organisation, prioritisation, time management'. These would all benefit an individual in their future career, allowing them to manage a varied workload efficiently and effectively.

The unique structure of the York music degree certainly improves these skills, as 'there is so much "free time" that you have to learn how to use this ... productively and wisely' (Respondent 4). Respondent 7 feels this is because students are 'taught to be very proactive – no music student ever seems to have a dull moment'. While they will likely choose to take full advantage of their unstructured time, students must remember that their academic work should remain a priority. This develops an ability to work flexibly – a skill valued by employers.

Another skill developed through creative collaborative learning is teamwork and co-operation, including working 'in a team with people I may not have chosen to work with' (Respondent 9). Team members may have interests or specialisms in a variety of areas, and students must learn to draw on all these influences to create a high-quality end result to which each person has contributed.

Music students also learn to be reflective, refining not only practical work, but also written and spoken assignments. Respondent 10 suggests that 'progression comes in the form of one's own learning, and being able to identify what the practical areas are in which one is weakest ... and how to develop that weaker ability'. Allowing students the opportunity to try different methods of assessment helps students gauge which method suits them best. The use of coursework rather than exams allows them to refine their work continually and identify clearly areas of weakness through their module feedback.

Development in all these areas leads to another important skill: confidence in oneself and one's own abilities. By having the freedom to choose the modules and assignment topics that interest them, students assume responsibility for developing their independent learning, through which they may identify their strengths. The sense of ownership this awareness can bring may then encourage a sense of pride in their work.

Of course, not all the skills that music students develop come from the classroom or coursework, as the vast majority also choose to be involved in many extracurricular activities. Respondent 3 believes that extracurricular activities differ from academic ones in that they are 'more likely to reinforce what you already think/learn from other people doing similar things', but they remain an excellent way 'to get creative through having fun rather than ... an actual aim'. Extracurricular activities also allow students the opportunity to develop their creativity further by applying their skills in new contexts. Respondent 10 aimed to use involvement in additional activities such as publicity and artist liaison to 'support my academic knowledge with practical knowledge of engaging other[s] in music'.

A number of skills gained through extracurricular activities which are identified in the survey, and also subsequently in our own reflections, are similar to those developed through the degree, such as organisation, time management and teamwork. Extracurricular activities, including society involvement and volunteering, also offer the opportunity to work and network with new people and organisations. These could include students or lecturers from other departments, or contacts from outside the university such as schools or local businesses. Extracurricular activities not only provide the social benefits of a widening friendship circle, but also allow students to form professional partnerships that may prove fruitful both during university and after graduation.

Similarly, extracurricular involvement can provide valuable work experience that may not be available through a degree alone. Respondent 6, a Master's degree student at York who studied elsewhere at undergraduate level, benefited not only from the 'social side' of running the university wind orchestra, but from gaining 'experience which has been invaluable in helping me to get work'. Such roles allow students to see their actions making an impact, increasing their confidence and providing new opportunities to solve problems and work creatively.

Students must be self-motivated in order to commit to projects which may gain no official or academic recognition, but will benefit them in other ways. Respondent 10 believes that 'creativity is encouraged more' when students are 'looking to learn from the activity' rather than treating them simply 'as a hobby'.

It is clear that music undergraduates are able to develop a wealth of creative skills while at university, many of which can help shape or benefit their future career path. In the final section of our chapter, we will reflect as individual authors on our own undergraduate experiences, aiming to highlight three different accounts of how creativity has aided our professional development.

Building a career path

Alice

While studying for my degree, I found that I became increasingly interested in the world of opera. This interest has led me to undertake internships with companies including Northern Ireland Opera. At York, I directed productions such as Britten's *Albert Herring*, and studied opera through my solo project (a dissertation on semi-staged operas) and in modules including 'Mozart Opera'. This academic and practical preparation was invaluable in terms of developing my knowledge of and interest in the subject.

During my third year, I began interning with English Touring Opera in the Easter and summer holidays, and was subsequently employed as a full-time artistic assistant. This role encompasses a large range of tasks, including assisting directors in rehearsals with dramaturgical research, preparing scores for future seasons, and assisting the company manager in producing and running the rehearsals and tours. The degree prepared me well for this role, in that I had a very varied experience and consequently am well versed in being open to new jobs and projects to work on! It has also given me a fantastic foundation for working with a busy and lively company, as I was involved with numerous different performing and academic groups. It taught me to work well in a team and think quickly and efficiently, and improved my people skills. I also learned to research thoroughly and always be prepared – skills that I am finding invaluable in this new role.

With regard to the future, presently I am not sure what I would like to do in terms of a career, but I am very happy working with such an exciting opera company, enabling people to experience the joy and magic of live opera. My degree – and York – have given me the passion and drive to work in the opera world, and I am very grateful to be a part of it.

James

My undergraduate experience led me to pursue postgraduate study in composition at York, first in an MA by Research, now currently in a PhD. My decision to remain at York for my MA was based partly in wanting to continue working with a wide range of people in the open, collaborative environment that the department allows (undergraduates and postgraduates also mix often). During my third year and MA, I began collaborating with musicians in Manchester as a freelance conductor. Towards the end of the MA, I decided that York would be the best place for me to remain for a PhD, to continue cultivating professional contacts and work in northern England.

During my BA, the modules I chose offered ample opportunity to experiment with interdisciplinary work and create music in alternative formats through practical tasks in modules such as 'Composition 2: Experimental Music, Theatre and Performance' and 'The Body in Musical Performance'. My PhD research now specialises in processes of devising music-theatre works collaboratively, and is influenced as much by live art and contemporary performance as it is by musical practices. The ideas that challenged me in my undergraduate degree have undoubtedly had a significant bearing on my path since.

My role as conference weekend manager for the student-run York Spring Festival of New Music over the three years of my BA gave me a wealth of managerial experience. The variety of work that I experienced in the role taught me the value of knowing your skill set and the benefits certain activities can give you. I am now able to use the organisation, planning, team management and artistic liaison skills I gained to develop my preferred career as a freelance composer-performer and conductor. Currently, I support my PhD with this freelance work (I have been very fortunate to gain some commissions and professional engagements) and with part-time work at the University of York Music Press and as an Education Support Worker. Although I know that I would most like to have a career as a creative artist, I am aware of the economic, financial and even political instability of work in this field. Knowing how to adapt your skills can allow you to keep your career options as open as possible. I have found that trusting and collaborating with other people can retain the focus and motivation needed to build the career you want.

Natalie

After graduating, I remained at York to complete a Master's degree in Community Music, and then worked for a year in the university's Widening Participation department, promoting higher education among under-represented groups (for example, students with no family history of higher education or from poorer backgrounds). This role, although not directly related to music, still required me to use many of the skills developed during my studies. Speaking in front of large audiences required me to use the confidence that I had gained through seminar presentations and recitals. Undertaking assessed group work during several modules ensured I was used to working as a team and could adapt to fit with the working styles of others. Involvement in volunteering projects, as well as part-time work as a student ambassador, outside my degree also provided valuable experience working with children and young people – a major part of the role.

At present, I am interning in education and youth theatre with a York-based theatre company. I was able to dabble in theatre several times throughout my degree, acting in several music department productions and writing and directing a short scene as part of the 2011 Practical Project. Again, it requires a great deal of creativity and confidence, whether I am planning a session, demonstrating an exercise in front of a group of schoolchildren or adapting my approach to support performers of varying ability. My long-term career goals are still undecided, but ideally I aim to work in arts education and outreach.

At university, I particularly appreciated the opportunity to adopt interdisciplinary approaches to my work, through taking modules such as 'Music and Gender' and writing a dissertation on the social, economic, political and (of course) musical impact of songs from the 1984–95 UK miners' strike. My dissertation supervisor in particular was extremely helpful, allowing me the freedom to explore the topic in my own way; I always left tutorials feeling confident and inspired about my project. Although the idea of choosing my own essay topics initially seemed daunting, I now understand that I am capable of creating interesting ideas and carrying out successful research independently and am much more confident in my own abilities.

One of the most important things university has taught me, however, is to strive to improve continuously, and not to give up if I do not succeed first time.

Through evaluating my progress throughout the degree and getting involved in every opportunity, I was able to develop not only as a student, but as a person.

Concluding remarks

Our survey has shown that students' perceptions of creativity are closely aligned, as demonstrated in their use of similar words to describe creativity as 'new', 'original' and promoting 'independent thought'. Despite their differences in opinion about the success of their course and perceived experiences, the sample, though small, has highlighted how creative teaching may be defined as flexible, adaptable and student-led. We have thus defined creative learning as autonomous and individual, but also as exploratory and shared. By learning creatively, the influences one is able to accumulate can only be more numerous and varied, thus offering greater potential for personal and professional development. The autonomy that students can discover through creative teaching, the flexibility of teaching styles, and the open-mindedness of lecturers gives them the freedom to choose their own path. Although we are only at the beginning of our careers, we feel that the skills taught to us through creative teaching and learning can maximise the opportunities available to us in the diverse world of professional work.

Appendix: 'How we learn creatively in music degrees' survey, 25 April to 23 June 2013

Q1: What does creativity mean to you?

Q2: How has your university experience differed to your musical education at school?

Q3: How do you think you are engaged creatively in your degree work?

Q4: What do you think is creative about how we learn?

Q5: Aside from the inherent creative aspects of music – performance, composition, analysis – what else do you feel you are taught in your degree?

Q6: How do you feel creativity is encouraged through academic activities, compared to practical or extracurricular activities?

Q7: The life of a music student is not solely made up of assessed degree work; are you involved in projects that won't count towards your degree, and, if so, what are the reason/s for getting involved with them?

Q8: Is there a relationship between your reasons and what you feel you are taught through the course and its structure?

Notes

1 The University of York Department of Music is one of the UK's leading music departments for teaching and research; it has a particular focus on independent practical study, as well as on academic excellence among its students.
2 See the Appendix to this chapter for the survey Squestions.
3 An online survey-making tool: http://www.surveymonkey.com (accessed March 28, 2016).
4 Boden (1996a: 2) describes 'conceptual spaces' as 'styles of thinking', the origins of which are 'largely social'.
5 An example of a practical assessment could be a performance of a devised piece or a recital.
6 Due to the anonymity of the survey, we do not know which projects are being referred to here. We believe the respondent is commenting on modules such as Music in the Community, where participants are encouraged to try out ideas for workshops and similar activities within the classroom environment.
7 It can be the case that the university, course or module was not the student's preferred choice. However, the shared investment remains even when a student may not be on their first choice of module.
8 Society categories range from politics, debating and campaigning to faith, performance, games and leisure pursuits.
9 The Student Union runs various ongoing volunteering projects, including working with children and people with disabilities, as well as arts, cultural, charity and environmental projects.

References

Boden, M.A. (1996a). 'Introduction'. In: M.A. Boden (ed.), *Dimensions of Creativity* (pp. 1–12). Cambridge, MA: MIT Press.
——— (1996b). 'What is creativity?' In: M.A. Boden (ed.), *Dimensions of Creativity* (pp. 75–118). Cambridge, MA: MIT Press.

3 Creativity in higher music education

Views of university music lecturers

Elizabeth Haddon

Creativity and creative skills are increasingly recognised as key attributes for music students, particularly concerning engagement with their studies (Brinkman, 2010) and subsequent employment (Burnard and Haddon, 2015). This chapter explores the views of a sample of lecturers working in the Music Department at the University of York, a department known for its creative ethos since its founding in 1965. As in other UK university music departments, the broad range of lecturers' interests and specialist areas of composing, performing, teaching and research create a rich environment for student learning which offers valuable possibilities for researching creativity. This chapter complements Chapter 2 by Natalie Edwards, James Whittle and Alice Wright, which details students' conceptualisations of creativity in the same music department. To avoid duplication of detail relating to the course structure, it is recommended that readers refer to Chapter 2 for an overview of the programme.

The subject of creativity has a rich and evolving literature (see, for example, Pope, 2005, for a detailed overview). Approaches to the concept have ranged from the behaviourist idea of individual creativity linked to notions of talent and giftedness (Gardner, 1993) to a 'democratic' perspective proposing that 'all people are capable of creative achievement in some area of activity, provided that the conditions are right and they have acquired the relevant knowledge and skills' (National Advisory Committee on Creative and Cultural Education, 1999: paragraph 25). Further perspectives involve recognition of creativity as 'a process by which a symbolic domain in the culture is changed' (Csikszentmihalyi, 1996: 8) and an understanding of creativity from a sociocultural perspective (Amabile, 1996) involving domain-relevant skills, creativity-relevant processes, intrinsic motivation and the social environment. The view of 'a sociology of multiple musical creativities' (Burnard, 2012: 4) recognises a fluid relationship between cultural and social systems, related capitals and habitus, acknowledging that real-world musical practice encompasses multiple creativities; for example, career and entrepreneurial creativities; improvisational, compositional, songwriting and digital creativities; communal creativities, critical listening creativities, and empathic creativities (Burnard and Haddon, 2015). Therefore, 'musical creativities assume many forms, and serve many diverse functions, and are deeply embedded in the dynamic flux and mutation of a musician's personal and sociocultural life' (Burnard, 2012: 213).

In higher education, creativity has been positioned as a 'wicked problem' involving issues of rapid change in the employment market and in societal and personal well-being (Jackson, 2008). Previous studies have identified ideas associated by academics with creativity (Jackson and Shaw, 2006) and considerations relating to creativity and curriculum design (Edwards, McGoldrick and Oliver, 2006). Jackson and Shaw (2006: 90) summarised academics' perceptions of creativity as being associated with originality, imagination, 'exploring for the purpose of discovery', innovation, adaptation and transference, and communication. In their synthesis of the findings of Edwards, McGoldrick and Oliver relating to creativity and curriculum design, the survey responses from academics were concerned with creativity as personal innovation; creativity working at and across boundaries; creativity within the 'holistic idea of graduateness – the capacity to connect and do things with what has been learnt and to utilise this knowledge to learn in other situations'; creativity as making sense out of complexity, and 'creativity as a process of narrative-making in order to present the "real curriculum" in ways that conform to the regulatory expectations of how a curriculum should be framed' (Jackson and Shaw, 2006: 91). A subsequent study by Kleiman (2008) involving interviews with 12 academics from a range of disciplines found five main categories of creativity: a constraint-focused experience, a process-focused experience, a product-focused experience, a transformation-focused experience, and a fulfilment-focused experience. These suggest complex and varied views of creativity across disciplines.

Within higher music education, issues of creativity are further complicated by the positioning of the subject within an institutional audit culture in which creativity may be constrained by the enforced application of ubiquitous policies and procedures imposed by a higher-level management team (Smith-Bingham, 2006; Haddon and Potter, 2014). Furthermore, the longstanding association of creativity with composing, improvising and arranging (Philpott, 2001) may not only hinder recognition of creativity in other areas, but may also impede discussion of the comprehensive needs of the discipline at managerial level.

This chapter explores these complexities through the views of a sample of university music lecturers concerning creative teaching in higher music education. Staff were asked whether they would be interested in participating in research, either through completing a questionnaire or taking part in a semi-structured interview. Nine full-time members of staff opted for interviews, which took 40–90 minutes, and two others returned questionnaires. Their specialist research areas included composition, musicology, world music, early music, performance, analysis and music technology, and their academic experience as lecturers ranged from fewer than 10 years to over 40 years. The interviewer asked how staff would define creativity; whether it had been explored during teacher training or professional development; how staff felt about creativity within the music department (if creativity was integral to the department, whether they felt there was a culture of creativity and, if so, how this might be conveyed to students); whether they taught for 'creative learning' and, if so, what they wanted the students to experience and learn; how creativity might be facilitated; whether it was modelled by staff; how creativity might operate in areas beyond composition, performance and improvisation, and how teaching for creative learning might benefit students, both now and in future employment. The interviews were transcribed and returned to the interviewees for comments and approval; subsequently, the collated data were thematically analysed through an iterative coding process. Participants were invited to comment on a draft of this chapter; this process provided the opportunity to check the interview and questionnaire data in context and to clarify comments.

Defining creativity

In response to the question 'How would you define creativity?', lecturers expressed divergent individual and collective perspectives. The elusive properties of creativity were noted in relation to its 'mystical' nature; one lecturer felt that 'to define it is in itself a restriction on the possibilities that creativity might offer'; another suggested avoiding defining it, as it is 'one of those things that you know when it's there, or you experience'; it could be 'intangible' in performance, the 'something extra that's not on the page ... in any type of activity, the thing that goes beyond the mechanics of just doing it'. Creativity was also problematic: context-dependent, and possibly 'value-laden' – sometimes 'entangled' with concepts of 'talent' or 'ability'. However, lecturers generally concurred that creativity meant the ability to make something new, involving 'the skills and the knowledge ... to enable you to move around in the space of possibilities'; this needed curiosity, confidence, imagination and invention 'to approach tasks, problems or issues in new ways' which could involve 'the ability to see potentialities – for example, what can be made with existing materials, what the medium is capable of in terms of the plastic arts, but also for the fusing of existing ideas in more abstract fields'. This could result in a 'change to a very small element of a task or problem or can be a complete overturning of what has been tried before'.

Several responses emphasised that while creativity might involve applying existing knowledge within 'old, established parameters', it was necessary to 'step outside the familiar and bypass routine', therefore utilising 'reflection and evaluation and real introspection' as part of an active process which 'prompts a kind of change or difference of perspective in some way'. It was also suggested that 'to do music well, that extra dimension is assumed as being part of what we do', and this idea of an omnipresent creative orientation was further enhanced through comments indicating that the subject was difficult to articulate – not necessarily part of any overtly conscious thought in relation to the individual's own areas of musical practice as it was implicitly embedded in working processes.

Evolving creative pedagogical practices:
Lecturers' previous experience

Only two participants had received pedagogical training addressing creativity. The others had either begun their careers before the establishment of training courses or noted that training focused on other areas. Therefore, they learned to teach 'the hard way, through making a mess of things, experimenting, seeing what worked and what didn't'; from observing others ('I followed certain kinds of models, or reacted against certain kinds of models that I'd experienced'), and from participation in and reflection on collaborative teaching.

The two lecturers whose training had included a focus on creativity discussed different orientations towards this. The first noted the inspiration of John Finney, at Cambridge University, who 'taught his [PGCE] students to think very widely about possibilities, and in a non-prescriptive way … getting different types of outcome from the same problem, the same set of parameters', which influenced 'different realisations and approaches on a creative issue' in teaching. The other lecturer detailed varied experiences of formal training which included training to teach composition, working as a composition animateur with children, and PGCAP training.[1] Three different foci were identified: first, 'talking around the problem … how do you teach creativity; how do you teach someone to compose?'; second, 'realising creativity, and stimulating creativity, and getting things happening with the children, and inspiring them', and in the PGCAP, 'it was more about how can we teach creatively, it was never actually teach creativity but how can we be creative teachers, I think, was the idea that would make things more inspiring, it would allow better learning … it's a useful way of solving problems'. It was recognised that reflection and analysis of these processes was vital for informing one's own practice as a lecturer.

These views were reinforced by other comments which suggested that lecturers' personal educational experiences strongly influenced their teaching philosophies, either through rejecting restrictive models of undergraduate training and rigid teaching in instrumental lessons which allowed little creative freedom, or through identification with positive practices – for example, not making 'a distinction between scholarly approaches to music and practical approaches to music', bringing in ideas from 'left field' in lectures which were 'absolutely inspirational', realising that 'understanding comes from exposure to all these different views and ideas and then trying things out for yourself', and therefore 'it's a really vital thing to set up those opportunities and allow synthesis'. Furthermore, the working processes of one composer, which involved writing for specific performers and enjoying developing material with them, led to a commitment to help students 'understand the social context of what they're making', and to a desire in teaching contexts to 'set up and enable a situation where people feel they can say what they want to say, and there is validity to it, worth the experiment'.

Aspirations for the learner

Lecturers provided a range of aspirations for the learner, which included enabling students to develop an 'informed view' through 'providing a really good set of exposure to context, in a really tangible way that's tied to actual work that goes on'. This could involve exploring material made by the lecturer, by the group, or from external sources. Lecturers stressed the importance of ensuring 'a diversity of teaching [through providing] options and choices, and also the rationale to help negotiate these options and choices'. Staff felt that it was important to communicate diversity of expectations to students, as one undergraduate project would inevitably have a different focus and modes of teaching from another: 'these things are often very context specific … our students are quite diverse in some ways, and their experience of creativity … and the extent to which they're willing to try things out is quite diverse';

therefore, the student will have 'certain expectations, and these are rightly quite different and so what works in one situation and what seems creative … might not be so much in another'. Within this breadth of experience, it was hoped that students would 'question assumptions and rethink the familiar', which 'should help them develop a more flexible mindset, and this in turn can create the conditions for creativity'.

However, this lecturer thought that a perceived separation of students' self-view as either composer or performer, promoted by choices in pre-university education, could be challenged by 'more opportunities to muddle all of that up a bit more', enabling 'a sense of what it is to explore ideas creatively and to make things', to 'take more risks' with more 'occasions where [students] can try out performance and composition in ways where they're not going to be judged in a conventional concert … or assessment situation, that they can use these modes as ways of showing understanding, developing understanding and out of that comes something creative'. This would also promote 'a way of understanding music … it becomes about working with other musicians … understanding each other's minds, spinning ideas off each other'. Opportunities for this type of engagement are provided in some of the projects, and in ensembles, but because students are able to select which projects and ensembles they participate in, not all students will benefit from these opportunities.

Lecturers were also keen to emphasise the aim of student ownership, not only through enabling students to 'work things out for themselves' rather than be given all the information, but also, in collaborative activities, to consider 'how ownership issues might play out across the piece', communicating that each student needs to make a contribution and therefore 'it's got to be very clear that there's a kind of open playing field for setting up different types of idea'. Furthermore, 'there does have to be an element of selection … rejection may be a time-limited thing and there may be other moments where that person's ideas are exactly what you need', and therefore lecturers were keen to guard against anything or anyone 'trying to shut people's creativity off'. Therefore, ownership further involves students in questioning process and product and in evaluating their own input and that of their peers in creative activities, and in staff-led ensemble settings involves acknowledging student contributions, allowing them to take ideas forward both within the particular group and by additionally supporting students in non-departmental ensembles or work in other contexts such as musical projects in the community.

Aspirational tensions

Lecturers' aspirations for the learner underpin every element of the design of their teaching, from structure and content to delivery and support. However, lecturers perceived some tensions between staff and student aspirations. Staff were keen to encourage students to engage creatively during project sessions and in their work for assessment, but thought that students were sometimes reluctant to engage with activities taking them outside their preconceived notions of ability, for example, mentioning resistance from 'non-singers' to singing and from those not identifying as composers to composing. However, 'it's only when you work with sounds that you really start to hear the relationships and you start to form creative relationships between one sound and another', thus students need to be involved in the practical making of their work. These difficulties appear to be entangled with longstanding student anxieties about outcomes, particularly as school education 'is more and more about getting things right, about understanding, having the right information, being able to put it together in the right way and ticking all the boxes ... to conform, to do things in the way that people are expecting', which can be 'quite damaging to the willingness to try out new things, or to push things in different directions'. Therefore, 'we're trying to help students in some ways unlearn a bit of that, or at the very least question it'.

However, while students have freedom to choose essay topics and programmes for performance, and receive guidance and support in preparation for assessment, it was felt that students do 'come to get the best mark ... they're strategic and have conflicting pools which have been ingrained in them since school and they therefore take a very conservative and safe and risk-averse attitude because they don't want to get low marks and they've invested a lot'. One lecturer thought that creativity was associated with 'the pressure to be original and people get terrified by that', proposing that 'if you can make connections and show critical thinking and a bit of research ... that should be enough'; however, it was also recognised that 'there's a desire to get a high mark which does not seem to translate into a desire to do things particularly creatively, whereas actually, precisely the way you get a first is by doing something creative'. Another lecturer suggested that through pressures of 'consumer culture' and institutional policy changes which inflicted modularisation on the department, 'education is coming second to assessment', and this affected both teaching and student engagement: summative assessment tasks were the focus of much student concern, whereas formative tasks were sometimes viewed as non-essential by students.

Sustaining and developing a creative culture

While these issues are relevant to most, if not all, music departments in higher education, participants also articulated the desire to sustain a highly creative departmental culture, conveyed through promotional material and open day activities: even 'the underlying principles by which we interview the students here enshrine the necessity of a creative attitude in the students'. This ethos encourages students to be proactive and independent, and provides possibilities for using initiative and displaying imagination and creativity even in the very first module, the Practical Project, in which all first-year students work with second- and third-year students to produce public performances, either of an existing piece or of material devised entirely by students, in the sixth week of the course. This project primes the students 'to be kind of dumped into unexpected problems or unexpected environments' and to respond creatively. In addition, 'from the day they arrive they see tons of stuff happening around them all the time and they quickly learn "ah, that's where the bar is set" ... and they just get on with it'. Students also notice 'manifestations of creativity in what goes on in the teaching spaces and the concert halls'; they can participate in a vibrant community of peer-led activities, they note the diversity of modules on offer and teaching methods, and also 'see the staff encouraging all sorts of unusual ways of setting about a topic'. The solo project (an independent study module taking place in the final undergraduate year, which is a project of the student's own choice, often involving practical work, editing, recording, community workshops and composition, as well as essays) offers many opportunities to embrace creativity; it was recognised that 'the way we encourage creativity is through the freedom of our course', which staff stressed must be defended against attempts to standardise academic practice with that of other departments within the university.

Staff clearly aspire to promulgate and develop the positive creative learning environment which has been a feature of this forward-looking department for fifty years, and also noted its effect on the reinvention of their own practice:

> the department as whole, puts itself ... in a position of having to invent new ways of doing things, the project system, the timetabling ... it's at least an invitation ... to find a different answer than the one you had last time you taught the module or thought about the structure of the course.

Another lecturer observed that each member of staff possesses an array of very varied personal research interests which inform their teaching; this helps students to 'have a much more open mind about what music is' and fed positively into the creative culture. While it was thought that there was no contradiction for lecturers in individually possessing such diversity of personal research interests, it was felt that 'if we, ourselves, as faculty, can be a [research] problem that the students have to solve, that's very useful'.

Creative teaching for creative learning

The following sections detail lecturers' discussions of ways in which they constructed teaching to promote creativity. These divide into comments concerning the structure of teaching and those relating to practice within taught sessions.

The structure and ethos of academic project teaching

Most undergraduate projects are taught for one full day and one half day each week during a four-week period, though some now operate on a 'long-thin' basis with more sessions equalling the same contact time (30 hours in total) over a greater number of weeks. One lecturer noted that:

> I might spend the first session [of a full project day] with quite a lot of more standard lecture/seminar type stuff, certainly lots of discussion, ideally bits of group discussion as well, but primarily I'm showing them stuff, getting across certain kinds of ideas ... I'm very much leading it.

Other lecturers agreed that the provision of knowledge was important: 'at the beginning you have to be a teacher and then you might move on to be a facilitator' as students need 'information and guidance' otherwise 'they can't progress the way you want them to'.

In composition projects, lecturers could 'feed in information all the time, so they're listening to things all the time that will surprise them … if I play them Diamanda Galás or something and they thought they were going to get Pierre Boulez it's also mind-blowing'. Another staff composer explained that while many processes could encourage compositional creativity and the development of an individual voice, it was essential to enable 'the student to clarify, for themselves, what it is they're trying to do', and that it was necessary for students to experience a broad range of music and therefore reach a stage where 'they're making [compositional] choices because of choice as oppose to a lack of knowledge'.

In projects concerned with historically informed performance, lecturers might provide information on the 'ground rules' relating to the composer's expectations and available information to lay the foundations for a process in which 'a performer has to think, "these are the boundaries; where do I creatively nudge them in order to be expressive and to communicate?"' because 'as performers, our creativity is taking the information which includes not just the notes that are there … but also things that the composer can't really indicate – rubato, tempo freedom, over-dotting, under-dotting, how to resolve a dissonance'.

In projects on music technology, providing a firm foundation was vital: 'I try and give people things to do in the studio which are quite directed … they get tasters of different activities and I try and construct things in such a way that there's a framework within which they're working, so that they're not going to come completely unstuck.' This participant discussed the tensions between building structured knowledge for sound engineering to enable 'a proper understanding of the instrument [the studio] and the right technique' versus a more experimental approach: 'go in there, and see what happens', which might 'lead to all sorts of bad habits and poor technique and lack of understanding … without the ability to transfer that knowledge and those skills to more difficult situations which have some unexpected problems'. Therefore, a certain amount of procedural knowledge is required as a foundation for creativity, and the educator has a responsibility to establish understanding of good practice and technical competence before imbuing an outlook described by another lecturer as involving 'doing things in an imaginative way and in a speculative way … wanting to resist things which are too systematised and processed'. This risk-taking outlook, in which the outcome may not necessarily be totally successful, could be transferable.

One participant recognised that 'there's two things: allowing people to be creative, and then there's preparing people for creativity'; however, if the latter 'goes on for too long you feel in a very uncreative kind of purgatory – "When are we going to get our hands on it?" "When are lectures going to stop and when can we do this?"', but 'if you go through that, then you arguably might be able to be more creative once you get there'. The importance of tools as well as knowledge was articulated:

> It's important that students also learn what perhaps feel like some uncreative tools. For instance, they need to be able to engage with the way ideas/ music are communicated through language/notation/performance, and

practise doing that themselves on a small scale before you can expect them to make any leaps (or perhaps to communicate any leaps they might be making). They need some models to look at ... and then practise the kind of process involved.

In the context of a project on musical analysis, structured activities were used to enable students to develop skills and tools through which creative understanding could be expressed:

> We looked in detail at a number of compositions. We explored analytical techniques that have been used to examine them. We looked at critiques of those techniques, and new responses to the problems they (the pieces and the techniques) posed – many of those were very imaginative, creative. We did some analysis ourselves – as a class/in breakouts [small groups]. We also did some compositional work that took those ideas and used them as starting points – as a way of understanding the processes involved, but also in order to make something new (as a class/in breakouts). We also thought about the way in which a reading or an analysis can make the piece 'new'.

This idea of 'starting points' was widely used in other projects:

> I've got various different workshop formats and different starting points ... in the project on the relationship between words and music ... there's quite a lot of potentially theoretical stuff ... but we also look at quite a lot of the ways in which composers have exploited that ... but I do find it's much more effective if I then find time to have a session where I have some starting points for them to do exactly that – to work with little bits of text ... as a little group they are effectively developing something – developing and making a composition for themselves that they will show to the whole group ... that is a way of exploring exactly the things and concepts and ideas we've been talking about and that will take them in different directions.

In 'Staging an Opera', students were invited to 'take a scene of an opera and stage it in two different ways ... to emphasise the possibilities for creativity within interpretation, and to show them how one starting point can be developed in very different ways'. In composition projects, it was essential to 'get people making stuff on day one, because the longer you let people sit there taking in ideas and watching what other people do the harder it gets for them to act'. This was enabled through setting 'the sort of exercises that they can take in any direction ... like ... "choose five notes; now make a piece for any two instruments in the group that we've got here"', affirming that any style would be acceptable, thus moving students away from preconceived notions of what was permissible, expected or legitimate, and towards greater self-belief and expression of their own creative individuality. Therefore, it was vital for students to be active participants; it was recognised that 'you could have all the ideas in the world', but through working with material, 'something creative happens ... [students] end up ... producing stuff which actually can be interesting and delightful and can help illuminate the concepts'.

Furthermore, this would require relinquishing traditional lecturing roles and the idea of control: while students needed to 'be willing to play with the stuff in the first place ... to try stuff and go down false routes ... to take risks ... with a sense of criti-cality about it', the lecturer also needed to deploy a similar mindset: 'a lot of it is about being willing to try things out ... not always being in control ... for them to know that they don't always have to have somebody who knows it all, who's going to tell them, but we'll find a way through'. While there is a danger that students might think 'this is a shambles, [the lecturer] doesn't know anything; I wonder what [they're] doing?', this participant saw the educational benefits: 'you want them to recognise that being directive isn't always going to get the best results, or just providing information or saying "do this, do that" isn't always positive'. Therefore, rather than model crea-tivity directly, lecturers model a creative mindset, encouraging students to be proac-tive in engaging with learning activities which extend their knowledge of a subject through creative practice and 'possibility thinking' (Craft, 2001).

In addition, lecturers were aware that labelling and defining how creativity was happening through various activities would detract from students' personal extrapolation of meaning from creative engagement: attempting 'to communicate specifically to people when they're being creative ... "we're having a very cre-ative piano lesson today" would have immediately destroyed it'; this participant said 'I clearly feel viscerally uncomfortable about this idea of highlighting it'. Another lecturer felt that 'if it's done well then it wouldn't need to be talked about ... the students have got it into their systems and it doesn't have to be artic-ulated or even explained in that way'. Therefore, lecturers were aware of the need for students to create their own understanding of learning, which might inform higher-level thinking and benefits to cognitive development beyond the particular learning outcomes defined for each project.

Teaching practices within undergraduate projects

In addition to the examples already mentioned, lecturers outlined further exam-ples of techniques for creative teaching used in undergraduate projects. It was acknowledged that different types of teaching were needed for different contexts and learning outcomes, and that the lecturer would often be 'up against all sorts of different factors, different pressures' that impinged on his or her consideration of the most appropriate form for the learning. This was also influenced by 'resources of time, space, practicalities' and the understanding that 'you can't force someone to be creative, and you do your best to create – to generate situations in which they have the opportunity to be creative, but they can choose not to be'.

The idea that 'creativity in whatever form usually involves some kind of original or unusual outcome that is inspiring in some way or prompts us to see, hear or think about something differently' suggests that it is frequently positioned by these lecturers as an active tool for learning which elicits a change in the learner. This could occur through a change in knowledge, for example, through the assimilation of discipline-specific information and from 'material that comes from outside the discipline of music … from psychology, from physics, technology' in studio-based projects and from phonetics and linguistics in others.

This change could also occur through putting students in a position where they encounter a new problem, or perhaps more powerfully, to put them 'in a position where you have to devise a new approach', which may involve imposing restrictions of some kind which mean that 'the thing that you wanted to do, the thing that you are creatively inclined to do, isn't possible because it goes against the rules, so you have to [find] a different kind of creativity'. This setting up of what might be termed 'playful constraints' was recognised by other lecturers, particularly in relation to composition. One felt that 'it depends which stage of the process you're at. Probably at the beginning constraints are good; as you get closer to the goal of creating whatever it becomes more tangible in your mind and therefore you are less comfortable having to make changes'; further on in the process, flexibility was needed, as boundaries 'can stop you being responsive to things that emerge as part of the creative process'. Another composer suggested that 'if you want people to really learn a lot quickly and develop quickly, the easiest way to do that is to limit them to a particular style … that's easier for everybody; they know exactly what's required'. However, this lecturer stressed that 'I don't teach that way, because for me it's not creative enough and it's not allowing people to follow their own heart and their own voice, to develop their own imagination.' The responses suggest that what is valued by both lecturers and students is the development and empowerment of the individual, and that teaching in this department is oriented towards discovery rather than imposition.

As noted earlier, the freedom to select essay topics and programmes for performance means that students invest in their own creative response to a subject. In a project based on sensation and perception, involving material from other disciplines, students were expected to 'write an essay in detail about a particular topic they've covered on the course, but they've also got to identify how they can use that knowledge from outside the discipline and demonstrate its applicability within the discipline'. Some examples included:

> compositional fragments where they've looked at theories of auditory streaming and how we've organised melodies … they might have created a short piece based on their knowledge of timbral perception … or they might think about vocal performing and clarity of vowels with high pitches, but it could also be a music therapy exercise or music in the community, whatever they want to do, provided they bring it back into the discipline … that's where they're asked to be creative – they're being asked to use their imagination, to think about how this often quite dry knowledge that's expressed in charts and tables … how they can bring it in and make use of it as musicians.

This approach, which could be defined as setting a very open aim and then creating an 'inquiry-based' learning culture, was endorsed by other lecturers, who advocated the facilitation of student initiative through promoting a questioning culture in which lecturers aspire to enable student ownership and encourage students to 'find an expression of what defines them, individually, and not to be clones, and not accept handed-down methodologies without question'. One other major concern for lecturers was to prioritise musical understanding; in projects on non-Western music, this could be through aiming to ensure that 'it feeds back into their regular music and makes them think about it in a different way', therefore building connections between what might seem to students like disparate practices and encouraging a holistic rather than compartmentalised sense of learning.

Creativity and future prospects

Lecturers identified that students benefited from creative teaching for creative learning through the experience of being individually and collectively creative, and thus developed 'blue-sky thinking, thinking out of the box, disruptive thinking'. It was noted that 'if a student has the ability to approach things without being bound to past practice, and is therefore in a position to find new solutions to problems, he or she has a transferable skill that is useful in any situation'. Not only was creativity viewed as 'one of the key components of a good student', it was also regarded as 'a way of approaching the world' which would have lasting benefits through graduates' future lives, and therefore, 'creativity is one of the most important skills we can help our students to develop'.

Concluding thoughts

Through the accounts of creative teaching for creative learning from music lecturers at the University of York, we can sense the complex interrelationships between the individual student, the lecturer and the student cohort, and knowledge, attitudes, processes and products. Creativity appears to be implicitly embedded in lecturers' working processes within their teaching as well as their own composition, performance and research: as one lecturer noted when asked about creative teaching: 'Isn't it to an extent just good teaching?' The responses from these participants suggest that creativity was not considered to be a special enhancement adding extra value; it was essential to teaching and to student learning, not least because 'we teach through doing as much as we can', imbuing the learning context with processes of active student involvement, student ownership and the pursuit of open-ended goals which could be approached with considerable freedom.

While it was recognised that 'creativity operates on different time scales' and therefore not all students would produce 'an exceptional piece of work' within the time frame for assessment, it was felt that the values imbued through the processes facilitated, supported and encouraged by staff would result in creativity being an ongoing preoccupation essential to students' future careers. Furthermore, a concern to position the work of the department as 'creating music that has relevance to culture and society and people' would also impart an ethos of social awareness to students. This idea of connectivity was also articulated in relation to school music education, as lecturers acknowledged the creative work of the student-led music education group, but also stressed the need for greater emphasis on creativity in pre-university education.

In delineating lecturers' concerns, aspirations and teaching practices, this chapter shows that this particular creative culture inspires reconsideration and refreshment of teaching practices which reinvigorate staff; in addition, students' realisation of these concepts provides further inspiration for lecturers: 'it's what keeps me here, simple as that'. While political, financial and managerial issues inevitably present constant challenges to higher education music departments, this chapter suggests that creative teaching for creative learning provides a fundamental reaffirmation of the value of the music degree, and is an inspiration both to staff and to students.

Acknowledgments

Sincere thanks to colleagues at the University of York for their generous participation in this research.

Note

1 The Postgraduate Certificate in Academic Practice is a UK teaching qualification for university lecturers, primarily aimed to support new academic staff with less than three years' full-time teaching experience.

References

Amabile, T.M. (1996). *Creativity in Context: Update to 'The Social Psychology of Creativity'*. Boulder, CO: Westview Press.
Brinkman, D.J. (2010). 'Teaching Creatively and Teaching for Creativity'. *Arts Education Policy Review*, 111(2), 48–50.
Burnard, P. (2012). *Musical Creativities in Practice*. Oxford: Oxford University Press.
———— and Haddon, E. (eds) (2015). *Activating Diverse Musical Creativities: Teaching and Learning in Higher Music Education*. London: Bloomsbury.
Craft, A. (2001). 'Little c Creativity'. In: A. Craft, B. Jeffrey and M. Leibling (eds), *Creativity in Education* (pp. 45–61). London: Continuum.
Csikszentmihalyi, M. (1996). *Creativity: Flow and the Psychology of Discovery and Invention*. New York: HarperCollins.
Edwards, M., McGoldrick, C. and Oliver, M. (2006). 'Creativity and curriculum in Higher Education: Academics' Perspectives'. In: N.J. Jackson, M. Oliver, M. Shaw and J. Wisdom (eds), *Developing Creativity in Higher Education: An Imaginative Curriculum* (pp. 59–73). London: Routledge.
Gardner, H. (1993). *Creating Minds: An Anatomy of Creativity Seen Through the Lives of Freud, Einstein, Picasso, Stravinsky, Eliot, Graham, and Gandhi*. New York: Basic Books.
Haddon, E. and Potter, J. (2014). 'Creativity and the Institutional Mindset'. In: I. Papageorgi and G. Welch (eds), *Advanced Musical Performance: Investigations in Higher Education Learning* (pp. 129–41). Farnham: Ashgate.

Jackson, N. (2008). 'Tackling the Wicked Problem of Creativity in Higher Education'. Background paper for a presentation at the *Australian Research Council Centre for the Creative Industries and Innovation International Conference*, Brisbane, June 2008. Retrieved 15 May 2015 from http://imaginativecurriculumnetwork.pbworks.com/f/WICKED+PROBLEM+OF+CREATIVITY+IN+HIGHER+EDUCATION.pdf.

———— and Shaw, M. (2006). 'Developing Subject Perspectives on Creativity in Higher Education'. In: N.J. Jackson, M. Oliver, M. Shaw and J. Wisdom (eds), *Developing Creativity in Higher Education: An Imaginative Curriculum* (pp. 89–108). London: Routledge.

Kleiman, P. (2008). 'Towards Transformation: Concepts of Creativity in Higher Education'. *Innovations in Education and Teaching International*, 45(3), 209–17.

National Advisory Committee on Creative and Cultural Education (1999). *All Our Futures: Creativity, Culture and Education*. London: Department for Education and Employment.

Philpott, C. (2001). 'Three Curriculum Issues in Music Education'. In: C. Philpott (ed.), *Learning to Teach Music in the Secondary School: A Companion to School Experience* (pp. 238–56). London: Routledge.

Pope, R. (2005). *Creativity: Theory, History, Practice*. London: Routledge.

Smith-Bingham, R. (2006). 'Public Policy, Innovation and the Need for Creativity'. In: N. Jackson, M. Oliver, M. Shaw and J. Wisdom (eds), *Developing Creativity in Higher Education: An Imaginative Curriculum* (pp. 10–18). London: Routledge.

4 Considering creative teaching in relation to creative learning

Developing a knowing–doing orientation for change in higher music education

Pamela Burnard

Learning the politics of academic culture in post-secondary publicly funded institutions is a complex business. Students and institutions are co-dependent. Higher music education institutions are increasingly challenged to improve how students learn to become successful musicians and navigate student-focused approaches (Kompf and Denicolo, 2013). The 'culture of specialism' (Perkins, 2013), a characteristic of conservatoires, often sees performers of classical music assume superiority over specialised performers of jazz, pop or folk. The ways in which students learn to navigate the learning site, as they seek to become professional musicians and performers, reflects social navigation practices which may be deemed deviant or compliant to particular cultural brokers. A complex dynamic of institutional expectation, peer influence, social capital and cultural capital – something which Perkins (2013) identifies as a kind of 'pecking order' of prestigious value – arrives 'in' music 'about' music, 'of' music and 'through' its performance, in terms of social positioning within the institution and alignment with social networks and musical hierarchies in contemporary fields.

What students come to know, learn to become and do, as musicians, of course, is not clear-cut. Reflecting on what makes for a 'creative musician' involves commitment to looking anew at things as they are, giving form to the idea that a consistent feature of tradition is that past practices are continually changing, as are the values and practices that make, one would hope, radical improvements to the processes and outcomes of any particular musical performance or project. Reflecting on what makes for 'creative teaching' in relation to 'creative learning' is only part of the picture for understanding and developing innovative practices in higher music education, since teaching for creativity, together with the mutual dependency of learning and teaching, also needs to be acknowledged. One of the biggest challenges for higher music education, particularly in the present climate of radical institutional reform, programme renewal, and changing standards of valuation and review, is in the *institutional* strategic planning and forms of practice that are given social and cultural recognition by conferring degrees. Building academic communities of practice with an ethos of creative teaching in relation to creative learning affords high value to curiosity and risk-taking, to ownership, autonomy and making connections (Bennett and Burnard, 2016).

The untold, unaddressed stories of academics, musician-artists and artist-researchers, in terms of identity-bearing signifiers of professional expertise within higher education academic cultures (Upitis, 2006; Sawyer, 2004), combined with the view of 'academics as their own agents of learning and change' (McAlpine and Åkerlind, 2010: 3), contribute to the complex labyrinth of expectations and change demands for academia in the twenty-first century (Wenger, 1998).

Whether your work identifies you as a scholar (that is, an academic), artist (professional musician), educator (teacher), researcher, or any combination of these, the range of work characteristics that effective higher music educators are either in possession of or are capable of acquiring include qualities of passion, driving curiosity, depth/range of knowledge(s), critical reflexivity and creativity. The name that we give an activity or process (such as 'teaching') acts as a 'frame' for how we put it into practice. As with 'unscripted theatre' and 'jazz music', where there is a body of accumulated knowledge built up around the terms, so too with 'creative teaching'. Creative teachers make a conscious effort to develop improvisational expertise, purposeful play characterised by risk-taking and learning through mistakes as effective educational practices that create improvisatory spaces where the teacher/learner power balance allows freedom for creativity. Within creative learning literature, the dialogical, reactive end of the spectrum is commonly foregrounded as a pedagogical strategy for encouraging creative learning, with teachers 'standing back' and positioning themselves 'off centre-stage' (Cremin, Burnard and Craft, 2006). Then there is teacher-generated criticality, which challenges students and encourages them to engage in critical struggle in relation to their own work and that of their peers. Proactive intervention, typically in the form of long-term initiatives between artists and scholars, and by artist-scholars, usually involves an arts organisation that both funds the project and has direct input in its planning and delivery. Local government arts offices have acted as major stakeholders in supporting and developing partnership initiatives. Research evidence highlights the impact of partnerships (involving professional artists and teachers in collaboration with pupils) in developing creative learners who can succeed in a twenty-first-century economy that rewards creativity and innovation.

In this chapter, I will explore some assumptions which underpin the concept of 'creative learning', what 'creative learning' is, and why promoting it is a necessity – not an option – to improve the level of higher music education and teachers' status as creative professionals. But what constitutes 'creative teaching' in higher music education remains ambiguous. The language is confusing, and it is common for slippage to occur between the terms 'teacher creativity', 'creative teaching', 'teaching for creativity' and 'creative learning'. I will discuss studies that explore partnership programmes which aim to foster and promote classroom creativities through the development of positive learning environments in which students can take risks, engage in imaginative activity, and do things differently.

One of Maurice Galton's many groundbreaking projects in educational research, the Oracle (Observational Research and Classroom Learning Evaluation) project, provided a detailed picture of the range of strategies observed in British classrooms. In Galton, Simon and Croll's study (1980), the pedagogic levels on which teachers operate were identified as: (a) *classroom practice* at the strategic level, which thematised teachers' intentions before the start of a lesson, and (b) *tactical decisions* in the 'moments of teaching', that is, minute-by-minute occurrences throughout the lesson. Galton, Simon and Croll identified a number of *teaching styles* which can be seen to be linked closely to different types of pupil behaviour – some being more effective than others. Studies conducted in the following decade have largely confirmed these findings (Galton, Hargreaves and Comber, 1998). Similarly, the ongoing debates about (a) the disciplinary specificity of musician-artists and (b) engaging institutional learning communities by activating diverse creativities recognise that the translation of educational policy into pedagogic practice in higher music education is neither straightforward nor unproblematic.

Higher music education teachers and learners have the option of co-constructing a *pedagogy* when the institutional learning community collaboration encompasses 'the act of teaching, together with the ideas, values and collective histories that inform, shape and explain that act' (Alexander, 2008: 38). For this to occur, the core acts of 'creative' teaching – namely, 'task, activity, interaction, and judgement' (ibid.: 78) – need to feature in the process of 'creative learning' within and across the higher education institutional and learning cultures. This is, of course, easier said than done.

In debates between academics and musician-artists, educators or students, different conceptions of the nature and practices of creative musical performance (such as forms of creative teaching and creative learning) can be institutionally bound up in the place and space that authorise the practice and cultures of learning in higher music education settings. Some artist-scholars typically use a more improvisational, open-ended approach in their teaching, while others often use a more structured style (Burnard and Swann, 2010).

This gives rise to a dilemma: How can the more unpredictable, improvisational approaches to teaching in higher music education be balanced against the more predictable, normative and accountable style of the higher education teacher? And how do we go about documenting and assessing creative learning? How are the politics of creative teaching in relation to creative learning institutionally bound up and valued within higher music education sectors?

Considering improvisational practices in relation to creative teaching

In higher music education, as in improvisation, creative teaching can be thought of as the discovery or invention and undertaking of musical experiments; this can take many forms and inflections while performing. As with improvisation, the notion of creative teaching, when defined as a performative act, moving flexibly and reflexively between scripted and unscripted sections – a kind of partly improvised and partly choreographed dance – tends to follow constructivist traditions of learning, in dynamic interaction with all those present.

Another relevant dimension of improvisation which is often referred to in music and theatre is 'going with the flow' or 'getting in the groove'. These skilled performances are based on a high degree of tacit knowledge and practice, just as is all professional expertise. Improvised behaviours involve 'ideas which leap to mind' (and to jazz players' fingers, according to Pike, 1974) and can be seen in the perceptual nature of responsiveness on the part of the teacher to students. This resonates with the notion of Nardone (1996), who considered the lived experience of improvisation to be a coherent synthesis of the body and mind engaged in socially valued conscious and pre-reflective activity. Similarly, when teachers and students work and learn creatively together, particularly if they are undertaking digital experiments, creativity and innovation become critical competences, and good practices are created (Thomson and Sefton-Green, 2011).

Berliner (1994: 216) offers a further understanding of the openness, uncertainty and improvisational practices and the conditions that allow individuals to be generative, adaptive and reciprocal. He says:

> The sense of exhilaration that characterises the artist's experiences under such circumstances is heightened for jazz musicians as storytellers by the activity's physical, intellectual and emotional exertion and by the intensity of struggling with creative processes under the pressure of a steady beat. From the outset of each performance, improvisers enter an artificial world of time in which reactions to the unfolding events of their tales must be immediate. Furthermore, the consequences of their actions are irreversible. Amid the dynamic display of imagined fleeting images and impulses – entrancing sounds and vibrant feelings, dancing shapes and kinetic gestures, theoretical symbols and perceptive commentaries – improvisers extend the logic of previous phrases, as ever-emerging figures on the periphery of their vision encroach upon and supplant those in performance … Few experiences are more deeply fulfilling.

The emergence of improvisational forms of creative teaching, of incorporating creativities in teaching performer-musicians in the context of university pedagogy classes, or of integrating creativity in the programme of study for instrumental music teaching, is a challenge for university teacher practice (Peters, 2014) and requires a shift in the paradigm of higher music education. Bennett Reimer (2003: 108–9), a philosopher and influential advocate for music education, insisted on the democratisation of creativity, in both teaching and learning, as this allows it to be something all people have to some degree, and he shows how creative teaching links to the co-construction of creative learning:

> Such a view of creativity as existing in degree, and as constituted of particular, identifiable ways of dealing with one's world, *provides a role for education.* Whatever the level of one's capacity to be creative at something, that level can be better achieved by educational interventions designed to improve one's thinking and doing so as to make them 'more creative'.

In higher education settings, when teachers and learners collaborate, their different conceptions of teaching and different paradigms of expertise must be resolved before they can construct an effective creative learning environment. Creative teaching represents the improvisational end of the paradox, while creative learning has been shown to help professional learning communities enliven and loosen up tightly scripted ways of teaching (Sefton-Green, 2008; Burnard and Swann, 2010). As one creative practitioner put it in Galton's (2010: 365) study:

> To me being here is about several things. One important thing for me is to look at a different model of working; of the ways artists can work with schools and teachers in a much more collaborative way rather than be expected to come in and deliver and then go away again. And another important thing is with the children. What we ... are trying to do here is to be a person who responds to ideas that the children are coming up with and then to bring our own practice to share.

In some cases, musician-artist university teacher identities are played out in particular professional roles where their pedagogy and values are regularly scrutinised and tested in the classroom, as behaviour managers fuelled/informed by an institutional dimension which often creates an inner conflict between skilfully modelling teacher attributes and pedagogic content knowledge (Kerchner, 2014). Musician-artists are stereotypically presented and seen as artists or arts practitioners, professionals involved in cultural production. Musician-artist university teachers can also see themselves as outsiders who come into an educational space and act as a catalyst for or challenger to learning – someone who provides ways of exploring the world which involve more sensory, immersive and improvisatory ways of working than are customary in tertiary classroom settings. Artist-musician university teachers can also see themselves as precisely *not* the teacher, but rather as the 'other' who is permitted to open up new contexts, new frontiers and challenges that are unfamiliar to the learners (Triantafyllaki, 2014).

It would seem, therefore, that higher music education institutions need to become spaces for creative teaching in relation to creative learning, where the affordances provided by diverse creativities, pedagogic experimentation and an emphasis on taking risks and allowing for the unexpected are deemed essential workplace practices.

Creative teaching for creative learning

In the decades following the publication of the influential report of the National Advisory Committee on Creative and Cultural Education (NACCCE, 1999), many subsequent government policies and advisory documents have indirectly increased the interest in partnerships and collaborations across higher music education and industry sectors. These partnerships are thought to have a direct impact on creative learning (Creative Partnerships, 2005), as well as an indirect impact on it by enhancing the teacher's ability to teach for creativity, even after the partnership has ended (Pope et al., 1999). In education, there is a small but growing body of research that identifies the potency of institutional and artistic collaborations (Burnard and Swann, 2010; Triantafyllaki and Burnard, 2010). The vision and the hope are that the creative learning of pupils and the creative pedagogic practices of teachers, alongside institutions as cultural and creative learning communities, will be changed by educational partnerships (McLellan et al., 2012).

The term 'creative learning' has been well documented, tracing back to policy, practice and research in creativity in education over the past two decades in the UK and elsewhere (NACCCE, 1999; Craft, 2005; Craft, Cremin and Burnard, 2008). Loveless (2008: 63) offers a useful summary in saying: 'Creative learning can be considered from different perspectives, either as the learning which enables creativity to be expressed, or the imaginative activity supporting learning and intellectual enquiry.'

In 2005, an International Symposium held at the University of Cambridge drew upon growing research and interest in creative learning; co-convener Anna Craft (2005: 5) concluded by saying that 'one of the outcomes of our thinking about how we document creative learning was a renewed focus on clarifying what it is we think we are capturing evidence about, and the urgent need for a flexible and evolutionary, and yet stable definition of "creative learning"'. The definition has continued to evolve. The Creative Partnership funded a *Progression in Creative Learning* (PiCL) study (reported in Craft, Cremin and Burnard, 2008: 77), which led to a further definition recognising the development of knowledge: 'Significant imaginative achievement as evidenced in the creation of new knowledge as determined by the imaginative insight of the person or persons responsible and judged by appropriate observers to be both original and of value as situated in different domain contexts'. While recognising the value of significant imaginative achievement in higher music education, in relation to creative learning we might still ask: What kind of practices should be 'known', and what are the 'knowing–doing' orientations needed for creative teaching to enable the development of creative learning?

If, as argued throughout this chapter, creative teaching dances between planned, scripted, deliberate, conscious episodes and opportunistic action, then how can teachers enact spontaneity in their teaching by yielding to the flow of its immediacy? From teacher expertise literature, we know that expert teachers master the structures of creative teaching – seen as a large repertoire of plans, routines and scripts – and do more than 'doing' music. In addition, creative teachers must master the practice of teaching – a range of teaching strategies which include improvisational forms. But what forms of pedagogy do these take?

Bernstein (1996) offers a helpful framework which differentiates between pedagogies in terms of *competence* and *performance*. Competence pedagogies focus on the learner and what the learner has achieved, and so tend to be 'active, creative and self-regulating'. Performance models of pedagogy place the emphasis upon clearly defined outputs so that learners are expected to acquire certain skills or to construct specific texts or products in fulfilment of the required outcome. The pedagogies of musician-artists tend to define themselves in terms of the specialist knowledge and skills they and others perceive they possess, and prioritise the development of learners' ideas and individual creativity, while encouraging them to reflect on the process and what has been achieved. The emphasis is on 'competence' pedagogies that pass a greater degree of control over learning to the learner.

The performance model of pedagogy, Bernstein (1996: 4) argues, 'places the emphasis upon a specific output of the acquirer [learner], upon a particular text the acquirer is expected to construct and upon the specialised skills necessary to the production of this specific output, text or product'. In any given teaching session, performance models might include, as a core act of teaching, improvisational forms which 'in the moment' promote learner independence and autonomy or require the teacher to spontaneously scaffold learning so as to help learners move forward. Higher music educators (that is, university teachers) are being pushed by two opposed agendas: they are being asked to promote creativity, while at the same time being required to meet accountability targets and research assessment outputs. The evidence from several studies is that there are many understandable tensions arising out of this paradox (Burnard and White, 2008).

Knowing and doing creative teaching in relation to creative learning: Introducing a knowing–doing orientation to change

The ways that student musician-artist-educators exist as creative learners provides an important clue as to how higher music artist-educators (that is, their teachers) can better negotiate a shift in paradigm of practice. In the same way that instruments are tuned on the basis of tension, so the success of pedagogic partnerships depends on the tension being maintained in balance. As teachers and students open themselves up to each other, they feel the pull of the other that demands respect. The point at which the pedagogic partnership results in the most effective learning environment is when improvisatory acts (of collaboration) and improvisations (in classroom activities) occur. When teachers and students attune to each other's ways of working, they render diverse classroom creativities in higher music education. These include practices which invite flexible thinking, risk-taking, multi-vocality or taking a new professional viewpoint. These practices are modelled on more improvised and less formulaic and fixed approaches to teaching. Creative teaching and creative learning are more likely to occur when the rigid division between teacher and student is relaxed, creating an improvisatory space where all members of the learning community jointly and authentically construct and reconstruct the improvisational flow and creativities in developing a knowing–doing orientation (Craft, Cremin and Burnard, 2008).

Being a musician-artist involves commitment to looking anew at things as they are, giving form to the idea that a consistent feature of tradition is that past practices are continually changing, as are values and practices that make, one would hope, radical improvements to the processes and outcomes of any particular musical project.

Being a musician-artist also involves working in those fields of music generally, and in music performance specifically. These are concerned with the
production and dissemination of an art form, with the art object being a form
of subjective reality and subjective knowledge. With subjectivism, meaning is
completely imposed on the object or constructed by the artist or audience. When
musician-artists work, they are seeking to understand experience and critically
examine and describe arts practice as the exploratory epistemology of subjectivism, aware of their own bias and reflexivity. This may entail developing new
understandings, new practices, new tools, and access to new forms of purposeful
activity inspired by contemporary fields of music. It may require a shift from a
narrowly specialised view of the 'subject' of music, through a new way of seeing
what musician-artists are doing and the application of what they have learned
by conducting research (Ball, 2012). This knowing–doing orientation champions
theorising practice, from a perspective that works within institutional parameters
while maintaining professional credibility – a position which is both distinctive
and defensible.

As stated earlier, what musicians know and do, of course, is not clear-cut. Yet
they do more than 'doing' music. The 'doing' or making or creating of music
is an object and subject of study which has been comprehensively explored by
historians, psychologists, sociologists and cultural commentators. If the goal
of musician-artists is to make music, then research by musicians about music-
making helps us to get a sense of how practices in the field can be conceptualised.
Furthermore, by positioning the way music is 'done' (that is, created and performed) in individual, historical and cultural contexts, discrete and comparative
approaches to musical performance inquiry 'in' music, 'about' music, 'of' music
and 'through' its performance become the premises of research in music. The
process of seeking explanations that can be captured in elegant yet powerful ways
carries high status as a goal of enquiry. What are the principles underlying how
creative teaching and creative learning are applied and viewed, and what is the
cultural impact of such practices? What rules and roles are carried within their
own legitimisation?

Creative and musical practices should be 'known' and the knowing–doing
orientation interrogated and studied as fields of music performance as diverse as
performance creating in original bands, as singer songwriters, as DJs and performance creating of composed musics and in live improvised musics. So why is it
that higher music educators find it difficult to equate the research coming out of
their advanced degree programmes with the measurements of research outcomes
maintained by others within and beyond the academy?

Addressing the knowing–doing gap: Orienting the development of creative teaching for creative learning

Our everyday academic conversations with colleagues inside and outside
music institutions suggest that the issue of getting artist-musicians involved
in and co-ordinating creative teaching in relation to creative learning in

diverse spheres is challenging. In the case of music, professional knowledge, researcher support, new tools for networking, and supporting networks and venues to disseminate findings are some of the institutional commitments that are essential for research sharing and evidence-informed policy decisions concerning creative teaching and creative learning. The growing complexity of teaching and learning practice imposes a range of responsibilities and priorities on the institution. These include: enhanced practice-based research education; engagement with the disciplinary specificity of musician-artists; the process of two-way interchange between the institution and its communities; engaging professional learning communities in the process of learning practice-based research strategies on long-term transformation as well as on immediate achievement gains, and being persistent about improvements in students' practice-based research as well as being patient in waiting for the outcomes. Acknowledgement of the need for these changes within and across the fields of music, the workplace and society leads to the creation of new knowledge that translates into economic, social and cultural innovation. This is the essence of what may be learnt from skilful performances by gifted musicians with extensive disciplinary knowledge.

The issue central to building, addressing and representing this knowing–doing gap can be represented as four models (as adapted from Arnetha Ball's American Educational Research Association Presidential Address; Ball, 2012):

1. The Research Development Creative Diffusion Model;
2. The Evidence-based Creative Practice Model;
3. The Boundary-crossing Creative Practice Model;
4. The Knowledge and Creative Communities Model.

These four models (see Figure 4.1) reflect different perspectives on promotion of and engagement with practice-based research in higher music education. They also offer solutions to some of the challenges of helping to foster cross-sector communication, networking and knowledge mobilisation to stakeholders.

1. **The Research Development Creative Diffusion Model** characterises practice-oriented research that draws on theories and practice in the dominant research field. Music needs to be understood as an agency of cultural production, construed as academic practice and as a mode of research. This model represents a framework which depends upon the institution playing the mediating role for promoting links between research and practice. Institutional practices are central in mediating the research–practice gap by developing, supporting and promoting creative teaching and learning programmes and published practices with explicit learning tasks, frameworks and materials. For example, the question of how creative teaching practice informs research and research informs creative learning practice is a pervading theme which involves two worlds through the notion of research activity and performance.

It is culturally located and often shared through institutional spaces, performances of research and practice forums describing the 'knowing' and 'doing' and portrayal of creative music learning and creative practice. The pervading theme of the event is 'multiple identities' and their portrayal of music and creative practices and how these practices inform research and advance knowledge by means of creative practice.

2. **The Evidence-based Creative Practice Model** values research and emphasises the central role of empirical evidence in translating findings from effective research into creative practice. The mediators can be institutions, organisations or professional societies which: determine what counts as impact; review and publish practices; provide activating materials; make explicit to practitioners 'what works', how 'results' of creative practice-based research work and what is 'best practice', and bring together what is effective. In this, what constitutes knowledge is seen within institutional structures as questions of theory and practice and forms of research which open up possibilities of how knowing and doing can be conceptualised and embedded in institutional practice. When considered this way, practice-based research is considered a codified form of academic enquiry that informs institutional practice. This provides an example of knowledge embedded in creative practice and the interdependent relationship between the creative musical work, the creative musician-artist, the research and the institution.

3. **The Boundary-crossing Creative Practice Model** emphasises the importance of collaboration in ensuring that research translates to creative practice, as with previous models. Institutions have diminished responsibility as mediators, and there is greater blurring of roles by policy-makers, musician-artists, researchers and practitioners (educators). The nexus of these roles is played out simultaneously by multi-skilled individual musician-artist-researchers whose approach to research and knowledge is to develop creative practice-based research in which they operate and move between creative possibilities as musician-artist, researcher, academic/scholar, industry innovator, educator and policy developer. The essence of this methodological position is to set up the conditions and parallel processes of research as creative practice.

4. **The Knowledge and Creative Communities Model** addresses the research–practice gap creatively through knowledge creation, transformation and impact by means of cross-sector collaborations, networks, website hubs and knowledge exchanges. It brings together knowledge mobilisation by specific stakeholder groups in the sectors to which research projects relate, which then take responsibility for the practical mobilisation of the knowledge they have generated from diverse occupational and theoretical locations. Knowledge mobilisation processes can be enacted in and mediated by institutional research programmes which combine authentic user engagement with high-quality science – appropriate outputs that are then targeted at contemporary issues.

Model 1 (The Research Development Creative Diffusion Model)

Model 2 (The Evidence-based Creative Practice Model)

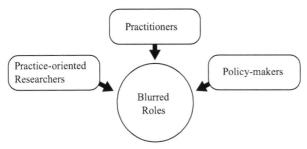

Model 3 (The Boundary-crossing Creative Practice Model)

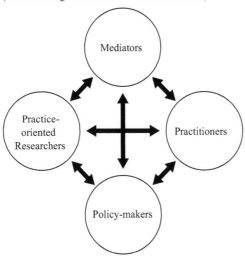

Model 4 (The Knowledge and Creative Communities Model)

Figure 4.1 Four models that represent how the knowing–doing gap can be addressed in defining creative teaching in relation to creative learning in higher music education.

Source: Adapted by author.

Concluding thoughts

Music institutions should regard creative teaching and creative learning as critical issues (of professional capital and knowledge creation) in higher music education, and orient their development and distribution in that direction. Thus, one of the principal roles of knowledge creation – an indispensable element in the functioning of society – is to define creative teaching and creative learning as creative 'know-how' (knowing how to teach creatively, and knowing how to learn creatively) through which the professional learning community's relationship to itself and its environment is played out. Communicated through the practice of creative teaching for creative learning are narratives which allow higher music education to effectively define its criteria of creativity and to evaluate, according to those criteria, what is performed creatively within it. This is an imperative for the development of twenty-first-century creativities and a culture of change in higher music education.

References

Alexander, R. (2008). *Essays on Pedagogy*. Abingdon: Routledge.

Ball, A.F. (2012). 'To Know is Not Enough: Knowledge, Power, and the Zone of Generativity'. *Educational Researcher*, 41(8), 283–93.

Bennett, D. and Burnard, P. (2016). 'The Development and Impact of Creative Human Capital on Higher Education Graduates'. In: R. Comunian and A. Gilmore (eds), *Higher Education and the Creative Economy: Beyond the Campus*. Abingdon: Routledge.

Berliner, P. (1994). *Thinking in Jazz: The Infinite Art of Improvisation*. Chicago, IL: University of Chicago.

Bernstein, B. (1996). *Pedagogy, Symbolic Control, and Identity: Theory, Research, Critique*. New York: Rowman and Littlefield.

Burnard, P. and Swann, M. (2010). 'Pupil Perceptions of Learning with Artists: A New Order of Experience?' *Thinking Skills and Creativity*, 5(2), 70–82.

Burnard, P. and White, J. (2008). 'Creativity and Performativity: Counterpoints in British and Australian Education'. In: *Creativity and Performativity in Teaching and Learning*, special issue, *British Educational Research Journal*, 34(5), 667–82.

Craft, A. (2005). *Creativity in Schools: Tensions and Dilemmas*. Abingdon: Routledge.

———, Cremin, T., and Burnard, P. (eds) (2008). *Creative Learning 3–11 and How We Document It*. Stoke-on-Trent: Trentham Books.

Creative Partnerships (2005). *First Findings – Policy, Practice and Progress: A Review of Creative Learning 2002–2004*. London: Arts Council England.

Cremin, T., Burnard, P. and Craft, A. (2006). 'Pedagogy and Possibility Thinking in the Early Years'. *International Journal of Thinking Skills and Creativity*, 1(2), 108–19.

Galton, M. (2010). 'Going with the Flow or Back to Normal: The Impact of Creative Practitioners in Schools and Classrooms'. *Research Papers in Education*, 25(4), 355–75.

———, Hargreaves, L. and Comber, C. (1998). 'Classroom Practice and the National Curriculum in Small Rural Primary Schools'. *British Educational Research Journal*, 24(1), 43–61.

———, Simon, B. and Croll, P. (1980). *Inside the Primary Classroom*. London: Routledge and Kegan Paul.

Kerchner, J.L. (2014). 'Razing Structures and Raising Creative Teaching and Learning in Institutional Program Curricula'. In: P. Burnard (ed.), *Developing Creativities in Higher Music Education: International Perspectives and Practices* (pp. 281–92). Abingdon: Routledge.

Kompf, M. and Denicolo, P. (eds) (2013). *Critical Issues in Higher Education*. Rotterdam: Sense Publishers.

Loveless, A. (2008). 'Creative Learning and New Technology? A Provocation Paper'. In: J. Sefton-Green (ed.), *Creative Learning* (pp. 61–72). London: Creative Partnerships, Arts Council, England.

McAlpine, L. and Åkerlind, G. (2010). *Becoming an Academic: International Perspectives*. Basingstoke: Palgrave Macmillan.

McLellan, R., Galton, M., Steward, S. and Page, C. (2012). *The Impact of Creative Partnerships on the Wellbeing of Children and Young People: Final Report*. London: Creative Partnerships and Creativity, Culture and Education.

NACCCE (1999). *All Our Futures: Creativity, Culture and Education*. London: Department for Education and Employment.

Nardone, P.L. (1996). 'The Experience of Improvisation in Music: A Phenomenological Psychological Analysis' (unpublished PhD thesis). Saybrook Institute, University of Michigan.

Perkins, R. (2013). 'Hierarchies and Learning in the Conservatoire: Exploring What Students Learn Through the Lens of Bourdieu'. *Research Studies in Music Education*, 35(2), 197–212.

Peters, V. (2014). 'Teaching Future Music Teachers to Incorporate Creativities in Their Teaching: The Challenge for University Teacher Practice'. In: P. Burnard (ed.), *Developing Creativities in Higher Music Education: International Perspectives and Practices* (pp. 162–74). Abingdon: Routledge.

Pike, A. (1974). 'A Phenomenology of Jazz'. *Journal of Jazz Studies*, 2(1), 88–94.

Pope, M., Fuller, M., Boulter, C., Denicolo, P. and Wells, P. (1999). 'Partnership and Collaboration in Teacher Education'. In: M. Lang, J. Olson, H. Hansen and W. Bünder (eds), *Changing Schools/Changing Practices: Perspectives on Educational Reform and Teacher Professionalism* (pp. 161–70). Louvain: Garant.

Reimer, B. (2003). *A Philosophy of Music Education: Advancing the Vision*. 3rd edn. Upper Saddle River, NJ: Prentice Hall.

Sawyer, R.K. (2004). 'Creative Teaching: Collaborative Discussion as Disciplined Improvisation'. *Educational Researcher*, 33(2), 12–20.

Sefton-Green, J. (ed.) (2008). *Creative Learning*. London: Creative Partnerships, Arts Council, England.

Thomson, P. and Sefton-Green, J. (2011). *Researching Creative Learning: Methods and Issues*. Abingdon: Routledge.

Triantafyllaki, A. (2014). 'Musicians as Beginning Music Teachers: Creative Transfer and Identity in Higher Music Education'. In: P. Burnard (ed.), *Developing Creativities in Higher Music Education: International Perspectives and Practices* (pp. 245–55). Abingdon: Routledge.

——— and Burnard, P. (2010). 'Creativity and Arts-based Knowledge Creation in Diverse Educational Partnership Practices: Lessons from Two Case Studies in Rethinking Traditional Spaces for Learning'. In: *Making the Case for the Arts*, special issue, *UNESCO Observatory Multi-Disciplinary Research in the Arts e-journal*, 1(5). Retrieved 20 October 2015 from http://www.researchgate.net/publication/264277033_CREATIVITY_ AND_ARTS-BASED_KNOWLEDGE_CREATION_IN_DIVERSE_EDUCATIONAL_

PARTNERSHIP_PRACTICES_LESSONS_FROM_TWO_CASE_STUDIES_IN_RETHINKING_TRADITIONAL_SPACES_FOR_LEARNING.

Upitis, R. (2006). 'Challenges for Artists and Teachers Working in Partnership'. In: P. Burnard and S. Hennessy (eds), *Reflective Practices in Arts Education* (pp. 55–68). Dordrecht: Springer.

Wenger, E. (1998). *Communities of Practice: Learning, Meaning, and Identity*. Cambridge: Cambridge University Press.

Part II

Developing the creative lecturer and teacher

5 Thinking, making, doing

Perspectives on practice-based, research-led teaching in higher music education

Louise Harris

This chapter was initially envisaged as a consideration of, and meditation on, just what research-led[1] teaching actually *is* when one's research is practice-based.[2] However, as the chapter has progressed, and the perspectives gathered extended and broadened, more pertinent and constructive trajectories have emerged, concerning effective teaching strategies applicable across all areas of creative practice in music, and indeed the creative arts, and how we can teach creativity without simply communicating knowledge in linear form or teaching students to 'do what we do'.

This chapter will consider lecturer and student perspectives on the nature of practice-based, research-led teaching within higher music education (HME), what the phrase 'research-led teaching' has come to mean for both the teacher and the learner, and how we can develop strategies to better facilitate the teaching of creative practice within HME through developing effective 'communities of practice' (Lave and Wenger, 1991). As this volume is concerned with creative teaching for creative learning, this chapter is also concerned with the consideration of what creative teaching and creative learning actually *are* within HME and how they relate to creative practice-based, research-led teaching.

Context and situation

Numerous authors and thinkers illuminate and influence the ideas in this chapter, both directly and indirectly. First, some of Sennett's ideas in *The Craftsman* (2008), particularly those related to the nature of Linux programming communities, find particular affinities to the author's own ideas and ideals in approaching the construction of learning communities within the teaching of sonic art. Discussing relationships between ancient craft and online programming workshops, Sennett states:

> We'd err to imagine that because traditional craft communities pass on skills from generation to generation, the skills they pass down have been rigidly fixed; not at all. Ancient pottery making, for instance, changed radically when the rotating stone disk holding a lump of clay came into use. … But the

radical change appeared slowly. In Linux the process of skill evolution is speeded up; change occurs daily.

(Sennett, 2008: 26)

The rapidity of the evolution of contemporary technology is a key issue in the author's own practice, both creative and pedagogic. However, parallels between traditional and contemporary 'craft' and the lack of rigidity in each can inform relationships between, for example, the teaching of composition for acoustic instruments and that which is technologically mediated. Further, the kinds of communities referenced by Sennett, though functioning within a somewhat different context, find resonance with concepts of collaborative learning advocated by (among others) Gaunt and Westerlund (2013). Indeed, the negotiation of technological developments discussed in their *Collaborative Learning in Higher Music Education*, though in many ways distinct to the Linux communities, nonetheless speak to the importance of collaborative learning in problem-solving, be that technical/technological or creative. For Gaunt and Westerlund (2013: 6), the conceptual basis of collaborative learning is positioned to 'capture diverse attempts at cultivating shared goals and joint problem-solving, to illuminate the complexities of interactions involved in collaboration ... and to provide inspiration through the improvisatory and creative aspects of collaborative learning'.

Closely allied to processes involved in collaborative learning are Lave and Wenger's (1991) ideas concerning the construction of communities of practice, particularly Wenger's definition of communities of practice as 'groups of people who share a concern or a passion for something they do and learn how to do it better as they interact regularly' (ibid.: 1). Wenger's codification of the three characteristics of a community of practice, *domain*, *community* and *practice*, will be discussed in some detail later in this chapter, and underpin the framework for effective practice-based, research-led teaching proposed. Equally important in the construction of this framework is Burnard's synthesis of her own work with the models of creativity proposed by Csikszentmihalyi (1999) and Bourdieu (1993) into a spectrum of musical creativities. This spectrum, underpinned by a consideration of a broad range of narratives of practice, also resonates with Stoller's conception of knowing as an emergent property of experience. Stoller (2014: 56) posits that:

> learning is not merely a form of cognition, but an act of making which takes artistic production as its paradigmatic case. The result is a view of learning which is deeper than brute cognition and closer to what artistic communities have termed *maker's knowledge* – a phrase which attempts to draw together cognitive knowings, moral, and aesthetic meanings under a form of habit: a capacity to act.[3]

Stoller's work considers the importance of the artistic community not only to thinking, making and doing, but also to the construction of an individual's creative identity. Andrew Hugill's ideas concerning the development of an individual's creative identity in *The Digital Musician* (2008) have also been hugely influential to the author's teaching to date, and the development of strategies for facilitating this process will be discussed further.

Finally, the initial premise for this chapter took influence from Aslaug Nyrnes. In *Lighting from the Side: Rhetoric and Artistic Research* (2006), Nyrnes problematises the tendency for discourse on research in the arts to use terms associated with scientific research, such as 'method', 'fact', 'content', 'objectivity' and 'truth', contending that art research instead explores a more nebulous field of materials and practices, rather than the pursuit and transmission of fact and objective knowledge. This more sensuous knowledge, drawn from across diverse fields of materials, practices and influences, implies the necessity for teaching in this area to reflect and indeed encourage this nebulousness through the construction of collaborative learning communities or, indeed, communities of practice.

Creative teaching, creative learning and the co-researcher relationship

It is useful at this point to better illuminate the relationships between creative teaching and/or creative learning and the creative practice-based, research-led teaching that will be discussed as this chapter progresses. As Burnard and White (2008), Gibson (2010) and others have discussed, there is considerable tension in language used to describe both creative teaching and the differences between *teacher creativity* and *teaching for creativity*. Jeffrey and Craft's (2004: 15) problematising of these two terms raised the question of whether these distinctions were helpful or, in fact, necessary, concluding that 'the constitution of creative pedagogic practices may be more transparent if the focus is on the teacher *and* on the learner'. This advocacy of the broadened focus on a culture of creativity for both the teacher and the learner (in this case, within primary and secondary education) foreshadowed burgeoning interest in creative learning within higher education.

'Creative teaching' and 'creative learning' in the literature are somewhat nebulous terms, defying rigid classification yet implying quite specific roles and conditions for the processes of creative pedagogy (see, for example, Sefton-Green et al., 2011; Burnard and White, 2008; Burnard, 2012b). For this author, the definitions, mechanisms and cultures surrounding creative teaching and creative learning as terms perhaps create a false sense of distinction and division between teacher and learner, advocating roles that are somewhat separate and insufficiently overlapping.[4] While this is, in the majority of contexts,[5] appropriate to the relationship between teacher and learner, this type of distinction does not resonate particularly well in the context of creative practice-based, research-led teaching in which the primary mode of assessment is via creative artefact. Instead, developing a mutually beneficial relationship of creative co-researcher, in the context of effectively scaffolding an individual learner's creative identity within a community of practice, could be considered a viable approach.

Methodology

The intention of this study is to interrogate the perspectives of both artists/lecturers and students in UK higher education institutions on their experiences of practice-based, research-led teaching. All respondents were current or former colleagues and students; consequently, participant research was deemed appropriate and relevant, and data were gathered through structured and semi-structured interviews where possible, and through open-ended questionnaires where not. Once gathered, the data were analysed for themes, key concepts and patterns, and each response was coded according to these criteria. This served to dictate the structure of the following research findings.

Lecturers' perspectives on creative practice-based, research-led teaching

Participants were asked a range of questions; these included whether they considered their research to be practice-based, whether they considered their teaching to be research-led, how any research-led teaching was manifested, and what strategies they had developed for implementing practice-based, research-led teaching in HME. They were also asked about the structure of teaching in HME, and the relationships and possible tensions between the rigidity of intended learning outcomes and the nature of summative assessment, and the teaching of subjects involving creativity. Certain themes emerged that were common to respondents based both within more traditional music practice (that involving instrumental performance or composition) and those involved in the teaching of technologically mediated creative practice.

Perspectives on the definition of participants' research as practice-based

Almost universally, participants felt their research to be practice-based as opposed to the act of practice itself being research in its own right; that is, they felt that simply writing or performing works didn't necessarily qualify as research, but that the research existed in the experimentation inherent in the processes underpinning the creative outcome. For example, one participant stated: 'within my own work, the research aspect is (a) characterised by a process of investigation, enquiry or discovery ... and (b) provides some 'thing' (an idea, tool, information, approach or methodology, etc.) that someone else can pick up and use'.

This was echoed by another participant, who considered the importance of the research context surrounding the research process:

> during the composition of works I engage deeply with questions concerning artistic process, compositional technique and form, collaborative relationships, performance practice and/or listener perception. Perhaps what differentiates research-led practice from 'practice' is this element of critical

inquiry, the act of interrogating aspects of the work and the practice in order to derive new insights. This also involves contextualising the work, and the processes that contribute to its form, as part of a broader research landscape.

These two examples are indicative of a general view that practice-based research comprises a number of complementary elements: the act of the practice itself (performance, composition, improvisation and so on) alongside the process of experimentation that enables the practice; the broader context surrounding the work (including related practice within the field) and the subsequent contribution to knowledge in the field. That knowledge, for practice-based researchers, while not easily definable as a linear argument attempting 'objectivity and truth' (Nyrnes, 2006), should nonetheless advance the field of practice through providing original thought concerning method, process, experimentation or outcome, and might also attempt to provide a framework for the shaping of future practice, either for the individual practitioner or the field more broadly.

Research-led teaching

Questions concerning research-led teaching were a little less conclusive. While most participants considered their teaching to be research-led, this was manifested in a variety of ways. There also seemed to be a distinction between teaching involving technologically mediated creative practice and teaching involving more traditional music practice.

The majority of participants felt that *some*, but not necessarily *all*, of their teaching could be described as being research-led. The most clearly defined form of research-led teaching was offered by composers whose classes directly dealt with methods and frameworks they were developing in their own practice; interestingly, several participants cited these not only as their most directly research-led teaching, but often as their most successful teaching, evidenced through feedback from students.

An interesting distinction was noted concerning classes in which participants were presenting examples of analysis or close engagement with particular works or practitioners. Some participants cited these as research-led sessions, in which the research was often concerned with the analysis of compositional method that in turn might inform their own practice. Other participants felt differently, citing this as being 'a form of learning closely linked to research', but not necessarily linking to 'original outputs' in the same way. There was no uniform consensus regarding which of these perspectives was more valid or more useful.

Research-informed teaching

Following on from this, one participant described their teaching as 'research-informed', which is perhaps a useful umbrella heading under which the majority of the forms of teaching discussed here might fall. Others joined this participant in articulating a difference between research-led teaching at undergraduate and postgraduate level, citing a greater ease in getting postgraduate students to engage in critical inquiry, largely due to these students having 'acquired at least competent technical capabilities, which frees up space for creative and aesthetic issues to be foregrounded during teaching'. Other participants echoed this perspective, and indeed it could be argued that the time spent teaching students particular skills presents both an opportunity and a barrier to research-led teaching.

One participant defined an important aspect of research-led teaching as being the development of a relationship with students of 'co-researcher' as opposed to the more traditional master–apprentice paradigm. This perspective, though not necessarily articulated in these terms by other participants, was nonetheless synergic with numerous responses and points perhaps to a close relationship between practice-based, research-led teaching and the development of collaborative learning advocated by authors such as Gaunt and Westerlund (2013).

Research visibility

Almost all participants discussed both the importance and the difficulty of engaging students with the nature of practice-based research and of making it clear what research within music actually *is*, what forms it takes, and what impact it has on their learning experiences. An essential part of this is increasing the visibility of the practitioner's own research, and indeed its value can be seen through participants citing examples of this as some of their most valuable and well-received teaching. However, perhaps this speaks not only to student unfamiliarity with the nature of music research, but also to a broader condition within academia concerning the nature of practice-led and practice-based research. Indeed, as one participant remarked: 'If practice-led research is commonly misunderstood, even by academics, we cannot expect students to engage with this kind of research themselves without some kind of introductory guidance.' A broader argument here could concern tensions surrounding the designations 'practice-led' and 'practice-based' research within music and research that are deemed as being neither of these. For this author, Candy's (2006) definitions of the differences between practice-led and practice-based research have served as a useful guiding principle, and can, I believe, effectively define all forms of research undertaken within music academia. Is it possible that greater application, acceptance and ownership of these terms within music academia could not only reduce confusion over what these forms of research actually *are* among academics, but also allow for greater accessibility of, and therefore engagement with, research from a student perspective?

Assessment structures and intended learning outcomes

Finally, participants were asked about the nature of practice-based, research-led teaching within higher education institutional contexts, particularly related to aims and objectives, intended learning outcomes and summative assessment. Many of the responses revolved around language, often considering appropriate terms with which to describe and discuss forms of creative knowledge in order effectively to define intended learning outcomes. One participant described a particular difficulty with defining these due to practice 'creating knowledge, but not in the verbal or literary sphere'. Many participants also pointed to the importance of formative assessment in preparing students for summative assessment, which will be discussed later in this chapter as part of developing strategies for teaching and learning. Finally, all participants felt that it was possible to enact practice-based, research-led teaching within these kinds of structures, but this required innovation in the content, delivery and forms of assessment undertaken. Indeed, as one participant remarked, this form of teaching requires 'scaffolding a learning environment that supports, and indeed encourages, the non-linear aspects of creative research'. This particular form of scaffolding will form a basis for the discussion of teaching strategies later in this chapter.

Viewed from the other side: The student perspective

Student participants were asked to give general feedback concerning what they felt had worked well and less well with respect to teaching in subjects in which a creative outcome was the primary form of summative assessment. Students are familiar with these types of evaluative feedback through module and course evaluation procedures. Questions were kept as open-ended as possible to avoid leading responses. There were a wide variety of responses, but as with perspectives gathered from practitioners, some of the themes that emerged were remarkably universal.

Critical engagement and the sharing of work in progress

First, almost all participants agreed that sharing work in progress was, although daunting, extremely helpful in shaping the trajectory and outcome of the creative process. One participant remarked that 'It is useful for the class to gain perspective on their work', with another agreeing that 'It helped me see what stage I was at compared to others, and gave me a bit of a kick!' This was true of both creative and analytical work, with some participants citing particularly the sharing of contextual work in progress, in the form of both presentations and written work, as helpful in shaping their approach.

Responses also indicated the importance of striking a careful balance between too much and too little learning being self-directed and enquiry-based. While the importance of giving students the opportunity and freedom to explore ideas and gather knowledge for themselves was acknowledged, particularly with the teaching of technical skills it was largely felt that to be most effective this needed to be balanced with enough specifically guided tuition. One participant remarked: 'For many terms, the format was basically "here is some software and some examples, go and create something" … this structure led to a drop off in engagement with the subject … I think the tutor has a responsibility to keep their students engaged throughout the course.' This was echoed by other participants, who felt that if too much learning was self-directed, particularly with respect to more complex technical processes, engagement with the topic suffered.

Interestingly, more participants than expected highlighted the importance of critical analysis and engagement with existing works. One participant remarked: 'performing critical analysis of previous student's work was an invaluable experience. I found it really opened my eyes to how a tutor views my work when marking it.' I have also found that students respond extremely well to evaluating the work of others, as this affords them a better understanding of how they themselves are performing, along with providing an opportunity to voice their own opinions, articulating, analysing and justifying their individual responses and allowing them to feel that their perspective is as valid as their lecturer's. This closely ties into the concept of student as 'co-researcher', which will be discussed in more detail later in this chapter.

The broader contemporary context

With regard to research and contextualisation, the responses were a little more mixed; many students felt that researching other artists/practitioners or reading around a topic was something to be done just before submitting a piece of work, as opposed to guiding the project throughout. Others, however, acknowledged the importance of situating their creative work within a field of contemporary practice, with one participant remarking: 'it was useful to think about how my own work related to the work of others, particularly of musicians whose work I enjoy. It made me think about how I could use this work outside my course.'

A variety of teaching methods was also almost universally agreed to be beneficial. One participant stated that 'individual tutorials are good for frank and open discussion about your work ... I also found one-on-one teaching helpful from a technical point of view' – a perspective echoed by many other participants. Group work, however, was generally perceived as problematic when it formed part of an assessment. Students seem to have largely felt uncomfortable with the outcome of any part of their assessment being in the hands of someone other than themselves, and some participants described negative experiences. However, pair and small group work within individual teaching sessions was, on the whole, well received, as was ongoing collaborative work which had limited impact on summative assessment.

Contact time

Finally, time was an issue that was discussed at length, with a number of students feeling that there was usually insufficient time available in class to cover everything. This is, of course, an unfortunate aspect of teaching within an institution with stringent demands on staff time. However, what seems key to negotiating this issue is the efficient use of contact time, often through the instigation of a variety of teaching methods and the establishment of learning communities that exist outside the formal class setting. This will be discussed in more detail in the next section.

Teaching and learning strategies – scaffolding a learner's creative identity

Developing effective teaching strategies is a highly personal process, informed by a lecturer's ideals, their background, the subject area and the context in which teaching takes place. Therefore, none of what follows is intended to apply across the board or attempt to lay claim to any form of universal truth concerning the 'correct' way to teach creative practice within music higher education. Instead, I hope to offer, on the basis of my own experience and the perspectives of respondents within this study, a framework for the effective teaching of creative practice across a range of subjects in HME. This is not intended to be specific to tuition within sonic arts, music technology or audiovisual composition, which is my particular area, but could, I hope, be equally applicable to the teaching of performance, improvisation or instrumental composition, or indeed to the teaching of creative practice in disciplines outside music.

One phrase which had particular resonance for me from the material gathered for this study was that of 'scaffolding a learning environment', for which I am indebted to a colleague who has had a profound impact on my practice, both as an artist and as a lecturer. Therefore, I use the phrase 'scaffolding a creative identity' as a heading under which to outline a framework for effective practice-based, research-led teaching within the creative arts.

Within the framework, there are a number of distinct areas, but all are interlinked and related. The non-linear nature of creative research demands a strategic framework that is itself non-linear, being perhaps instead more closely allied to models such as Burnard's (2012a) spectrum of creativities, and the underlying structure for this framework is informed by Wenger's (2006) three characteristics of communities of practice, which are usefully summarised as follows:

1. *The domain* – A community of practice has a domain, an area of knowledge, experience or practice that renders the members of the community distinct from those outside it. Within HME, this domain might be instrumental composition, sonic arts, performance practice, installation art and so on, and might to some extent be established before the learning activity takes place, while also being informed by the nature and the context of the learning environment.
2. *The community* – Within the community, members build strong relationships based on discussion, on sharing and on developing mutually beneficial learning environments. Essential to this is the sharing of perspectives and practice, of collaborative learning and of continuing dialogue and interaction, both within and outside the formal learning environment.
3. *The practice* – 'Members of a community of practice are practitioners. They develop a shared repertoire of resources: experiences, stories, tools, ways of addressing recurring problems – in short a shared practice. This takes time and sustained interaction' (Wenger, 2006). For our purposes, this might be the development of skills and shared knowledge to facilitate creativity, or might be the eventual outcome in the form of creative practice.

Table 5.1 The five components of the framework

Domain	Community	Practice
Laying the Groundwork		
		Internal and External Reflection
		Collaborative Learning and the Construction of Communities of Practice
Planning Time and Teaching Methods		
		Forming Professional and Individual Creative Identity

The five components of the framework, and their situation within the characteristics of communities of practice, are shown in Table 5.1.

For the purposes of clarity, lecturer/artists will be referred to below as tutor-practitioners, though it should be assumed throughout that the ideal relationship developed between student and tutor-practitioner should be that of co-researcher. It should also be noted that this is a framework for teaching and learning, and therefore is not tailored to the delivery of specific content. It is intended to facilitate practice-based, research-led teaching within the creative arts, and is not directed towards the successful completion of summative assessment; rather, it is directed towards the successful generation of creative practice that is engaging and relevant to students and the context and the community of practice in which they are working.

Laying the groundwork

Within this, there are two essential components – conceptual/theoretical and practical/experiential – which overlap considerably. Whatever the field of practice, forming a solid basis of knowledge concerning existing works in the field or existing artists and practitioners is essential, as is understanding how these existing works and artists connect to creative practice more broadly. This needs to be done in two interlinked ways: (1) conceptual/theoretical engagement with the ways in which practitioners and theorists have discussed and documented works, surveying and critiquing relevant conceptual and theoretical frameworks and the impact of those on the creative process, and (2) practical/experiential engagement with the works themselves, not just those identified by the tutor-practitioner as important, but also those identified as interesting and relevant by the student. These need to be discussed, critiqued and evaluated, with students articulating their own responses to works and questioning 'Why have I responded in this way? What components of the work have elicited this response?' Ideally, this should involve engagement with works and concepts both within and outside a class setting, and it is essential that students both are pointed towards and seek out opportunities to engage with relevant practice outside the institutional setting, becoming part of the artistic life of the broader community they inhabit.

Internal and external reflection

This is essential at all stages of the teaching and learning process, and can be encouraged through a variety of mechanisms. One of those I particularly favour is engaging students in critical engagement with and analysis of existing works, both written and creative, and in the sharing of creative works in progress. This takes place, for example, through mock assessment of existing pieces of work as though they had been submitted for the same course, in order to allow students to better understand and relate to marking and assessment processes. I have also asked students to act as a mock panel for conference and festival submissions, both of papers and creative work, to encourage them to consider and articulate their critical perspectives in some detail and to view their own responses and reactions to works as being as valid as my own. This ties in, again, to the building of a co-researcher relationship.

Collaborative learning and the construction of communities of practice

These aspects can be facilitated by the tutor-practitioner sharing their own practice; this is essential not just in building trust between tutor-practitioner and student, but also in making the tutor-practitioner's own work more visible to students. It also helps students to understand better the relationships between research and teaching, and what practice-based research actually *is* within HME. Students should also be encouraged to work in a variety of configurations, such as in pairs and small groups, when conducting practical exercises or enquiry-based learning both during and outside class time. Social media are particularly useful for this kind of activity and for facilitating the building of communities; as an example, a sonic arts class I teach have been sharing their Max patches with each other through Facebook, which has not only encouraged them to share and respond to each other's work, but has also facilitated a much higher percentage of students engaging in homework tasks outside class.

Planning time and teaching methods

Time is always against us in teaching, but what is most important is innovation and flexibility with the time available – that is, not always sticking to a lecture/ seminar format if something else would be more relevant or useful. The responses showed that students did not always feel tutors made the best use of time, and that often an individual or small group tutorial as opposed to a lecture for 30 people might have progressed the class more effectively. Constantly varying the type of teaching, the activities undertaken within a teaching session and the nature of the student learning experience, which is essential when teaching such multifaceted subjects in any case, has proved to be the most successful approach for the author.

Forming professional and individual creative identity

In forming professional and individual creative identity, it is vital to make students feel that their ideas and work are relevant and valuable within and outside the context in which they are produced. The danger inherent in summative assessment within higher education, and in many ways the saddest thing about creative work as a form of assessment, is that so much of it ends up going unseen/ heard/experienced, except by the student and the tutor-practitioner. There are several ways to counter this. The first is to provide numerous opportunities to share work in progress within class. This is always an essential part of any of my practice-based teaching, and although a number of students can initially find it daunting, I find that the benefits by far outweigh the drawbacks. The second is to encourage students to see their work as a contribution to a professional portfolio of work as opposed to an isolated creative event. Encouraging students to submit work to festivals, open calls and so on can be a really good way to facilitate this. The final way is to attempt to, at least in a small way, replicate the degree show-style model of arts schools by encouraging students to publicly share their work, particularly that which signals the culmination of their course of study. This is important in making students feel that their work is valuable, but also provides something other than the assessment to aim for, and allows them to assess critically their own work in relation to that of their peers.

As Boden (2004: 271) has argued, creativity 'involves not only a passionate interest but self-confidence too. A person needs a healthy self-respect to pursue novel ideas and to ... make mistakes, despite the criticism from others.' Similarly, Black, Castro and Lin (2015: 117) suggest: 'Rather than the creative process being about individual expression and identity development through a visual media, the kind of identity formation ... is fundamentally shaped by the relationship linkages of the individual to the group identity.' This framework should facilitate the essential components for effective practice-based, research-led teaching.

Reflection

As discussed at the outset, this chapter attempts to draw on the perspectives of both artists/lecturers and students to help illuminate what might constitute effective practice-based, research-led teaching within HME. In so doing, questions have arisen concerning the nature of practice-based research and research-led teaching within the creative arts, and although no single strategy or approach has emerged as universally successful, particular themes and synergies have suggested possible strategies which might be applicable across disciplinary boundaries and a broad range of approaches. In proposing a framework for effectively scaffolding a creative identity within students, and in developing the relationship of co-researchers within a community of practice, I hope not only to help facilitate effective practice-based, research-led teaching, but also to encourage the sharing of the wealth of creative work that takes place within higher education contexts but which is rarely seen outside the summative assessment for which it is designed. Indeed, as Burnard (2013: 85) has stated: 'it is our remit to empower students to be all they can be and to position creative musicianship as the essential currency for crossing borders in their musical worlds'. I am hopeful that effective practice-based, research-led teaching can be an important contributing factor in this.

Notes

1 Research-led teaching, in this case, being teaching which is directly informed by or communicates aspects of the academic's research.
2 I find Linda Candy's (2006: 1) definitions of the differences between practice-based and practice-led research most useful here: *Practice-based research* is an original investigation undertaken to gain new knowledge partly by means of practice and the outcomes of that practice. *Practice-led research*, by contrast, is 'concerned with the nature of practice and leads to new knowledge that has operational significance for that practice'.
3 'Maker's knowledge' here being closely allied to the mindset of Sennett's Craftsman.
4 Though this is by no means the intention, the simple separation of the terms as entities has this almost subliminal semantic suggestion.
5 Certainly in the primary and secondary educational contexts in which these terms first gained prominence.

References

Black, J., Castro, J.C. and Lin, C.-C. (2015). *Youth Practices in Digital Arts and New Media*. New York: Palgrave.

Boden, M.A. (2004). *The Creative Mind: Myths and Mechanisms*. London: Routledge.

Bourdieu, P. (1993). *The Field of Cultural Production: Essays on Art and Literature*. Edited and introduced by R. Johnson. Cambridge: Polity Press.

Burnard, P. (2012a). *Musical Creativities in Practice*. Oxford: Oxford University Press.

———— (2012b). 'Rethinking Creative Teaching and Teaching as Research: Mapping the Critical Phases that Mark Times of Change and Choosing as Learners and Teachers of Music'. *Theory into Practice*, 51(3), 40–52.

———— (2013). 'A Spectrum of Musical Creativities and Particularities of Practice'. In: P. Burnard (ed.), *Developing Creativities in Higher Education: International Perspectives and Practices* (pp. 77–86). London: Routledge.

———— and White, J. (2008). 'Creativity and Performativity: Counterpoints in British and Australian Education'. In: *Creativity and Performativity in Teaching and Learning*, special issue, *British Educational Research Journal*, 34(5), 667–82.

Candy, L. (2006). 'Practice Based Research: A Guide'. *CCS Report*, 1, 1–19.

Csikszentmihalyi, M. (1999). 'Implications of a Systems Perspective for the Study of Creativity'. In: R.J. Sternberg (ed.), *Handbook of Creativity* (pp. 313–35). New York: Cambridge University Press.

Gaunt, H. and Westerlund, H. (eds) (2013). *Collaborative Learning in Higher Music Education*. Farnham: Ashgate.

Gibson, R. (2010). 'The "Art" of Creative Teaching: Implications for Higher Education'. *Teaching in Higher Education*, 15(5), 607–13.

Hugill, A. (2008). *The Digital Musician*. New York: Routledge.

Jeffrey, B. and Craft, A. (2004). 'Teaching Creatively and Teaching for Creativity: Distinctions and Relationships'. *Educational Studies*, 30(1), 77–87.

Lave, J. and Wenger, E. (1991). *Situated Learning: Legitimate Peripheral Participation*. Cambridge: Cambridge University Press.

Nyrnes, A. (2006). *Lighting from the Side: Rhetoric and Artistic Research*. Bergen: Kunsthøgskolen i Bergen.

Sefton-Green, J., Thomson, P., Jones, K. and Bresler, L. (eds) (2011). *The Routledge International Handbook of Creative Learning*. Abingdon: Routledge.

Sennett, R. (2008). *The Craftsman*. New Haven, CT: Yale University Press.

Stoller, A. (2014). *Knowing and Learning as Creative Action: A Reexamination of the Epistemological Foundations of Education*. New York: Palgrave.

Wenger, E. (2006). *Communities of Practice: A Brief Overview of the Concept and its Uses*. Retrieved 11 May 2015 from http://wenger-trayner.com/introduction-to-communities-of-practice/.

6 Practice-as-research

A method for articulating creativity for practitioner-researchers

Martin Blain

What is a composer doing in a conservatoire, and what is a performer doing in a university? In 2007, the Polifonia Third Cycle Working Group, which was established to explore the potential for doctoral study within the conservatoire sector, reported that 'conservatoires traditionally offer vocational training that leads to a career as a professional musician … [and] universities have been seen as the locus of research activity' (Polifonia, 2007: 9), so to respond to the question, we might suggest that the composer is pursuing a 'professional' career as a musician, and the performer is developing a career as an 'academic'. Indeed, this formulation assumes that one institution constructs practical environments where the focus of study is on the 'making' of work, while the other institution is concerned with constructing modes of thought to articulate issues and ideas concerning the making of the work (normally the work of others) – this might be seen as constructing environments for 'thinking' about art. However, as John Dewey (1934: 14) reminds us: 'The odd notion that an artist does not think and a scientific inquirer does nothing else is the result of converting a difference of tempo and emphasis into a difference in kind.' Research where practice constitutes a significant element of the inquiry is now well established within the university sector, and following the recommendations of the Polifonia Third Cycle Working Group, conservatoires have been developing third cycle doctoral programmes for practitioner-researchers. PhD students wishing to develop their creative practice, not only as a researcher 'making' work but also as a practitioner 'thinking' about the theoretical, contextual and critical implications of the work within a research inquiry, can do so through the structures of a conservatoire and/or a university. However, how the detail of the research inquiry is formulated, what methodologies and resulting methods are used to carry out the research, and the development of skills required to recognise when moments of significance occur through the research process and how this is documented remain points of contention.

This chapter will consider the position of practitioner-researcher doctoral students within higher music education. It will consider recent developments in practice-as-research (PaR) methodology, a research methodology that has developed in other performing arts disciplines, but has only recently been taken up within the music community. The chapter will discuss how the work of the Department of Contemporary Arts at Manchester Metropolitan University (MMU) has contributed to the development of PaR methods in relation to the performing arts with a particular focus on practical music PhD projects, and will then consider the collaborative partnership it has with the Royal Northern College of Music (RNCM) in relation to its PhD programme and how the PaR methodology is being used to generate methods appropriate to individual projects. The chapter will use two case studies, one from MMU (a jazz improviser/performer) and one from the RNCM (a composer), and will draw on my role as director of studies for practitioner-researchers registered at both institutions. The chapter will conclude with a review of the work achieved so far, as it considers the development of a method for PaR within the higher education (HE) sector.

While precise definitions of the term 'creativity' remain elusive, most commentators agree that creative teaching and learning occur when conditions prevail. Klausen (2010: 347) claims the 'standard definition of creativity as the production of something that is both novel and appropriate' remains 'problematic', and Burnard (2012: 213) reminds us that 'musical creativities [can] assume many forms'. Nagy (2015: 69) has suggested that 'to investigate the apperception of musical creativity is, first and foremost, an exploration of the structure of musical imagination', and that to do so 'offers a direct link between creativity and a path of self-critical development, gradually evolving a personal attitude to musical creation'. Sullivan offers a similar articulation of how creative environments might be constructed when he identifies three dominant strands of activity in his work that he sees as necessary for creative learning to manifest. He suggests that creativity might be explained through the cognitive processes of 'thinking in a medium ... thinking in a language ... [and] ... thinking in a context' (Sullivan, 2011: 115). This resonates with my own approach to developing creative environments for students where the thinking and making of practice is exposed through the medium of the artwork, through a range of performative and compositional languages that contextualise and critically evaluate the final product as well as the working processes that have come to generate the work, and through the external constraints imposed on arts practices by institutional, professional and commercial need. Artistic medium, contextual/critical reflection and institutional/professional contexts are explored as pathways through which musical creativities flow.

PaR within HE

The practice-as-research initiative, begun over two decade ago in the wider performing arts community, has enabled practitioner-researchers to position their practice within an academic context. The construction of appropriate contextual frameworks, the implementation of embodied practitioner/professional knowledge acquired through training as a practitioner and the development of practitioner skills in critical reflection have each encouraged academic practitioners to expose creative insights into the making of their work as well as making these insights into creative practices available to both academic and non-academic communities. For some, practice may stand alone as evidence of a research inquiry, with its research imperatives clearly articulated through the practice – for example, through the production of a notated score and/or a performance of the work. For others, as suggested by Robin Nelson (2006: 112), 'it may be helpful, particularly in an academic institutional context where much rides on judgement made about research worthiness, for other evidence to be adduced'. Here, there is a suggestion that the production of new knowledge and/or substantial new insights within a research inquiry may not only be an outcome as evidenced within the product, but may also reside in the processes that have led to the making of the work.

As the UK higher education research communities prepared for a research audit in Autumn 2013, the Higher Education Funding Council for England (HEFCE) published criteria for its Research Excellence Framework (REF)[1] on the articulation of practice-led research. The criteria included the statement that research outputs '*may* include a statement of up to 300 words in cases where the research imperatives and research process ... might *further* be made evident by description and contextualising information' (REF, 2012: 87; my italics). While this statement is welcomed and offers some guidance to practitioner-researchers on how to make the results of a research inquiry explicit for the purpose of the REF exercise, and by implication allows those outside this practice to gain access to the key stages of the creative process that have led to the making of the final product, it only partly addresses the issue of how practitioners working within an academic institutional context can best disseminate their research insights for the benefit of their respective research communities. In 2015, when the HEFCE have made the decision to bring together the research communities of music and the research communities of drama, dance and the performing arts for the REF process, I would suggest that it is pertinent for music practitioners working within academia to consider the relationship between arts PaR and methodologies for research dissemination; doing this can shed new light on the workings of a creative process.

While there have been some initiatives within the music academic community to develop methodologies for practice-led research, much has centred around performance practice, and the community has not dealt specifically with the development of appropriate methods for the dissemination of research resulting from the practice of composition. In 2007–2009, the University of London ran a project, Practice as Research in Music Online (PRIMO). One of the outcomes of the project was to provide a resource for 'capturing and disseminating what was once an ephemeral event'. It also, however, assumed that 'traditional modes of dissemination, for musical scores ... are well developed' (PRIMO, 2007). In England, within the wider context of arts practice, the PaR initiative over the last two decades has begun to establish new practice-led methods for practitioner-researchers across the arts communities. Practice as Research in Performance (PARIP) was a five-year Arts and Humanities Research Board project that ran between 2001 and 2006 aiming to 'develop national frameworks for the encouragement of the highest standards in representing practical-creative research within academic contexts' (PARIP, n.d.). More recently, an Arts and Humanities Research Council project, Practice as Research Consortium North West (PARCNorthWest), led by MMU, has invited postgraduate research students, project partners and other interested parties to share experiences, exchange knowledge and explore the development of appropriate methods for the dissemination of research where practice remains a substantial element of the research inquiry. This has resulted in arts practitioners from across a wide range of arts disciplines coming together to share their research insights and discuss issues in research dissemination. By doing so, practitioner-researchers are capturing and documenting key moments of a creative process that would otherwise pass unnoticed.

Articulations of PaR

At the core of the PaR initiative, debates have focused on what constitutes knowledge in arts research where practice is used as the dominant methodology, and how what is understood as knowledge can be captured and disseminated within academically established research methodologies. Of course, this debate remains ongoing, continues to challenge the dominant research methodologies established within the sector, has generated a variety of bespoke approaches and is discipline-specific.

Haseman (2007: 147) has challenged established quantitative and qualitative research methodologies as being inappropriate for what he describes as 'practice-led research', using Gray's (1996: 3) term for 'research which is initiated in practice, where questions, problems, challenges are identified and formed by the needs of practice and practitioners'. Haseman (2007: 147) suggests that this approach 'captures the nuances and subtleties of their research process and accurately represents that process to research funding bodies'. His use of the term 'practice-led research' suggests something very similar to the concerns of the PaR initiative.

Haseman suggests that the established research paradigms of quantitative and qualitative research do not resonate with practice-led research, therefore new methodologies are required. He points out that practice-led researchers normally construct 'experiential starting points from which practice follows' (Haseman, 2006: 100), and that this conflicts with the established positivist research paradigm whereby researchers begin their research inquiry by first constructing a 'problem' and then working through that problem towards a solution; in practice-led research, problems (or what might better be described as research questions) normally emerge after the practice element has begun.

From this position, Haseman suggests that a third paradigm is emerging, which he calls 'performative research', whereby practitioner-researchers develop research methods appropriate to the individual needs of specific practices. Although these methods are likely to be project-specific, Haseman (ibid.: 104) has suggested that these might include a reinterpretation of some of the practices currently exploited within qualitative methodology, such as 'reflective practice, participant observation, performance ethnography, ethnodrama, biographical/ autobiographical/narrative inquiry, and the inquiry cycle from action research'. In performative research, practice is seen as the principal activity for the research, and researchers desire to express its findings in 'forms of symbolic data other than words in discursive text' (ibid.: 103). For Haseman, both the process of creation and the final product are positioned as research.

Barbara Bolt (2007: 29) offers a different perspective: she suggests that arts researchers can 'demonstrate a very specific sort of knowing, a knowing that arises through handling materials in practice'. For Bolt (ibid.: 30) this form of knowing occurs when materials and processes of production 'come into play in interaction with the artist's creative intelligence'. Bolt (ibid.) uses Carter's terminology when she calls this process 'material thinking' (Carter, 2004: xi), and suggests that this process is pivotal to the creative process. Drawing on the philosophy of Heidegger, she states that 'we come to know the world theoretically only after we have come to understand it through handling' (Bolt, 2007: 30). She suggests that the resulting praxical knowledge that this approach may produce is likely to take a number of different forms, and it is the teasing out of the subsequent knowledge to form relationships exposed through the handling of materials and processes that gives 'practice-led research' its distinctive quality.

Bolt's formulation of the term 'practice-led research' resonates with the concerns of the PaR initiative. Of relevance to our discussion, Bolt regards the articulation of praxical knowledge exposed during the process of creating practice as an essential element of the research inquiry. While she believes that an artwork can be 'imminently articulate and eloquent in its own right' and that 'tacit knowing and the generative potential of process have the potential to reveal new insights' (Bolt, 2007: 31), she concludes that these are best articulated through written text. Furthermore, she sees the articulation of the research processes that have been exposed through material thinking as being of significant benefit to the wider community. When relating her argument to postgraduate research study, for example, she argues that 'research can disable practice-led research by confusing practice with praxical knowledge and severing the link between the artwork and the work of art' (ibid.: 34).

Hazel Smith and Roger Dean (2009: 4) suggest that '[arts] knowledge can take many different forms and occur at various different levels of precision and stability'. In an attempt to tease out these forms and give a general overview of the potential for the PaR methodology within HE, Smith and Dean have developed the iterative cyclic web. The model presents as a map of potential starting points for developing ideas. The model suggests that arts research has the potential to move between, and be located in, three specific areas of activity: practice-led research, research-led practice and more traditional forms of academic research. In this particular model, practice-led research is defined as practice that generates 'research insights which might then be documented, theorised and generalised' and research-led practice is defined as 'scholarly research [that] can lead to creative work' (ibid.: 7). As the name suggests, the iterative cyclic web offers the practitioner-researcher a complex network of pathways, potential methodologies and subsequent opportunities for constructing a research inquiry; of course, it is important to emphasise that a research journey for arts practitioner-researchers must be led by the concerns of the project under consideration. However, the iterative cyclic web is a useful tool for locating practice within the wider context of research; the concept of iteration within the cycle is offered as a way of developing and refining the work and is seen as 'fundamental to both the creative and research processes' (ibid.: 19).

Focusing specifically on the articulation of a research inquiry where practice is a substantial element of the research output, Nelson's formulation of PaR has much to offer. He suggests that:

> Poststructuralism fosters a sceptical and radical mode of thought which resonates with experimentation in arts practices insofar as *play* is a method of inquiry, aiming not to establish findings by way of data to support a demonstrable and finite answer to a research question, but to put in *play* elements in a *bricolage* which afford insights through deliberate and careful juxtaposition.
>
> (Nelson, 2006: 109; my italics, except *bricolage*)

From this position, Nelson offers a model that combines three specific areas for consideration: practitioner knowledge, conceptual framework and critical reflection. This tripartite structure encourages the practitioner-researcher to move freely between these positions as the research unfolds, and suggests that the model may encourage the production of new knowledge and/or substantial new insights through the interplay of encounters exposed throughout the research inquiry, what Nelson refers to as 'Praxis (theory imbricated within practice)' (ibid.: 115).

Nelson's triangulation is conceived within a larger portfolio of evidence. For Nelson, 'a PaR submission is comprised of multiple modes of evidence reflecting a multi-mode research inquiry' (Nelson, 2013: 26). This is of particular significance for a practitioner-researcher exploring approaches to the dissemination of research intended for both specialist and non-specialist audiences, as it requires the practitioner-researcher to go through the process of selecting, exposing and refining key moments from the inquiry. Communicating with diverse audiences is an important skill for practitioner-researchers to develop – for example, when approaching potential funders and promoters to support the development of creative work. The portfolio should include a product (score or performance) providing a durable record for further reference, and a contextual document that draws out and further articulates the insights present in the product. Nelson suggests that PaR dissemination is also likely to include some documentation of the process. The presenting of documentation is also inferred from the dissemination models suggested by Haseman (2006; 2007), Bolt (2007) and Smith and Dean (2009). I see the use of a variety of contextual frameworks as being pivotal for the practitioner-researcher to expose the material thinking embedded within the creative practice using an insider's perspective on the work. I am not suggesting that practitioners should be required to develop the specialist skills associated with other specialist areas of musicology, although this may be possible; I am suggesting that practitioners draw on these areas as contextual frameworks to articulate a practitioner-informed position, or material thinking through practice.

As part of a research journey, it is important for practitioner-researchers to be able to position their practice within the wider context of a research community. Nelson defines this area of exploration within his model as the conceptual framework, and suggests that 'one way in which creative practice becomes innovative is by being informed by theoretical perspectives, either new in themselves, or perhaps newly explored in a given medium' (Nelson, 2006: 114). Here, I would suggest, the researcher and the research community have a responsibility to each other to disseminate the results of research, allowing the community to engage fully with current thinking in creative music practice. While the 300-word statement required by the assessors for the REF exercise to draw out the 'research imperatives and research process' (REF, 2012: 87) may provide sufficient information for the panel to make an informed judgement regarding the quality of the research, I would suggest that this particular method of research dissemination may not be of significant benefit to the wider research community. This is where elements of Nelson's model may be of value, and I would suggest that practitioner-researchers consider alternative ways of disseminating their research to their research community. Critical reflection in the form of attention to the processes that have contributed to the making of a work is an important element of the research journey. This may include reflection, using a specific conceptual framework drawing on the subcomponents of the practitioner knowledge element of the model. However, it is important to stress that in Nelson's model, the triangulation and the relationship between each element should remain fluid.

PaR at MMU

While there have been many significant achievements in the development of PaR as a methodology for practitioner-researchers working in higher education institutions, for some practitioner-researchers there remains confusion, for example, regarding what a submission for a practitioner-researcher might look like and what evidence should be presented to validate the new knowledge claims. A decade ago, Schippers (2007: 2) raised concerns that 'although music making involves research [this] does not necessarily qualify all music making as research', and feedback from the REF 2014 panel suggests that the articulation of PaR projects remains problematic. In relation to PaR, the REF panel stated that 'generally, the 300 word statements too often displayed a misunderstanding of what was being asked for and provided evidence of impact from the research, or a descriptive account akin to a programme note, rather than making the case for practice as research' (REF, 2015: 100).

So what should we expect from practitioner-researchers, and how might this be aligned with PhD training and supervision? The UK Quality Code for Higher Education is the definitive reference point for all UK higher education providers; it takes its definitions of research from both the *Frascati Manual*[2] and the REF audit. The *Frascati Manual* defines research as 'creative work undertaken on a systematic basis in order to increase the stock of knowledge, including knowledge of man, culture and society, and the use of this stock of knowledge to devise new applications' (Quality Assurance Agency for Higher Education, 2015: 6); for REF, research is 'defined as a process of investigation leading to new insights, effectively shared' (REF, 2011: 48). Working within these and similar definitions of research within the UK and beyond, practitioner-researchers are continuing to develop appropriate methods of inquiry and dissemination strategies for PaR projects.

At MMU, within the Department of Contemporary Arts, the PaR methodology is embedded within the curriculum at all levels. Research training in PaR is delivered through the MA in Contemporary Arts programme to postgraduate students and practitioner-researchers registered for PhD projects; it provides a contextual understanding of PaR as a methodology for practitioner research before students go on to explore the potential of the model within their own practice. Similar to Sullivan's construction of creative thinking, students at MMU develop 'thinking' strategies in the 'medium' and 'languages' of their arts practice tradition, and this is contextualised within the wider remit of institutional, professional and personal directives. At MMU, practitioner-researchers working within and across art forms develop research methods appropriate to their specific inquiry. In addition to the PaR work that is developing at MMU, since 2008 the Royal Northern College of Music has entered into a collaborative partnership with MMU for the validation of its MPhil and PhD programmes. The collaboration provides opportunities for university and conservatoire practitioner-researchers to come together to share good practice. To offer a flavour of how the PaR methodology is being applied by practitioner-researchers at both institutions, I offer two case studies as exemplars. Each case study will identify the methods used within the research project and will align with current definition(s) of research.

Creative teaching of research methods aligns with the four key areas embedded in the Frascati and REF definitions of research: that the research inquiry (1) must be a systematic study and/or an investigative process, (2) must produce new knowledge or establish new insights, (3) must be applied to practice and (4) must be effectively shared. Both case studies map an individual student's research journey through the four areas of research as defined by Frascati and REF and aligned to the musical creativities exposed within the development of appropriate languages (contextual frameworks, critical reflection) and media (composition, performance). Each case study identifies a specific practice 'problem' relevant to the student's own creative work. Through the development and application of a PaR method, both students have been able to engage with the process of developing and articulating their own creative identity.

Case study: Adam Fairhall (2008): *Intertextuality and the Dialogic Principle in Jazz*

Adam Fairhall is a performer/improviser working in a university. His doctoral study 'examines the central issue of intertextuality and dialogism in jazz from a range of critical, analytical and practical perspectives' (Fairhall, 2008: iii). Fairhall was well placed to undertake this research: his inquiry had been taking shape for some time before he decided to register for the programme, so he was able to navigate the drafting of a research proposal early in the process; at the time of enrolment, he was an accomplished performer/improviser; and through his practice, he was familiar with some of the academic 'issues' he wanted to explore.

Locating his practice within the performance traditions of jazz and contemporary improvised music, Fairhall identified a disparity between how music of this particular genre was being discussed in academic texts and how he understood the music to work in and through his practice. As a practitioner with experience of developing improvisational strategies for performance in this genre, he was aware that analytical accounts of how this music was being positioned, read and understood did not align with his own understanding. Therefore, developing an 'insider' music analysis of particular works from the genre already discussed within the academic literature provided a useful starting point for this research. From this 'insider' position, Fairhall, pursued three lines of inquiry: (1) developing more appropriate analytical techniques to understand how this music might be operating by placing the music within its cultural context and by considering theories of code-mixing already established in some areas of jazz studies, but not fully appropriated into the design of traditional music analysis at the time of study; (2) locating the practice within the wider context of contemporary arts with particular attention given to theories of intercultural and hybridic practices afforded across the arts to further inform this practitioner's improvisational performance strategies, and (3) the development of a personal practical improvisational performance vocabulary that emerges from the previous two strands.

The outcomes of the research have had a direct impact on the professional development of Fairhall as a performer/improviser. Through contextual, critical and musical analysis, Fairhall identified particular performance and compositional strategies embedded within the practices of others working in related fields, and has incorporated and further developed these insights into his working practices. Fairhall's research into the use of intertextual and dialogic principles in jazz has resulted in a body of performance work. His improvisations explore and combine the mixing of jazz styles both sequentially, as differently coded blocks of material set in opposition with each other, and vertically, where blocks of material are performed as independent simultaneous layers each with identifying musical elements from different musical styles. In addition, Fairhall uses the vertical alignment of coded blocks of material to develop further the notions of hybridity within his practice. Here, musical parameters of one music tradition are processed through the musical parameters of another tradition: for example, Fairhall (ibid.: 74) discusses how Eric Dolphy explores hybridity in his work through '[Charlie] Parker's idiom providing the rhythm, and a non-Parker idiom providing the harmonic-intervallic content'. We can hear this process operating in Fairhall's practice – the opening section of *Cow Cow* from the CD that accompanies his PhD submission combines the 'recognisable shapes and accent patterns derived from bop-related jazz with a pointillistic type of texture' found in contemporary improvised music (ibid.: 87).[3]

This PhD submission contains a written thesis and a CD recording of the final performance that took place the evening before the viva voce examination. The thesis positions the research and practice within the wider context of contemporary arts, and provides a contextual and musical analysis of the practice of others through what Fairhall defines as 'Rhetorical Formulae' – that is, a combination of 'syncretic' and 'hybridic' practices used by jazz and contemporary music practitioners. The final performance (documented on the CD recording that accompanies the submission) is an articulation, through practice, of the research findings. The research findings have informed Fairhall's practice. While the performance/improvisation was for the purposes of the examination team, Fairhall was keen to allow the public to attend the event. The examiners had read the thesis before attending the concert, and so would have been aware of what Fairhall was attempting to achieve through this performance; the audience (and the examiners) were also provided with detailed programme notes written for a general concert audience. The thesis, the concert and the programme notes were used to disseminate Fairhall's research and practice to a specialist and non-specialist audience.

Case study: Jacob Thompson-Bell (2014):
Deconstructed Narratives: A Composer's Perspective on Form, Process and Review

Jacob Thompson-Bell is a composer working in a conservatoire. His doctoral study directly related to and informed the work he was undertaking as a professional practitioner. While undertaking the research, a variety of organisations commissioned him to develop work, he initiated collaborative interdisciplinary projects that explored non-traditional forms of musical notation, and he devised installation works and curated exhibitions of works he had produced as well as the works of other emerging composers within his community. Each of these activities had a significant role to play in the development of his research project.

Thompson-Bell's research inquiry takes three distinct but interconnected pathways. These can be defined as narrative, non-narrative and anti-narrative articulations of musical time through compositional practice. The inquiry begins from a structuralist approach to composition where 'narrative' is defined as 'temporal syntax – its presence, or absence, and [their] implications for reception and critical discourse' (Thompson-Bell, 2014: ix). Developing the work of Jonathan Kramer, for this particular strand of inquiry Thompson-Bell identifies two types of narratives at work in his compositions: multi-linearity, where time is experienced as a series of dislocated events, and non-linearity, to be experienced as cyclic structures. Further compositions are developed to test these constructions of time, and are then problematised within the second strand of inquiry where non-narrativity in music is explored from a poststructuralist position. In this strand, scores are developed in a variety of non-temporal media and are to be negotiated in performance as collaborative projects between performers and this composer. Here, process and product are the focus of the inquiry; the relationship between them is explored and contextualised within poststructural and performance studies frameworks. The third pathway considers sound as a non-temporal structure, what

Thompson-Bell (ibid.: xiii) defines as 'a tangible, sensate medium that implicates all of us in its production'; here, the creative relationships that develop between the composer, the performer/interpreter and the listener are explored through curated and other performative events.

Thompson-Bell's research into how time works in musical structures has directly influenced his compositional practice. Within the narrative/structuralist strand of his inquiry, *Waiting For You* is an example of how groups of interlocking textures, some constructed as multi-linear units and others constructed as non-linear units, are integrated into his work.[4] While at the local level of operation this work appears to juxtapose blocks of contrasting material, at the global level similar blocks of material presented within the work are perceived as being connected through a process of implied voice-leading techniques. The resulting knowledge gained through the manipulation of multi-linear (dynamic) and non-linear (static) structures is then further developed within the non-narrative and anti-narrative strands of the research inquiry. One example of this is in the development of the *Songmaking Project*, where traditional notation, transcribed from images of museum artefacts, a graphic score derived from photographs and an Alaskan traditional song are combined and used as source material for a collaborative performance project. The resulting realisation of this work presents elements of both multi-linear and non-linear structures. Commenting on this project, Thompson-Bell (ibid.: 41) reports that 'given the apparent open qualities, *Songmaking* has provided me with fresh approaches to [the composing of] fixed structure'.

Thompson-Bell's PhD submission contained a portfolio of practice and a written thesis. The portfolio of practice includes musical scores, CD recordings of performances, and DVD recordings, presented as documentaries, articulating the process of making some of the works. The thesis claims to document 'significant activities and insights as they arose during the course of the investigation. The documentation aims to mimic the compositional techniques employed in the scores referenced, and is consequently delivered through a mixture of media – this includes written word, graphical analysis, illustration and audio deconstruction' (ibid.: ix).

The narrative pathway is documented through the medium of text. Multi-linearity and non-linearity are critiqued, drawing on the writings of Kramer and others. Within this section, Thompson-Bell disrupts his text by inserting descriptions of his work *Waiting For You*. When reading the critique of narrative structures, the interjection of musical descriptions of the work being discussed recalls the experience of listening to this particular music. Graphical analysis demonstrating compositional processes is offered as part of an Analytical Sketchbook, and used to disseminate the findings of works explored within the non-narrative section of the research. For example, personal reflections on the works of others are offered as potential starting points for new compositions. The processes and methods of constructing works are then transcribed into visual forms. Finally, the work undertaken exploring anti-narrative structures is documented through contextualised video documentaries. Following Haseman's suggestion that practitioner-researchers may express their findings through non-text media, Thompson-Bell's video documentaries are artworks in their own right.

Initial conclusions

PaR is now an established methodology used by practitioner-researchers working in higher education. While some remain unconvinced by the methodology and suspicious of the resulting methods that have emerged from individuals articulating the outcomes of their research for the benefit of both specialist and non-specialist audiences, arguing that the research outcomes are evident within the artwork and need no 'further' articulation from the maker of the work, others are embracing the opportunities PaR affords in articulating the complexities of arts research projects. All this has far-reaching consequences for the status of so-called objective knowledge generally, particularly for those who value the positivist research ideology developed through the sciences, not to mention the political implications regarding *who* knows and *how* they know *what* they know. As Thompson-Bell (2014: 23) suggests:

> Much institutionalised research is conducted as though the researcher is generating a commodity that can be 'sold' on to would-be 'knowers'. ... [PaR] is a direct challenge to this kind of product, operating instead in a grey area between action and reflection, blending together the carrying out of research and its dissemination. The responsibility of the researcher is thus shifted from producing a sealed (hopefully unassailable) product, to providing a means for others to engage in a process of open-ended investigation.

For both Fairhall and Thompson-Bell, developing individualised models of PaR has been a liberating experience which has enabled specific practice-focused 'problems' that have emerged in their work to receive critical attention and has provided personal practical solutions that have enabled their professional work to develop. One of the key guiding principles of this process for both students is that through the designing and application of an appropriate PaR method, practitioner-researchers need not do anything very different from their work as professional artists (Blain, 2013: 132). As Burnard (2012: 238) suggests when discussing musical creativities, 'different paths can be taken to reach to the same place ... [but] there is no need to be a slave to them'. Fairhall's inquiry began with a specific 'problem' related to his own practice; he developed and applied analytical and critical reflections on both the practice of others and his own work, and this led to aesthetic discoveries in his own thinking about his practice that was manifested in the making of new work. For Thompson-Bell, compositional 'problems' and solutions emerged throughout the period of inquiry through a process of iteration similar to the model proposed by Smith and Dean; this compositional work had the potential to follow other creative paths. For me, in my role as director of studies for both Fairhall and Thompson-Bell, drawing on the achievements of Haseman, Carter, Gray, Bolt and Nelson has provided opportunities to examine the relationship between making work and thinking about it. The PaR methodology and the resulting PaR methods proposed by each practitioner-researcher provide one way to develop, implement and reflect on creative strategies that directly affect the development of practice. So, returning to but refining our initial question: what is Thompson-Bell doing in a conservatoire, and what is Fairhall doing in a university? We might suggest that they are doing something very similar. They are developing methods through the PaR methodology to disseminate the exciting creative practices their work engages with. By doing this, they are also contributing to a research culture where knowledge of 'doing' and 'thinking' is celebrated.

Notes

1 REF is the system in the UK for assessing the quality of research in UK higher education institutions.
2 An internationally recognised document on research practices prepared and published by the Organisation for Economic Co-operation and Development.
3 More information about Adam Fairhall can be found at http://www.adamfairhall.co.uk (accessed March 28, 2016).
4 More information about Jacob Thompson-Bell can be found at http://jacobthompson bell.com (accessed March 28, 2016).

References

Blain, M. (2013). 'Composition-as-research: *Connecting Flights II* for Clarinet Quartet – a Research Dissemination Methodology for Composers'. *Music Performance Research*, 6, 126–51. Retrieved 5 June 2015 from http://mpr-online.net/Issues/ Volume%206%20[2013]/5.%20MPR0053%20Blain%20FINAL%20126%20-%20 151.pdf.

Bolt, B. (2007). 'The Magic is in Handling'. In: E. Barrett and B. Bolt (eds), *Practice as Research: Approaches to Creative Arts Enquiry* (pp. 27–34). London: I.B. Tauris.

Burnard, P. (2012). *Musical Creativities in Practice*. Oxford: Oxford University Press.

Carter, P. (2004). *Material Thinking: The Theory and Practice of Creative Research*. Carlton, Victoria: Melbourne University Press.

Dewey, J. (1934). *Art as Experience*. New York: Perigee.

Fairhall, A. (2008). 'Intertextuality and the Diologic Principle in Jazz' (unpublished PhD thesis). Manchester Metropolitan University, UK.

Gray, C. (1996). *Inquiry Through Practice: Developing Appropriate Strategies*. Retrieved 5 June 2015 from http://carolegray.net/Papers%20PDFs/ngnm.pdf.

Haseman, B. (2006). 'A Manifesto for Performative Research'. *Media International Australia Incorporating Culture and Policy: A Quarterly Journal of Media Research and Resources*, 118, 98–106.

——— (2007). 'Rupture and Recognition: Identifying the Performative Research Paradigm'. In: E. Barrett and B. Bolt (eds), *Practice as Research: Approaches to Creative Arts Enquiry* (pp. 147–57). London: I.B. Tauris.

Klausen, S.H. (2010). 'The Notion of Creativity Revisited: A Philosophical Perspective on Creativity Research'. *Creativity Research Journal*, 22(4), 347–60.

Nagy, Z. (2015). 'The Apperception of Musical Creativity: Performance as Ritual, Composition as Self-realization'. *Creativity Research Journal*, 27(1), 68–75.

Nelson, R. (2006). 'Practice-as-research and the Problem of Knowledge'. *Performance Research*, 11(4), 105–16.

——— (ed.) (2013). *Practice as Research in the Arts: Principles, Protocols, Pedagogies, Resistances*. New York: Palgrave Macmillan.

PARIP (n.d.). 'Practice as Research in Performance'. Retrieved 5 June 2015 from http://www.bris.ac.uk/parip/introduction.htm.

Polifonia (2007). *Guide to Third Cycle Studies in Higher Music Education*. Utrecht: Association Européenne des Conservatoires, Académies de Musique et Musikhochschulen. Retrieved 5 June 2015 from http://www.aec-music.eu/polifonia/polifonia-2004–2007/3rd-cycle-studies-in-music.

PRIMO (2007). 'Practice-as-research in Music Online (PRIMO)'. Retrieved 5 June 2015 from http://www.jisc.ac.uk/whatwedo/programmes/reppres/sue/primo.aspx.

Quality Assurance Agency for Higher Education (2015). 'Part B: Assuring and Enhancing Academic Quality. Chapter B11: Research Degrees'. Retrieved 5 June 2015 from http://www.qaa.ac.uk/assuring-standards-and-quality/the-quality-code/quality-code-part-b.

REF (2011). *Assessment Framework and Guidance on Submissions*. Retrieved 5 June 2015 from http://www.ref.ac.uk/media/ref/content/pub/assessmentframeworkandguidanceon submissions/GOS%20including%20addendum.pdf.

—— (2012). *Panel Criteria and Working Methods*. Retrieved 5 June 2015 from http://www.ref.ac.uk/media/ref/content/pub/panelcriteriaandworkingmethods/01_12.pdf.

—— (2015). *Research Excellence Framework 2014: Overview Report by Main Panel D and Sub-panels 27 to 36*. Retrieved 5 June 2015 from http://www.ref.ac.uk/media/ref/content/expanel/member/Main%20Panel%20D%20overview%20report.pdf.

Schippers, H. (2007). 'The Marriage of Art and Academia: Challenges and Opportunities for Music Research in Practice-based Environments'. *Dutch Journal for Music Theory*, 12(1), 34–40.

Smith, H. and Dean, R.T. (2009). 'Introduction: Practice-led Research, Research-led Practice – Towards the Iterative Cyclic Web'. In: H. Smith and R.T. Dean (eds), *Practice-led Research, Research-led Practice in the Creative Arts* (pp. 1–38). Edinburgh: Edinburgh University Press.

Sullivan, G. (2011). 'Artistic Cognition and Creativity'. In: M. Biggs and H. Karlsson (eds), *The Routledge Companion to Research in the Arts* (pp. 99–119). Abingdon: Routledge.

Thompson-Bell, J. (2014). 'Deconstructed Narratives: A Composer's Perspective on Form, Process and Review' (unpublished PhD thesis). Manchester Metropolitan University and Royal Northern College of Music.

7 Perspectives on research-led teaching

John Robert Ferguson

This chapter draws on my artistic work and experience teaching computer music and multimedia (Brown University, USA), music and creative music technology (Kingston University, London) and popular and contemporary music (Newcastle University, UK). I suggest that a discussion around practice-as-research can usefully contribute to creative teaching for creative learning in higher music education. My aims are: (1) to solidify practice-as-research as a valid academic method; (2) to provide idiosyncratic answers to the question, 'What is research-led teaching when the research is based around practice?', and (3) to consider broad differences and similarities at the above institutions.

Introduction: Exploring practice-as-research

I would like to begin by exploring practice-as-research. When Borgdorff (2006: 7) queries 'whether a phenomenon like research in the arts exists', he suggests that research in the arts revolves both around art objects and around creative processes, which are at once aesthetic, hermeneutic, performative and mimetic. Kjørup suggests that the concept of 'sensuous knowledge' is essential to the origins of the term 'aesthetics', which, in contrast to 'the science of beauty' or 'the philosophy of art', can be traced back to Alexander Gottlieb Baumgarten: 'To Baumgarten, aesthetics was to be the name of a kind of logic or epistemology for a specific type of knowledge, "cognitio sensitiva" in his 18th century Latin, a kind of intuitive knowledge or what we might render as sensuous knowledge' (Kjørup, 2006: 8).

Considering Baumgarten's thinking, Kjørup (2006: 20) suggests that, although not all artistic practice can or indeed should be configured as a kind of research, some of it 'may be'. I read this emphasis on 'may be' research as highlighting that art-based practitioners do not have such an established history of discursive tools and methods compared with scientific or more traditional scholarly researchers:

> The natural sciences have an empirical-deductive orientation; that is their methods are experimental and are designed to explain phenomena. ... The social sciences are likewise empirically oriented ... primarily designed to

> describe and analyze data. ... The humanities are as a rule more analytically than empirically oriented, and they focus more on interpretation than on description or explanation.
>
> (Borgdorff, 2006: 22)

What excites me about science is the emphasis placed on experimentation, but the formulation of precise universal laws is not my aim. I align myself with Nyrnes (2006: 7), who claims that artistic research is often discussed using vocabulary from traditional scientific theory, which tends to artificially focus on 'objectivity and truth', but does not capture what researchers in the artistic field 'experience as the most fascinating and even essential aspect':

> [Baumgarten] makes it clear that we must be able to discuss not only scientific knowledge, but also the one that is created and formulated through the arts. We have to develop ... new concepts and theories with which we can grasp that other way of knowing that we meet in the arts.
>
> (Kjørup, 2006: 20)

What I find most exciting here is the word 'grasp', which I take to mean grasping an idea or material object and thinking or making with it through speculative experimentation. Klaus Jung (2008: 12) states that 'artistic practice aims to grasp', which might be read as implying that it somehow never quite grasps. This could be further read as suggesting an (ironically) intangible aesthetic of the art object; the tangibility of the object does not completely equate with its aesthetics, which, however much we attempt to grasp them, we can never completely hold on to. Perhaps artistic practitioners, situated as they are on the sidelines of mainstream academia,[1] are well oriented to offer a unique form of illumination:

> the French philosopher Michel Foucault ... once wrote that it is not always climbing the highest peak that will give the most interesting view. On the contrary, light from the side will be the most alive and life giving. ... Foucault distinguishes between top light and side light as a means to obtain a clearer view of a situation.
>
> (Nyrnes, 2006: 7)

It is clear to me that any conceptualisation of theory and practice that configures their relationship as binary or oppositional will withstand little interrogation. The fact that material objects and artistic practices are often understood through theory suggests a conditional interdependence. Nyrnes (ibid.: 13) suggests that 'we can gain a better understanding of art research when we also talk about it in spatial or topological terms'. She defines three main topologies – 'own language', 'theory' and 'artistic material/field/artistic expression' – and claims that an appropriate balance of all three is needed for a successful project. Nyrnes suggests that 'own language' is organic and natural to us, but we need to question it and be inquisitive in order to articulate beyond it, thus highlighting the importance of critical reflection:

> This topos [own language] is a circle in the model to stress that this kind of language is organic; that it depends on the situation. ... to be able to identify the different bits and pieces of this own language is an important step towards more precise expressions both verbal and artistic.
>
> (ibid.: 15)

Theory is considered an ideology or 'a set of notions combined to form a reasonable cluster'. Nyrnes (ibid.: 16) draws this as a square 'to indicate that it is in some way an artificial language'. Artistic material/field/expression comprises the field or material that one wants to explore. Nyrnes (ibid.: 17) considers this the 'energy centre of artistic research', suggesting that 'the artistic material is in command of the situation' and that 'often the material at hand demands a new kind of tool': 'Artists all know that this topos is the heart of the artistic research process. This often goes unacknowledged in more traditional research projects ... only facts, in the singular, not reflections themselves, make us think. In this way the artist will challenge the whole field and notion of research' (ibid.: 18).

Finding my way through these ideas, I suggest that 'own language' is what we do before we consciously reflect upon it, whereas 'theory' is a more conscious process – what we think about what we do, or what we come to understand about what we did. Theory remains external and separate to the doing of what was done, but is instructive in establishing the horizons in which the feasibility of making theory manifest as part of 'own language' can be tested. Crucially, 'own language' emerges through a process that includes 'theory', so each of the three topoi can be, and are, enriched by the other two. Nyrnes (ibid.: 19) suggests that one topos can 'rest while exploring the connections between the other two and vice versa. The important thing is to move on when one direction is blocked.' Idiosyncratic topological manoeuvring is the basis of this method. At this point, I find it useful to note a difference between method and methodology:

> method is here considered not as a systematic path to knowledge available to all, but as a singular mode of progressing tied ... to an individual life ... unlike a methodology in which rigorousness is measured against the organization of thought around a têlos that allows the fullness of this thought to fulfil itself as truth, method delays the attainment of truth through a movement that both Heidegger and Blanchot describe as erring: a rigorous error always maintaining a distance from truth and its allure.
>
> (Peters, 2009: 6)

Borgdorff (2006: 21) is similarly critical of methodology, especially in so far as 'as one criterion for sound academic research is a fundamental indifference as to who performs the research'. For the purposes of artistic research, I suggest that a rejection of the methodological establishment of universal laws, in favour of methods that embrace the unique insights afforded by an individual's prejudices, would seem to be suitable. This to me is what practice-as-research is all about, and also the premise upon which both hermeneutics and phenomenology are based. To bring this section to a close, I quote Borgdorff on when art practice should qualify as research:

> Art practice qualifies as research if its purpose is to expand our knowledge and understanding by conducting an original investigation in and through art objects and creative processes. Art research begins by addressing questions that are pertinent in the research context and in the art world. Researchers employ experimental and hermeneutic methods that reveal and articulate the tacit knowledge that is situated and embodied in specific artworks and artistic processes. Research processes and outcomes are documented and disseminated in an appropriate manner to the research community and the wider public.
>
> (ibid.: 23)

Practice-as-research as a strategy for creative learning – a summary

My overarching argument is that rigorously exploring music, art practice or whatever else you might call it *as* research is a productive strategy for creative teaching and learning. My experience working with new technologies in the field of music technology and computer music as well as my interest in the relationship between popular music and higher education means that, for me, it is useful to perceive 'art practice' and 'music' as one and the same. To summarise my main points: art-based practitioners do not have such an established history of discursive tools and methods compared with their scientific or more traditional scholarly counterparts, and such methods may be inappropriate. Resisting the allure of 'truth' or methodological correctness can avoid over-reliance on inappropriate means. Thinking about Jung's discussion around grasp and the intangibility of an art object raises the question: How do we teach our students to accept the intangibility of ideas and of material things and to value experimentation itself as a worthy aim? I believe that risk, experimentation and the sort of edge-of-current-knowledge research practice that exposes latent contradictions and broader issues within a subject should be at the foreground of teaching methods. In this regard, I find useful Nyrnes's topological manoeuvring, which highlights the interdependence of theory and practice, as well as the manner in which one informs and becomes the other, and I frequently use this as a framework to find momentum in my own work, and to inspire and encourage my students.

What is research-led teaching when the research is based on practice?

A statement such as 'I strive to make my teaching as innovative and research-led as possible' is easy to make, but what does it mean? Simply being in touch with contemporary thinking/practice and communicating this in a traditional linear form may not be enough. Following Sennett's (2008: 1) 'making is thinking' and

Fiske's (1992) 'thinking is for doing', learning is an active process that involves intellectual ideas and practical experimentation; thus, I strive to embed practical activity at the heart of theoretical learning, and vice versa. Borrowing from Gadamer (2004), I suggest that knowledge is an ability to apply, translate or interpret, so one only *really* knows something when one can apply or interpret it; creativity is an inherent but often intangible component within this. As an example I point to Fink's 'Teaching Music History (After the End of History): "History Games" for the Twentieth-century Survey Class' (2002). Rejecting techno-essentialism, he suggests that music history should not be taught 'in terms of the steady, inexorable development of purely musical technique' (ibid.: 44) and discusses three of his courses that deal with the rise of modernism and its collapse, an awakening from and unravelling of this collapse, and finally 'music now'. At the outset, he asks:

> how are we to ignore the fact that 'postmodernism', the collapse of these master narratives, happens within the period of music history that we are trying to teach? And that one of the narratives that collapses with the biggest bang is the self-congratulatory narrative of musical progress that twentieth century musicians and composers have consistently mistaken for 'music history' itself?
>
> (ibid.)

Fink introduces the idea of the 'history game: a complex, idiosyncratic, pragmatic, often self-reflexive performance of musical history that foregrounds its own contingent nature' (ibid.: 45). This approach asks students to make non-linear connections through history and emphasises the application and translation of ideas. Explaining 'music now', he writes:

> lectures took the form of multiple excursions back from the present moment into various possible historical contexts and ancestries. The game here was explicit: to use the self-conscious artifice of a historical narrative, turned entirely upside down, to range as widely and as promiscuously as possible through the entirety of the de-historicized eternal present.
>
> (ibid.: 57)

In short, students do not just encounter history, but are taught to interpret creatively and construct history 'as players, not just spectators in the ongoing game of telling stories about the past' (ibid.: 45). I am convinced that jamming with ideas in this way is at least as important as jamming with instruments, and the emphasis on learning as a form of active interpretation resonates with my central argument. Thinking about 'History Games' and Nyrnes's topological manoeuvring, I believe that teacher and student should learn from and be challenged by each other, that group interaction and peer feedback are vital, and that a teacher's role as an active participant in learning should range from reflexive guidance to provider of creative catalyst. As Jamie Allen once put it, the goal is to offer 'the right amount of information at the right time'.[2] I am reminded that so much music-making is collaborative, yet as Ginsborg and Wistreich observe in *Promoting Excellence in Small Group Music Performance* (2010: 6): 'The development of music curricula in university music departments and conservatoires has been dogged by the inability to address the assessment of group performance.' During my time as a tutor at Newcastle University, I was involved in research that fed into this project and was particularly excited in September 2009 to encounter Wilkinson and Hardy's approach to tutoring collective performance on the Folk and Traditional Music degree. As reported by Ginsborg and Wistreich (ibid.: 42):

> [the tutors] began by chucking the students virtually at random into a series of 'instant bands', giving them perhaps a tune and half an hour to prepare an arrangement, present it to the class, have a lot of feedback from both peers and tutors, before it's all change and on to the next combination. After some weeks, as the various musical personalities, strengths and weaknesses become more evident, the tutors eventually assemble permanent bands that seem, at least from the outside, to have the best chance of working out and these stay together for the rest for the year.

Around this time, Bennett Hogg and I were co-teaching 'Practical Studies in Popular Music' to students on the Popular and Contemporary Music degree at Newcastle University. As well as guitarists, vocalists and drummers, this course was compulsory for studio composers, who were often more used to working alone and in 'non-live' scenarios, so contributing to an ensemble was challenging. Previous versions of this course had streamed students into ensembles using a short survey/audition, and then 'expected ... [them] to work [their] way through the challenges and crises – dis-bandment [was] strongly discouraged!' (ibid.: 42). Although this encouraged real-world professionalism typical of a working band and was successful for most, if artistic differences emerged it was occasionally catastrophic.

In light of this, Hogg and I implemented a version of Wilkinson and Hardy's 'instant bands', but the basic premise was that popular music is not repertoire based. So although we formed ensembles and assigned each group a song, we asked for a creative interpretation in a genre unrelated to the original or any known cover version. The second week revolved around performance, feedback and critique, then new bands were formed and the exercise repeated. During the third and fourth week, each ensemble wrote original material, broadly following on from the aesthetic they had arrived at with the previous cover. In short, they were asked to identify and further the characteristics of whatever band identity had begun to emerge. Hogg and I would offer practical and theoretical guidance and allocate listening assignments as potential 'jumping off points' for future work. By the third project, we sought to establish a 'final line-up' for each ensemble, which was expected to create its own material; at this point, we were confident that exciting work could emerge. The emphasis placed on creative interpretation and application seems to me similar to Fink's 'History Games'. Further to emphasise relevance to research-led teaching I return to Ginsborg and Wistreich (ibid.: 41–2):

> The principle underlying pretty well all conventional educational curricula is the concept of additive or teleological processes – working outwards by

measured steps from simple skills towards increasingly complex ones ... in the case of ... 'chamber music', from individuals reading their own notes and getting them right, towards coordination, cooperation and precision, with demarcated progressive stages of private practice, communal rehearsals. ... And yet folk and pop bands often *start* by creating their musical materials, either composing them from scratch or collectively arranging tunes, passing ideas around and developing them, often haphazardly, and in a state of constant flux.

From my perspective, these remarks highlight that popular music and creative music technology are relatively young fields of study, and appropriate research and pedagogical methods remain a work in progress. Perhaps the most research-oriented undergraduate course I have taught to date originates in Hogg's concept of 'post-vernacular composition', which is something he defines as 'developing a practice beyond the confines of the vernacular expectations of that practice' and 'making something new with a set of old skills'.[3]

Drawing from these ideas, my 'feral pop' course at Brown University, USA, explored the fertile creative territory found around the more adventurous edges of popular musics and sought to extend and build upon the inherently experimental dimensions of much vernacular musical practice. The open-endedness of this course, and the suggestion that genuinely new musical paradigms are emerging in bedroom studios and underground venues through the experimental appropriation of vernacular and popular music, means that practice-as-research was at the absolute foreground. Thinking about this description and the 'other way of knowing' that Kjørup (2006: 20) proposes, the course that I was most proud of at Brown is 'Circuit Bending and Hardware Hacking as Musical and Artistic Expression'. Basic principles were introduced via a range of simple electronic circuits, and students then explored strategies to animate and interpret pre-existing electronic devices. The aesthetics of do-it-yourself and the handmade were at the foreground and the final events featured solo and collaborative projects with idiosyncratic instruments. This course negotiated the edge of my technical knowledge; the research needed to teach it is what Nyrnes would characterise as 'theory'. However, it also provided opportunities to develop my 'own language' and explore 'artistic materials' because I built new instruments as part of the class and performed in class concerts. It is interesting to note feedback from students regarding what they valued most: 'The appreciation of art I do not fully understand or can quantify. The pursuit of improvement in spite of an absence of a quantifiable art form'; 'This class has surprisingly been the most effective in my pre-dental education. The motor skills and attention to detail with soldering has helped me prepare for a future holding dental tools and operating on patients'; 'It was inspiring to see him working alongside the students as well, showing us examples of what could be done with the course material.'

Apart from showing that performing alongside students means they learn from how you use the space and react to the pressure of a performance situation, the third comment demonstrates the value of incorporating exploratory research in a teaching context. The 'pre-dental' comment was a surprise, but speaks to Brown

University's Open Curriculum (see Bergeron, 2012) and against those who might insist on a more methodologically attuned or industry-focused pedagogy. Returning to the question, 'What is research-led teaching when the research is based around practice?', and thinking about Nyrnes's topological map, the first comment is perhaps the most telling. Research-led teaching in this case is asking students to engage with aesthetic repertoire and technical knowledge (theory), to work with new materials, tools and collaborative scenarios (artistic field/material), filtered through whatever inspires them/existing skills (own language).

Section summary

My aims in this section were to highlight interpretation and application (both of ideas and practical skills) as a useful strategy for creative teaching and learning. Examples include (1) Fink's approach to creatively interpreting history, which empowers students to creatively construct the future; (2) Ginsborg and Wistreich's suggestion that collaboration itself, especially within folk and popular musics, is an issue that university music departments and conservatoires need to address, and (3) the incorporation of technology in performance-based work *as* a research question – that is, expecting a studio composer to play in an ensemble, or expecting a student to build new instruments or work with forms of composition that do not have a culturally established history. In support of this, I point to the student who valued 'The appreciation of art I do not fully understand or can quantify' and 'The pursuit of improvement in spite of an absence of a quantifiable art form'. This, to my way of thinking, speaks to the value of rigorous/idiosyncratic method over the apparent certainty of methodology.

Interviews with Rovan and Winkler

To further and broaden the discussion, I am grateful for the input of Professors Rovan and Winkler, who co-direct Multimedia and Electronic Music Experiments in the Music Department at Brown University. This section is based upon two wide-ranging conversations that go some way to highlight broad differences and similarities in pedagogy in the UK and the USA. Considering the question, 'What do students get from research-led teaching?', Rovan replied:

> They get the passion for something that really matters to you, and that fuels the classroom. It's one thing to teach a topic, but when you're completely inside something, living and breathing that thing, you have this incredibly intense perspective, and I think that's a pretty amazing window for students to have.

Discussing related ideas, Winkler touched upon the importance and role of collaboration and highlighted the significance of practice/repetition and embodied learning:

> I always want to teach what I'm doing my research on … I have this class Performance in Virtual Worlds and I'm working on a theatre piece … so I show

them what I know, we'll look at what other exemplary artists have done in the field, I'll show them some techniques and see what they come up with in collaborative groups. The best part of learning in that class is the three people working together; I'm convinced of that. … I say 'you're all really good at something or you wouldn't be here', we have writers, experienced filmmakers, actors, a lot of people that know some technology, I tell them 'you all will make together a project much better than you can do by yourself, if you collaborate well. If you don't it'll be a nightmare.' … If, for example, one student already knows *Final Cut* [movie editing software], I ask them to sit with the person that doesn't know it and show them what to do, but let them do the cutting. Their job is to teach the other people what they know.

It is clear that learning by doing is valued, and this conversation highlighted the importance of opportunities for repeated practice, hence making the person who does not know the software 'do the cutting'. Although not the fastest way to achieve a goal, this method has two advantages: (1) the student for whom the software is new gains fluency, and (2) the more expert student sharpens their skills because knowing how to do something and being able to teach it are different things. On this subject, and thinking about classes that focus on technology, I have often felt that too much time is typically wasted demonstrating skills in specialist resources such as a recording studio. This can lead to a lack of time for practical learning in the sense of 'doing'. In light of this, at Kingston University I developed a method whereby students would attend a weekly lecture introducing what they would be doing in a small group studio session later that week. I would then steer the studio session by offering guidance and asking questions, but would not operate any of the equipment myself. Although this sometimes meant more initial mistakes, I have found recurrently that it is much more valuable to get something wrong but understand why than not really understand how or why one has got something correct. Mistakes are thus an important part of the learning process. Rather than feel as though they were arriving at a studio session to be shown something, students demonstrated 'ownership' of their learning experience by arriving with ideas to practically experiment, interpret and develop. This approach seemed to resonate with Rovan:

It's something we wrestle with a lot – skill versus concepts, it's a balance. Presenting tools and techniques is OK as long as you don't present the suggested application of the tools too much. Because if you do that you close down the whole creative process. … Some of the way I teach has been described as teaching from the middle out, instead of starting at the absolute beginning, you start at a middle point and get going quickly.

When discussing with Winkler the danger of closing down the creative process, the subject of assessment arose, and he stated: 'most of my classes I make mandatory pass/fail, there are no grades, but if you miss more than three classes you won't get credit for the class'. If students fully participate in the class, they will learn the maximum amount that they possibly can: 'I tell them we're making difficult and interesting work in this class and we're going to do it together, in groups.' What I like about this approach is the broad mix of accepted experiences and abilities; it is great to have students from different year groups working together, and at Brown there seems to be an acceptance that students will have different skills and abilities. Students are graded on the extent to which their work develops, not the extent to which it matches external criteria, as Rovan comments: 'Assessment should be calibrated to the individual student, it's not a science class where there are a set number of formulae that everyone has to learn and it's very easy to see if they did this of if they didn't ... it's very, very different.'

Some scenarios do require a compartmentalised approach to grading. One example is 'Computers and Music', a course that examines the history of music technology within popular and experimental musics and teaches practical skills in computer music. Winkler explains, 'I want students to study and learn the facts and the background technical knowledge'; this class is assessed via two written exams, four audio projects and a short research paper. Asked about typical grades, Winkler said usually 'a little less than half get an A, most of the remainder get a B, there are a few Cs, and some do fail'. Grading and grade inflation is a contentious topic (see Zappa, 2014; Thomas, 2013). However, I find the system at Brown to be very healthy; students are not obsessed with grades, and unlike my experience in the UK, little importance is placed on quantitative ranking of students against each other or external criteria, meaning more time is spent on teaching and research. Rovan comments: 'Personal feedback takes precedence. Grades can be detrimental if they get in the way of personnel connection. There seems to be a global desire for more assessment, the UK is clearly way ahead [or behind] in that path; it's a little bit scary.'

At Brown, there seems to be much less need for professors to spend time writing detailed formative feedback than in the UK. This is because contact time with students is generous. One of my practical classes ran in two 90-minute blocks per week with an additional lab for an hour and two 'office hours', which I ran as an informal drop-in. This meant I would supervise students on four separate occasions per week for a total of six hours, and often considerably more in the run-up to concerts. When asked whether this amount of contact time was common at other institutions in the USA, Winkler, who has also taught at California Institute of the Arts and Oberlin College Conservatory of Music, suggested that this was 'pretty typical'. This seems very different to my experience in the UK. In thinking about a specific example of this open-ended approach to teaching and discussing the interdependence of theory and practice, and how one becomes the other, Rovan articulated his approach to teaching gesture:

> with gesture there's the technology aspect, but we're also thinking conceptually and physically moving and performing gesture and then we're trying to understand it from many different levels ... making a creative work that

takes all that and synthesises it into something else that's like a translation, and you can read in that translation the traces of all the various different angles that were put into it.

Furthering this, Rovan said: 'I trust students' innate creativity to find interesting things and I think that's maybe something we don't do enough.' In addition, he suggested that some schools 'tend to produce people who are very similar because they've somehow embedded a concept of what is correct or what's right'. Leaving the outcome open and having high expectations can result in 'amazing stuff', but 'you will get stuff that fails dramatically too and you have to accept that'. Further discussing the various tensions and differing skillsets/levels of prescription in different music-making traditions, I asked Winkler about friction between popular musics and art music and how he thought this might develop. He replied, 'a broad look at culture in all its forms is important', adding that:

> *Thriller* is the best-selling album of all time and *Dark Side of the Moon*, the longest charting. ... I think there's an understanding that whether you like it or not Michael Jackson is important, he's important to the culture, he's important to the world, if Michael Jackson hadn't existed everything would be a little different.

Like Fink, Winkler emphasised the need to teach contemporary music history in an open-ended and non-linear way: 'the development of the computers and music class is so interesting to me because it shows how much [and how fast] the situation has changed'. A similar conversation with Rovan led in a different direction, towards the future creative mix of art and technology:

> innovation remains tightly coupled with Science, Technology, Engineering and Math – the STEM subjects. Art + Design are poised to transform our economy in the twenty-first century just as science and technology did in the last century. We need to add Art + Design to the equation – to transform STEM into STEAM.
>
> (Rhode Island School of Design, 2015)

Highlighting STEAM, Rovan emphasised how contemporary music pedagogy is already ahead of the curve in terms of innovation, suggesting that 'our students may become entrepreneurs and innovators in this new art/tech space', which is why it's so vital to keep that spark of the student's individual creativity alive:

> In an instrument building class, we're not making products, we're making something that is going to be used in performance, but performance is the ultimate test of a concept. You could not make a better proof of concept. It's more than that. Whatever you've done exists and has this creative effect on people. So there is an amazing connection between what we do and what these other people are calling innovation and entrepreneurship.

Summary of interviews with Rovan and Winkler

Although something of a generalisation and not representative of the entire higher education system in the USA, it is clear that students at Brown benefit from a significant amount of contact time and a less 'assessment-focused' culture than their UK counterparts. At the foreground of Rovan and Winkler's comments, as well as my own experience of music at Brown, is the fact that students are trusted to choose their own curriculum, learn from each other and take responsibility for their own progress. Professors are free to change course content in light of their current research, which, combined with the inherent choice offered by the Open Curriculum (see Bergeron, 2012), seems to produce highly innovative and entrepreneurial students. The freedom to experiment and the possibility of failure, and the opportunity to work collaboratively with students from diverse backgrounds and across multiple year groups of a single concentration, are all valuable when considering creative teaching for creative learning in a higher education environment.

Conclusion

Summarising conversations with Rovan and Winkler revolved around how, as researchers, musicians and artistic practitioners function within Nyrnes's interpretation of 'lighting from the side'. Her tripartite topological thinking, which argues for the interdependence of theory and practice, as well as the manner in which one informs and becomes the other, also highlights the importance of open-ended teaching methods that nurture student creativity. If any conclusion was reached, it was that artistic research revolves around a multiplicity of approaches and angles that illuminate something from many different perspectives. Various practical interpretations of Fink's 'History Games' and the idea of simultaneous linear and non-linear teaching were also considered important. There was general agreement that the aim of research-led teaching is to foster and create a space for students to inhabit an evolving landscape that has no clear bounds. Additive or teleological processes have their place, but methods that involve application, translation and interpretation were considered most fruitful.

Whether Russell Group, post-92 or Ivy League, I see many opportunities for research-led teaching, and have experienced more similarities than differences at these very different institutions. Although I offer no definitive answer to the question, 'What is research-led teaching when the research is based around practice?', my work will continue to be driven by this, and I hope to have emphasised a need to further practice-as-research as a valid academic method.

Notes

1 See Borgdorff (2006: 8) for a more in-depth discussion.
2 Personal communication.
3 Personal communication.

References

Bergeron, K. (2012). 'A Tradition of Reform: The Curriculum at Brown University'. In: P. Blackmore and C.B. Kandko (eds), *Strategic Curriculum Change: Global Trends in Universities* (pp. 34–40). London: Routledge.

Borgdorff, H. (2006). *The Debate on Research in the Arts*. Bergen: Bergen National Academy of the Arts.

Fink, R. (2002). 'Teaching Music History (After the End of History): "History Games" for the Twentieth-century Survey Class'. In M. Natvig (ed.), *Teaching Music History* (pp. 43–68). Aldershot: Ashgate.

Fiske, S.T. (1992). 'Thinking is for Doing: Portraits of Social Cognition from Daguerreotype to Laser Photo'. *Journal of Personality and Social Psychology*, 63, 877–89.

Gadamer, H.-G. (2004). *Truth and Method*. Translated by J. Weinsheimer and D.G. Marshall. 2nd, rev. edn. London: Continuum.

Ginsborg, J. and Wistreich, R (2010). *Promoting Excellence in Small Group Music Performance: Teaching, Learning and Assessment*. Retrieved 1 May 2015 from https://www.heacademy.ac.uk/sites/default/files/smallgroupmusicperformance.pdf.

Jung, K. (2008). *Enabling Knowledge*. Bergen: Bergen National Academy of the Arts.

Kjørup, S. (2006). *Another Way of Knowing: Baumgarten, Aesthetics, and the Concept of Sensuous Cognition*. Bergen: Bergen National Academy of the Arts.

Nyrnes, A. (2006). *Lighting from the Side: Rhetoric and Artistic Research*. Bergen: Bergen National Academy of the Arts.

Peters, G. (2009). *The Philosophy of Improvisation*. Chicago, IL: University of Chicago Press.

Rhode Island School of Design (2015). 'STEM to STEAM'. Retrieved 4 May 2015 from http://stemtosteam.org/.

Sennett, R. (2008). *The Craftsman*. London: Penguin.

Thomas, E. (4 December 2013). 'Harvard Professor Slams College for Handing Out Too Many A Grades'. *Huffington Post*. Retrieved 1 May 2015 from http://www.huffingtonpost.com/2013/12/04/harvard-grade-inflation-_n_4384848.html.

Zappa, J. (12 March 2014). 'Fighting Grade Inflation: A Cause without a Rebel'. *Brown Daily Herald*. Retrieved 1 May 2015 from http://www.browndailyherald.com/2014/03/12/fighting-grade-inflation-cause-without-rebel/.

8 Teaching the supreme art

Pre-service teacher perceptions of creative opportunities in the higher education music class

Kari Veblen, H. Elisha Jo and Stephen J. Messenger

It is the supreme art of the teacher to awaken joy in creative expression and knowledge.

Albert Einstein

Introduction

This chapter explores the role of creativity in higher education through perceptions of pre-service music educators.[1] In a Canadian university elementary methods class, pre-service music educators develop strategies and skills for teaching music to children. This chapter examines the attitudes of nascent music educators after two semesters immersed in creative endeavours in an elementary methods course in which 15 students engaged in a variety of musical activities, created portfolios of their work for discussion and reflected on their development.

Canadian music education

Cultural assumptions about the nature and value of creativity are naturally embedded within educational systems. Therefore, we provide a brief background of the Canadian context. A large country extending across upper North America, Canada is a nation of immigrants. By law, ethnic groups are encouraged to maintain their individuality within a multicultural mosaic overlaid on a grid of indigenous peoples and settlers with European historical connections. The country is officially trilingual, increasingly secular in values and outward-looking. Canada ranks eighth in the UN Human Development Index – a composite statistic of education, per capita income and life expectancy indicators used to rank countries.[2]

The Canadian educational system – including music education – is decentralised at the national level. There is universal access to education. Each province or territory determines curricular guidelines, teacher education and other particulars of schooling, often with reference to other provinces. Canadian music educators value creativity;[3] however, valuing is often different from teaching. Canadian composer R. Murray Schafer wrote: 'You can't tell people *how* to become creative, but you can reveal the excitement of creative activity and hope that it may encourage them to try something on their own. Allowing children to become creative does not require genius: it requires humility' (Schafer, 2012: viii).

Children's musical creativity

Few researchers dispute that creativity is an essential factor in children's musical development (Barrett, 2006; Campbell, Scott-Kassner and Kassner, 2010; Hickey, 2009), and studies of natural musical play suggest that children are both innovative and conserving in their practice (Campbell, 1998; Marsh, 2008; Harwood and Marsh, 2012).

Research extols the benefits of composition and improvisation in the music classroom (Burnard and Fautley, 2014; Coulson and Burke, 2013; Leong et al., 2012; Odena, 2012; Robinson, Bell and Pogonowski, 2011; Wiggins and Espeland, 2012). This phenomenon is especially notable in small-group, collaborative creative work (Beegle, 2010; Beineke, 2013; Burnard and Younker, 2008; Harwood and Marsh, 2012; Lapidaki, De Groot and Stagkos, 2012).

Research with music teachers in the field

Although definitions of creativity vary, most music educators value qualities such as originality, independence, imagination and divergent thinking skills in teaching and learning music (Burnard, 2012; Burnard, 2007; Diakidoy and Kanari, 1999; Elliott and Silverman, 2014; Leong et al., 2012; Odena, 2012). Studies indicate that the teacher's own comfort and familiarity with a variety of creative practices are pivotal in furthering learners' musical explorations (Bernhard, 2013; Burnard, 2012; Diakidoy and Kanari, 1999; Stavrou, 2013). Odena and Welch (2012) conducted a four-year case study of English secondary school teachers which noted the importance for practitioners of having grounded knowledge of different musical genres and composing to engage with their students' efforts.

The nature and extent of improvisation in the classroom has been studied in very different settings. Gruenhagen and Whitcomb (2014) surveyed US elementary music teachers and found that they were most likely to incorporate (1) spontaneous rhythmic patterns, (2) melodic improvisation on pitched percussion instruments and (3) call-and-response singing. The authors noted: 'These teachers stated they were most interested in the quality of the improvisational process rather than with the product and indicated that sequencing was crucial in the instruction of improvisation' (ibid.: 379). In an investigation of the collaborative practices of three Norwegian music teachers with their primary level students, Sætre (2011) found that each teacher had a unique approach to compositional engagements. Regardless of the elements incorporated into a teacher's pedagogy, the teacher may be the vehicle by which the instruction is transmitted.

Research with pre-service teachers

Creative habits of mind are considered desirable attributes for teachers in training, and are embedded in many music education methodology courses as attitudes, approaches and techniques (Robinson, Bell and Pogonowski, 2011; Whitcomb, 2013; Wiggins and Espeland, 2012; Younker, 2013). While some research examines musical encounters in a university setting (Bujez and Mohedo, 2013), other studies seek to capture pre-service teacher assumptions. Cypriot music education majors defined creativity using the attributes of imagination, independence and divergent thinking skills (Diakidoy and Kanari, 1999). These students felt that 'creative outcomes are not necessarily appropriate outcomes' in a school context (ibid.: 239).[4] In addition, Kokotsaki (2011) found that her English pre-service music educators believed that creativity could be developed as a by-product of instruction, rather than an element of a systematic curriculum. Bernhard (2013) investigated undergraduate instrumental music majors in the USA, finding that those specialising at the elementary level were less confident in their abilities to teach improvisation than those training to teach at the secondary level.

Current research indicates consensus that creativity plays an important role in children's musical development. While most music educators understand the importance of imagination and divergent thinking skills in music-making, a teacher's familiarity with creative practices and personal ease is essential for furthering musical explorations. A university-level methods course presents an ideal space to cultivate both strategies and attitudes. Previous studies have found that music majors questioned the value of creative work in formal schooling, or believed that creativity could be developed, but might emerge as an indirect result. The study detailed in this chapter sought to engage pre-service teachers with activities and readings to promote metacognitive thinking as well as collaborative music explorations and to learn whether their perceptions reflected their evolving facility and comfort level.

Context

The setting for this research is an elementary methods class for pre-service educators, operating as part of 'Music 3850: Elementary Music Education' at the University of Western Ontario in Canada. In this one-year course, students develop strategies and skills for teaching music to children. The class is conceived as a community of practice shaped through connected engagement and relevant learning experiences (Lave and Wenger, 1991). The instructors assume the role of facilitators,[5] and the students initiate and collaborate, taking responsibility for their learning. At the beginning of the course, students list their expectations and requests, which are balanced with established course requirements and integrated into the curriculum.

The classroom is arranged as an intentional, interactive and safe space. Research-based formal and informal approaches to transmitting music are utilised in the class. Emphasis is placed on participatory music-making, holistic and multi-modal learning, collective decision-making and exploratory play (Burnard and Younker, 2008; Harwood and Marsh, 2012; Lapidaki, De Groot and Stagkos, 2012; Marsh, 2008).

Participants sing, move, play instruments, arrange, generate and perform as part of every class. Each opportunity for creative play through composition, improvisation or integration becomes a cyclical event. As Beineke (2013: 288) writes:

> The process of creative learning is not linear, ... each work produced, presented and analyzed by children can generate its own dynamic. ... Each of these moments in the composition activities contributing to the dimensions of creative learning were articulated in a process that changes and updates in a cyclic spiral movement, i.e., in a repeating cycle that renews, transforms and updates itself in this process.

This process is seen in relation to the particular cohort of students who participated in our research. Students are also challenged to explore cognitive and artistic possibilities in their initial music teaching via metacognitive strategies. During the course, each student chose and presented on two topics, taught several songs, reported on four structured observations of music classrooms, read systematically and attended outside events. Students interacted with five guest lecturers who shared songs and games and discussed music therapy, motivation in the classroom and composition. Students were challenged with both structured and unstructured creativity projects. For example, in one exercise, the class broke into groups of four, each with a different task:

Group 1: Choose percussion instruments and a $\frac{7}{8}$ metre. Over this, generate a repetitive melody with or without words, try harmony, improvised parts.

Group 2: Using three Orff instruments and recorders, choose a familiar song to arrange. Incorporate an improvised section.

Group 3: Using recorders and voices, perform Paul Fleishman's poem 'Fireflies' for two parts. How else can you convey this poem? Movement? Lights? Sound effects?

Group 4: Choose a leader, choose your topic and the limitations for your composition. Select instruments. Have leader direct activities. Then switch leaders.

You have 15 minutes. Perform for class. Then critique in group and reshape, refine. Perform again for class. What was the difference? Did you like this better the first or second time, and why? In groups, write your thoughts down in a composition reflection and submit reflections to the course instructor (no names).

Other structured activities included listening and moving to music, composing songs following a process facilitated by a class member, improvising skits with puppets and instruments, and using recorders to generate harmonies. Leslie Linton visited with student teachers from University of Western Ontario Althouse Faculty of Education, and generated rounds with varying kinesthetic and ostinato patterns. Composer Sean Kim played his emerging musical compositions, and then facilitated soundscapes. Two creative, individual project options were scheduled at the beginning and end of the second semester and shared with the class; students also submitted a portfolio of work. Other activities are constructed in response to the particular cohort's needs and interests, meaning that the course content will vary from year to year.

Methodology

This chapter focuses on pre-service teachers participating in the course detailed above, examining their perceptions of creative opportunities and their evolving abilities to create these opportunities. The participants comprised 15 music education majors in their third and fourth years of study at the Don Wright Faculty of Music, University of Western Ontario (13 female and two male, mostly in their early twenties, with two older students). In Ontario, students attain their undergraduate degrees and then apply to teachers' college for licensure.

This investigation employed structured interviews[6] balanced with observations and portfolios. The participants were interviewed after completion of an elementary music methods class (an interactive seminar with multiple opportunities to sing, move, play instruments and generate compositions) in the summer of 2012. Participants addressed questions inspired by our class text:[7]

1. What role does composing, improvising and/or arranging music play in your life?
2. Do you think that it is important to include opportunities to compose, improvise and/or arrange to develop full musicianship in children? Did you have these opportunities in your early schooling?
3. How comfortable do you feel with your ability to guide children to improvise, compose and/or arrange music? Do you feel more confident now that you've had these experiences?
4. How able are children to compose on their own with minimal guidance from their teacher? How motivated do you think children are to do this?
5. When you think of planning a curriculum in music, what kinds of musical activities should you plan for, and what should be the balance between them?

Information was compiled and analysed thematically, with supporting data from extensive field notes and portfolios.[8]

Interview findings

1. What role does composing, improvising and/or arranging music play in your life?

These pre-service teachers described themselves at three levels of expertise: (a) novice, (b) learning or (c) adept. Mary considered herself a novice: 'I personally find myself a very creative person (mainly through visual art and crafts) but when it comes to improvising, I find myself lacking.' Katie S. stated she had previously found little occasion to compose or improvise: 'I have never felt that I have much talent in this area and have not had time to develop the skills. However, in my future career as a teacher, I will likely spend time arranging music and will find that it is a rewarding experience.'

The next level of capability is typified by Katie B., who recalled childhood experimentation, but said: 'Now that I am older, I rarely try to compose or arrange music unless I have to for an assignment. I don't feel as though composing is my strongest skill; therefore, it seldom plays a role in my life anymore.'

Eight of the respondents described themselves as adept. Amie perceived creativity as freedom, as self-exploration and development of her 'inner ear'. She had composed since childhood, choosing notes first and then gradually adding rhythmic changes and building up chords. At university, Amie was studying clarinet to a professional level, always playing from notation. However, in her leisure time, Amie improvised from memory on guitar and ukulele. Melyssa also elaborated on her creative musical engagement:

> I improvise more than anything … in dance when I hear music, change some notes when I'm singing along to a song, and I make up different harmonies when singing with others. Composing to me occurs when I intentionally sit down to make music and then write it down. This happens every now and then and is never planned.

Jeryl-Anne grew up listening to her mother play popular music on piano by ear, fostering her connection to creativity:

> As a teenager I perfected my left hand accompaniment skills so that I was able to improvise a chordal base to any of the popular melodies that I wanted to play. … Setting up a rhythm with some well-blended chords can be very exciting. Transitioning chords, composing a melody to complement the chords, sinking into a colour chord to highlight your effort all the while feeling the rhythm with a thundering base line oscillating between the chord tones is all very delightful but totally instrumental – no lyrics. … Without [improvisation] I wouldn't be who I am.

Students regarded musical creativity as an enjoyable leisure activity, rather than serious study or formal music education. Not surprisingly, they consistently chose popular music over classical or other genres for exploration. Meghan commented:

> I find that composing/arranging tends to be what I do when I need to relax. Sitting at the piano and coming up with my own way to play and sing my favourite pop songs is something I look forward to doing. I can spend hours practising, but because it is something I enjoy, it doesn't feel like I'm practising.

Matt also noted the 'outside' nature of composition and improvisation, even though these activities held a significant place in his life:

> I think composition and improvisation are often found outside these traditional roles in my life as well, and I often find myself improvising new and

adapted melodies (or lyrics) to existing music around me or composing new ideas in my head or out loud as I go through my daily life.

2. Do you think that it is important to include opportunities to compose, improvise and/or arrange to develop full musicianship in children? Did you have these opportunities in your early schooling?

All students agreed that creative opportunities are valuable and that the earlier the opportunities are made available to a student, the better. However, most stated that their own schooling did not include these experiences. Parental influence and encouragement were important factors in early exposure, as Matt commented:

> Developing a creative mindset, and creative freedom in children is crucial … I had many opportunities to compose and improvise, but these were provided at home … and thankfully for me, I had a creative musical father who could encourage and direct that creativity.[9]

Although most collaborators came to creative work informally, for some, the groundwork was laid through formal schooling. Katie B. said:

> Though my schools never had any theoretical approaches or methods of musical education, I felt like I was always given many opportunities and was encouraged as a child to improvise music. I remember being able to experiment with different instruments such as sticks, bells, maracas, etc. I loved experimenting with these sounds and was always eager to try different instruments. In grade 4, I learnt to play the recorder and was constantly experimenting with the sounds and creating my own songs. … The environment was always welcoming and comfortable, I always felt that I could be free to express myself and always felt like there was no limit to my music.

But regardless of whether creative musicking was part of a formal curriculum or part of an individual's own musical journey, the vulnerable and personal nature of this experience resonated through the class members. Jeryl-Anne considered:

> I believe in the comfort factor. If it is not comfortable, it may not happen, especially when you are looking for something as personal as musicianship. It's like asking someone for a piece of their heart. Children need to know that it's ok to try things in music. They need to get familiar with the feel, the sound and even the sight. … Making music available and easy for children to experiment with is important. The earliest of experiences generate actions many years down the line.

Several students reported having opportunities for creative music-making in high school music class settings, but that these were one-off activities structured within a formal context. They considered these infrequent opportunities as irrelevant, and would have preferred a systematic immersion and training throughout schooling. Those who incorporated composition and improvisation actively into their lives regarded musical creativity as an approach and a personal choice. Those who wished to become creative were inclined to consider it as a skill.

3. How comfortable do you feel with your ability to guide children to improvise, compose and/or arrange music? Do you feel more confident now that you've had these experiences?

A few students voiced discomfort with their abilities to guide children in improvisation or composition: Mary felt that 'The question I ask myself is: how can I bring out musical creativity in my students, when I have a hard time bringing it out in myself?' Melyssa volunteered that this course provided her first and only opportunities to create. Matt agreed: 'It is not every day that university students are given this flexibility with a project, and I think the varying interpretations displayed the uniqueness of us as individuals, and our ability to truly be creative.' Cynthia added:

> [O]ne half-credit course on 'Improvisation in the Classroom', being the only experience I've had with improvising, I am not comfortable with composing or improvising on either of my main instruments. ... I do recognise the challenge in elementary music classes, where music class is only provided once a week or, if lucky for some, twice a week, providing teachers limited time and pressure to teach certain topic areas over others. But, time should be made for creative opportunities.

Those who were the most comfortable with generating musical ideas also felt ready to take on the teaching role. Half the class noted that they felt unprepared generally, but were certain that they could guide their students' creativity.

4. How able are children to compose on their own with minimal guidance from their teacher? How motivated do you think children are to do this?

There was general consensus that children could compose spontaneously, but that impulse and motivation varied. Matt opined: '[C]hildren are often natural composers and can be found making up songs or humming their own tunes outside a regimented class. Unlike any talent or subject in school, motivation to grow that ability varies from child to child.' Jeryl-Anne believed that children were very able to compose on their own without guidance, but that 'they need to take the whole exercise seriously'.

About half the students advocated structuring creative opportunities. Several noted that while children have an innate creative capacity, sequenced and comprehensive instruction with ample time for experimentation produce the optimal setting for success. Katie S. remembered working with children at summer camp when she had not had prior experience, but quickly realised the need to structure improvisation:

> I was given a group of eight mini campers (ages four and five) and a box of percussion instruments (bells, triangle, small drums). As a music major, I was assumed to be well able to direct their activity for the next 20 minutes. When I let them just pick instruments and bang them around for a bit, most of them got bored fairly quickly. I decided to sing some easy songs that they knew and could sing along to if they chose, like 'Jingle Bells', and asked them to play the percussion instruments along with the song. This kept their attention because it gave them some guidelines with which to focus their improvisation … it is easier for the children to come up with ideas if there is some broad outline, like a theme, or certain required elements, from which to start the process.

Not all class members agreed with the need to structure creativity. Katie B. recommended fewer guidelines:

> [C]hildren need very little guidance from teachers to be creative with music … a teacher needs to provide the child with a safe and comfortable environment to experiment within, the materials to make music, and simple guidelines. … I don't believe that children should be forced or given a strict set of rules when creating or improvising music, this will discourage them and not allow them to reach their full creative potential.

5. When you think of planning a curriculum in music, what kinds of musical activities should you plan for, and what should be the balance between them?

The class as a whole endorsed balancing a variety of musical activities. Valerie specified 'a balance between structure and freedom (enough structure and task knowledge and freedom to explore and able to create)'. Cynthia saw the music curriculum as part of a bigger picture:

> Creativity in the classroom is directly related to intelligence, achievement motivation, divergent thinking, and to attributes such as unconventionality, risk-taking, and imagination … it is our work as educators to encourage students to try new things and experiences, to make self-discoveries, not always being given the one and only 'right' answer.

Activities in a music class, according to Jeryl-Anne, should include 'singing, movement, creativity, individual opportunity, and … fundamentals of music. All activities are important and … should be given equal weight as long as musical fundamentals are being reinforced.' Other suggested class activities included playing composed music, drama, dance, listening, performing and integrated studies. Cynthia considered transferable skills:

> It needs to be about fostering an enjoyment and appreciation for music, and through music, the ability to develop creative thought, as well as learning

basic music fundamentals. If teachers are solely teaching music fundamentals (for example, music theory, music history, how to sing 'properly' and in tune, and what is considered 'good' music) then music becomes nontransferable for many students ... music should also focus on techniques that can be considered transferable to other subjects of study, such as creativity, imagination, and discipline.

Discussion and conclusion

This study took impetus and direction from the collective energies of this specific class and the context of a Canadian setting of a university elementary music methods class. While some aspects of the course are relatively stable from year to year, content such as songs, listening examples, activities, points of departure and readings change in response to the stakeholders. This particular class quickly manifested a playful, resourceful and responsive disposition which prompted more experimental projects. A visitor observed how easily these students generated and integrated musical ideas with other subject areas. Early on in the year, individuals initiated projects, freely improvised piano accompaniment and volunteered movement games.

The group dynamic propelled the class to take risks, even as individuals reported varying degrees of comfort in doing so. As the interviews indicate, there was unanimity of opinion that children have innate abilities and potential to be creative. This consensus is in agreement with other research from North America and the UK, but in contrast to research into teacher attitudes in Cyprus and Greece. Larger studies, including longitudinal and metastudies, are needed to examine further this cultural variation.

All participants agreed that it is important to provide opportunities for composition and improvisation for elementary and secondary students. However, the class members varied in their interpretation of what constituted creative opportunities and how they should be structured within the classroom – a finding that echoes Sætre's research (2011). The class was uniformly enthusiastic about composition and improvisation for children, believing that these activities should find a place along with singing, moving, playing and listening within the elementary music curriculum. However, the class members also stressed the importance of fundamentals and transferable skills.

As these pre-service teachers grew more adept at envisioning themselves in their futures, the role of the teacher frequently trumped the role of the creative musician, as if the teacher role was restricted while the role of a creating musician was as free from constraints as an improvisation. Some members of the class had not experienced systematic and comprehensive elementary music education, but regardless of their levels of music education, most reported few opportunities for innovative musicking in formal school settings. Although individuals could make musical decisions freely in the context of their own private music-making, when creativity was included in an academic context with an emphasis on future teaching, they saw their choices as being limited. The constant tension between freedom and structure imposed both internally and externally is logical given the constraints of their musical schooling and the demands of the academic institution.

During the course of the study, a number of themes and motifs surfaced. The class considered aspects of creativity as (1) natural and innate characteristics needing minimal guidance, and (2) creativity as process or processes. Creativity was linked with self-expression and childhood activities. Some class members noted a sense of loss for the lack of experiences in their earlier years, having missed something important in their development as musicians. Others regarded creative music-making as a pleasurable pastime and a choice for self-expression, but not one that should overrule or interfere with the serious work of a music major in a competitive academic setting. At the same time, creativity was ever-present: there were many brief and incandescent moments in this short year-long class.

For pre-service teachers, fostering relationships and creating environments where creative teaching can be the springboard for creative learning helps ameliorate the impact of risk-taking. The constant tension between freedom and structure inherent in the creative classroom fosters the creative spark, but an environment where familiarity, comfort and collaboration are the foundation of pedagogy is indispensable if learners are to begin and pursue their musical journeys.

Notes

1 We are very grateful to our collaborators in this investigation, Nadine Anyan, Katie Bekking, Jeryl-Anne Churchill, Rebecca Fernandes, Amie Haines, Hayoon Kim, Valerie Kipfer, Vanessa Lau, Cynthia Lussier, Melyssa Owens, Matthew Piché, Kayla Schnarr, Katie Spurgiasz, Richard Swan and Mary Wilson, for their creative spirits and insights.

2 http://hdr.undp.org/en/countries/profiles/CAN (retrieved 22 October 2015).

3 Music educators Elliott, Bowman, Younker, Willingham, Beynon, Beatty, Griffith, Bolden, Veblen and Russell, among others, are currently active in this area.

4 This corresponds with Zbainos and Anastasopoulou's (2012) survey of Greek music teachers, who believed that creativity is an innate gift and can only be partly taught in a formal setting.

5 The teacher-as-facilitator model is an ideal. Striving for this ideal does not negate the unequal and weighted roles of professor and student, nor does it counteract very real pressures for grades or responsibilities of all involved in an academic institution.

6 In accordance with the University of Western Ontario Ethics Review, interviews were conducted after the class ended and grades were submitted. Class members elected to use their names and complete questions via email.

7 The class text was Campbell, Scott-Kassner and Kassner (2010); interview questions were adapted from Chapter 10, 'The Creating Child' (pp. 248–69).

8 The portfolios include circles exercises which prompt students to review music in their lives. See Barrett, McCoy and Veblen (1997: 1–7). A complete analysis of portfolios is beyond the scope of this chapter.

9 Matt also stated: 'I was never taught to be creative in a school music setting until high school jazz class.'

References

Barrett, J.R., McCoy, C.W. and Veblen, K.K. (1997). *Sound Ways of Knowing: Music in the Interdisciplinary Curriculum*. New York: Schirmer.

Barrett, M.S. (2006). 'Inventing Songs, Inventing Worlds: The "Genesis" of Creative Thought and Activity in Young Children's Lives'. *International Journal of Early Years Education*, 14(3), 201–20.

Beegle, A.C. (2010). 'A Classroom-based Study of Small-group Planned Improvisation with Fifth-grade Children'. *Journal of Research in Music Education*, 58(3), 219–39.

Beineke, V. (2013). 'Creative Learning and Communities of Practice: Perspectives for Music Education in the School'. *International Journal of Community Music*, 6(3), 281–90.

Bernhard, H.C. (2013). 'Music Education Majors' Confidence in Teaching Improvisation'. *Journal of Music Teacher Education*, 22(2), 65–72.

Bujez, A.V. and Mohedo, M.D. (2013). 'Creativity in the Music Classroom'. *Procedia – Social and Behavioral Sciences*, 141, 237–41.

Burnard, P. (2007). 'Routes to Understanding Musical Creativity'. In L. Bresler (ed.), *International Handbook of Research in Arts Education* (pp. 1,199–214). Dordrecht: Springer.

——— (2012). *Musical Creativities in Practice*. Oxford: Oxford University Press.

——— and Fautley, M. (2014). 'Assessing Diverse Creativities in Music: A Spectrum of Challenges, Possibilities and Practices'. In: M. Fleming, J. O'Toole and L. Bresler (eds), *The Routledge International Handbook of Arts and Education* (pp. 254–67). London: Routledge.

——— and Younker, B.A. (2008). 'Investigating Children's Musical Interactions within the Activities Systems of Group Composing and Arranging: An Application of Engestrom's Activity Theory'. *International Journal of Educational Research*, 47(1), 60–74.

Campbell, P.S. (1998). *Songs in Their Heads: Music and its Meaning in Children's Lives*. Oxford: Oxford University Press.

———, Scott-Kassner, C. and Kassner, K. (2010). *Music in Childhood: From Preschool Through the Elementary Grades*. 3rd edn. Boston, MA: Schirmer.

Coulson, A. and Burke, B. (2013). 'Creativity in the Elementary Music Classroom: A Study of Students' Perceptions'. *International Journal of Music Education*, 31(4), 428–41.

Diakidoy, I.N. and Kanari, E. (1999). 'Student Teachers' Beliefs about Creativity'. *British Educational Research Journal*, 25(2), 225–43.

Elliott, D.J. and Silverman, M. (2014). *Music Matters: A Philosophy of Music Education*. 2nd edn. New York: Oxford University Press.

Gruenhagen, L.M. and Whitcomb, R. (2014). 'Improvisational Practices in Elementary General Music Classrooms'. *Journal of Research in Music Education*, 61(4), 379–95.

Harwood, E. and Marsh, K. (2012). 'Children's Ways of Learning Inside and Outside the Classroom'. In: G.E. McPherson and G.F. Welch (eds), *The Oxford Handbook of Music Education, Volume 1* (pp. 322–40). Oxford: Oxford University Press.

Hickey, M. (2009). 'Can Improvisation be "Taught"? A Call for Free Improvisation in Our Schools'. *International Journal of Music Education*, 27(4), 285–99.

Kokotsaki, D. (2011). 'Student Teachers' Conceptions of Creativity in the Secondary Music Classroom'. *Thinking Skills and Creativity*, 6(2), 100–113.

Lapidaki, E., De Groot, R. and Stagkos, P. (2012). 'Communal Creativity as Sociomusical Practice'. In: G.E. McPherson and G.F. Welch (eds), *The Oxford Handbook of Music Education, Volume 2* (pp. 371–88). Oxford: Oxford University Press.

Lave, J. and Wenger, E. (1991). *Situated Learning: Legitimate Peripheral Participation.* Cambridge: University of Cambridge Press.

Leong, S., Burnard, P., Jeanneret, N., Leung, B. and Waugh, C. (2012). 'Assessing Creativity in Music: International Perspectives and Practices'. In: G.E. McPherson and G.F. Welch (eds), *The Oxford Handbook of Music Education, Volume 2* (pp. 389–407). Oxford: Oxford University Press.

Marsh, K. (2008). *The Musical Playground: Global Tradition and Change in Children's Songs and Games.* New York: Oxford University Press.

Odena, O. (ed.) (2012). *Musical Creativity: Insights from Music Education Research.* Farnham: Ashgate.

—— and Welch, G. (2012). 'Teachers' Perceptions of Creativity'. In: O. Odena (ed.), *Musical Creativity: Insights from Music Education Research* (pp. 29–48). Farnham: Ashgate.

Robinson, N., Bell, C. and Pogonowski, L. (2011). 'The Creative Music Strategy'. *Music Educators Journal*, 97(3), 50–55.

Sætre, J.H. (2011). 'Teaching and Learning Music Composition in Primary School Settings'. *Music Education Research*, 13(1), 29–50.

Schafer, R.M. (2012). 'Foreword: Questioning Traditional Teaching and Learning in Canadian Music Education'. In: C.A. Beynon and K.K. Veblen (eds), *Critical Perspectives in Canadian Music Education* (pp. vii–x). Waterloo, ON: Wilfrid Laurier University Press.

Stavrou, N.E. (2013). 'Fostering Musical Creativity in Pre-service Teacher Education: Challenges and Possibilities'. *International Journal of Music Education*, 31(1), 35–52.

Whitcomb, R. (2013). 'Teaching Improvisation in Elementary General Music: Facing Fears and Fostering Creativity'. *Music Educators Journal*, 99(3), 43–51.

Wiggins, J. and Espeland, M.I. (2012). 'Creating in Music Learning Contexts'. In: G.E. McPherson and G.F. Welch (eds), *The Oxford Handbook of Music Education, Volume 1* (pp. 341–60). Oxford: Oxford University Press.

Younker, B.A. (2013). 'Composing with Voice: Students' Strategies and Processes, and the Influence of Text on the Composed Music'. *The Phenomenon of Singing*, 2, 247–60.

Zbainos, D. and Anastasopoulou, A. (2012). 'Creativity in Greek Music Curricula and Pedagogy: An Investigation of Greek Music Teachers' Perceptions'. *Creative Education*, 3(1), 55–60.

9 Pre-service teachers converting motherhood into creative capital through composing with sound

Clare Hall

Singing a different tune about pre-service teachers' musical capabilities

This case study of generalist primary school pre-service teachers' higher music education is driven by the recurring challenge of educating teachers to feel capable and motivated to include music in their future teaching. This is a challenge I share with many others in higher music education, and the picture painted by research in this area is somewhat grim. The educational discourse on pre-service schoolteachers' musical creativities rings loud with teachers' lack of confidence and competence to teach music, compose, improvise and involve creative pedagogies in their own classroom practice (Hallam et al., 2009; Hennessey, 2000; Russell-Bowie, 2009). Include technologies in the mix, and we have a more complicated view of teachers' capabilities (Partti and Karlsen, 2010) that suggests that in many instances music in schools is in the hands of graduate teachers lacking much experience and many essential qualities.

Using this lens through which to view pre-service teachers, I learn that the majority of the students in my university arts education classes label themselves as having below-average musicality and rarely describe themselves as musically creative. Their self-perceptions about music echo the findings of Lamont's (2011: 372) study of musical identity in adult amateur music makers: a 'fundamental outcome of their music education was to learn that music was not for them'. The repetition of symbolic distinctions that silence the creativities of those without specialised music education is alive and well in many educational institutions (Moore, 2012). Changing the perceptions of those – like the majority of my tertiary students – who regard music as 'not for the likes of me' seems to require interventions beyond the school, as wider community participation in the arts, in Australia at least, continues to be stratified according to social class and economic and gendered categories (Costantoura, 2001).

While my students agree music is important to their everyday lives and should be a key part of children's schooling, most believe that people other than themselves are better able to provide an education in music, and therefore these more 'capable' people should be responsible for music in the curriculum. Perhaps this is true in many regards, particularly if one is referring to an instrumental education and specialist performance skills. However, much of my time as an educator of generalist teachers is spent troubling the students' self-limiting sense of deficit. We do this in a sociological way by deconstructing the 'discourse of derision' (Burnard, 2003) and the associated 'terminal prestige' (McClary, 1989) of European art music traditions on the basis of the students' own music education experiences – issues of equal relevance to generalist and music specialist educators. It is within the norms of the European art music field that my students find justification to self-identify as 'unmusical' because they do not play an orchestral instrument to an expert level and they do not read conventional music notation. These are the two most common competencies which my students associate with being a 'musician' and being 'musical', which is consistent with research in this area (Lamont, 2002). Contrary to this commonplace understanding of musicality, research shows the increasing multiplicity and transdisciplinary evolution of musicianships and musical creativities that ought to be reflected in school music education (Burnard, 2012).

I argue that more can be done to disrupt the structures that segregate children according to musical abilities and 'dis-abilities' and those which render pre-service teachers competent or incompetent in the first place. I move beyond thinking about the ways in which pre-service teachers' deficits need to be improved by looking at my students through another lens: one focused on their capacities and on how to work productively with what each student brings to our musical exchanges. To do this work in pre-service teacher education, my teaching approach is what I refer to as musical sociology, as opposed to a sociology *of* music, whereby I aim to bring together a fusion of music education sociology, arts-based scholarship and performance ethnography (Hall, 2015). While the concept of *doing* sociology *with* music is not new (Bell, 2011; DeNora, 2003; Prior, 2011), it would appear to be under-explored in research. For this reason, musical sociology is a creative teaching approach to higher education that I suggest also has purchase beyond music education, and therefore warrants further scholarly discussion. The sections that follow describe what this creative teaching looked and sounded like in my university classroom and how it was put into operation by some of my students. First, I will explain the pedagogical underpinnings of my research-led teaching.

Music composition as performance ethnography

The discussion that follows and the accompanying digital asset (see below) relates to a small-scale ethnography of the musical experiences of my university students engaged in the Bachelor of Education degree at Monash University, Australia. These pre-service primary school generalist teachers, ranging in age from late teens to mid-thirties, participated in a single unit of music education (24 contact hours) over the course of their degree that I designed and delivered. I talked with 11 students from the cohort of 63 about their experiences. This is not a music teaching methods unit per se, but an introduction to the issues and practices relevant to the inclusion of music in the generalist primary classroom with the aim of students questioning what musicality is and what it means to be a musician, to carry out research and to educate musically. This unit places group performance, digital musicianship, music composition and arts-based research methods as pillars of its pedagogies for creativity. The students' experiences culminate in a group performance of an ethnodrama that problematises and attempts to resolve issues relating to the teaching and learning of music in childhood that the students are most passionate about.

The unit as a whole has an autoethnographic focus whereby playing and composing music together is a way of constructing and doing embodied narrative inquiry (Bresler, 2006). The promise of performance ethnography is the use of performance – in the sense of self-making presentations – as a method of understanding the ways people create and re-create themselves through 'communicative action' (Denzin, 2003: 7). Students construct and interrogate their personal musical life stories in relation to music and education discourses through writing and discussion groups. These are intended to prompt a critical perspective and reflexive vocabulary with which to examine the intersections between music and gender, class, race, indigeneity, sexuality, disability and creativity in regard to schooling and education (Hall, 2015).

Regardless of the students' artistic and educational backgrounds, I position them as musician-researcher-educators inspired by a/r/tography's commitment to contiguity between selves and ways of being (Irwin and Springgay, 2008).[1] I set up an expectation that we will playfully and reflexively explore this together through the creation of music – these musical processes and products are framed as autoethnographic performances as much as their verbal and written expressions. One task the students complete is a music composition of approximately three to five minutes' duration, which they digitally record. They are free to create music in any form, and we briefly workshop examples to inspire them with some additional online resources: songwriting, beatboxing, mash-up, remix, soundscape, DJing.

Inspired by the sound-based music composition work of Leigh Landy and R. Murray Schafer, I aim at least to disrupt my students' conceptions of what constitutes music and the diverse values we place on different sonic materials. I introduce the students to electroacoustic and sound-based music through the work of Australian artists[2] to investigate the aesthetic affordances of sound-based as opposed to note-based music. Landy defines sound-based music as 'the art form in which the sound, that is, not the musical note, is its basic unit' (2012: xi–xii). Individuals' everyday interactions with acoustic materials become resources for music creation, and many of my students take the opportunity to compose their own sound-based music. In doing so, my students question the possibility of there being different 'rules to the game' of music, whereby hierarchical conceptions of one's access to musical materials determined by one's level of formal education are inverted.

This composition forms part of the students' assessment for the unit, and the creative process, which the students critically reflect on through a 'process journal', is of equal importance in the evaluation as the final musical product. For the majority of the students, this is the first time they have ever produced their own music and/or used music technologies in the process of creation. The students' music composition work is largely self-directed, and depending on the form their music will take, they must research how to work effectively and experimentally within this genre. I act as a resource for their creative problem-solving, giving advice and suggestions about where to find further information throughout the process. Perhaps many of the pre-service teachers in my courses do not overcome their self-doubt to have a positive experience like those in this chapter, and their stories are important too. But here I am interested in examining how those students do overcome their negative self-labels and their anxieties about not being 'good enough' to create their own music.

The discussion that follows shares the experiences of three students who chose to compose digital soundscapes, how they went about this creative process, and what this afforded their sense of self as an educator.

Musical creativity and anxiety: Overcoming feelings of ineptitude

Following the conclusion of one cycle of this course, I invited students to speak with me in a one-on-one interview for an hour to tell me more about their musical life stories and to reflect on their experiences across the course, particularly the process of composing. Using narrative analysis methods, this chapter reports on the experiences of three individuals who have been selected because they are examples of higher education students who overcame their anxiety and negative self-identity to go on and produce their own often novel, meaningful and poignant music. I focus on the questions 'What sociocultural and emotional conditions act as enablers for these pre-service teachers' musical creativities?' and 'What creative teaching strategies were critical in this enabling process?'

On learning that the task required them to produce and submit for examination their own music in digital form, the majority of the students I interviewed reported reacting with high levels of anxiety, self-doubt and confusion. Some said they initially weren't sure what it even means to compose music, and they all told a version of what I call the 'surviving the baptism by fire' story. The task to create one's own music – like a symbolic ritual fire – has the potential to overwhelm and produce feelings of harm and threat. Jackie said that when she learned of the task, she was 'absolutely *mortified*, I was like "Oh how am I going to do that? That's not going to happen. I can't compose anything!" 'cause at first I thought we needed to play music so I was thinking, "What? I don't know any music."' Despite Jackie being a keen instrumentalist and music student at school, she initially made a negative appraisal of her abilities to create music based on her level of musical knowledge.

Likewise, Hannah, a very creative person in regard to visual arts and dance, judged her abilities on the basis of presuppositions about the kind of music expected. She said:

> When I initially thought, 'Oh, my God, I've got to compose something!' I'm thinking it had to actually sound like some professional track and I couldn't –'cause I downloaded *GarageBand* straight away and I was like, 'Okay, let's figure this out.' And it's just like, 'No. I know I don't work like this.' I've never used that. I've never been drawn to compose anything or make my own music.

Karen's reaction to the task of composing music was fuelled by her focus on the potential audience for her work, which she automatically doubted whether she could please. She said:

> I just thought, 'I've just got to give this a go and this is really killing me!' It really, really was like torture [laughs]. All I kept thinking of was what everyone would think of it. … I wanted it to sound like a proper piece of music, not just something that's been stuck together by a student [laughs]. I was so self-conscious about the result and I had to just keep quashing those feelings and just going, 'You have to get this done. This is an assessment. You have to do it. Come on.' I made myself do it. … I seem outgoing, but underneath it all, I'm a very big judge of myself, very hard on myself [laughs]. That's my demon, my criticism of myself.

The task to create music was in conflict with the women's supposed musical ineptitude. We get a strong sense of the high levels of emotional labour and the intense inner struggles induced by this unfamiliar expectation. The emotional work here seems to involve an insecure and threatened self, which the pre-service teachers indicated needs to be suppressed to present a competent and confident self. In class, I aim to counterbalance the negative dimensions of musical identities through group music-making experiences that emphasise improvisation, composition games, percussion playing, expressive movement and story-making, which I refer to as adult play-based pedagogy. These experiences that we share through laughter and humility open up the conversation I have directly with the students in class – and the conversation I hope they will begin to have with themselves – about who has permission to call themselves 'musically creative' if not them. After building up a repository of positive experiences, it is hoped that students will find it less difficult to dismantle the discourses of derision about musical creativity, despite the durability of such dominant cultural narratives (Hall, 2015).

The intersection between these pre-service teachers' experiences of music and mothering (and parenting) in everyday life emerged as a key theme in the way they survived the baptism by fire to get on with composing music in a productive way. I am curious about the emotional resources these students possess and how they are deployed for creativity. In the following section, I will discuss the ways these particular women's mother–child relationships provide significant emotional capital that funds their musical creativity.

Releasing the musical imagination through soundscapes of motherhood

Hannah, Jackie and Karen broke through their fear of composing by basing their creation on their own mother–child relationships, and they each used a different form of soundscape. Karen said that she overcame her confusion about how to get started by dedicating her project to her mother, who had recently passed away. She said:

> I thought I wasn't doing it for me. I was doing it for her memory so then I've got another reason to do this project. Not just you're doing this for a result. I was doing this for my mum. 'Okay, you're gonna make something to honour your mum,' and then that would be a way of making myself keep going.

Karen explained that 'music was always there' in the bonds of her family life and fondly recalled dancing to music in the kitchen with her mother each night as they washed the dishes together. Singing in the car together was a particularly happy family ritual right up to her mother's death. Being able to 'speak' to her absent mother through her music clearly gave Karen a great sense of comfort. She said after receiving her feedback and results for her project: 'I just felt awesome. I felt peaceful about it. Mum would be proud. Because it's kind of caught up with what my mum wanted me to do with my life. [Studying at university,] I'm doing something that I know that she wanted me to do.'

Like Karen, Jackie combated the fear of music composition by externalising her motivations and taking a playful approach to her everyday family life. She explained that her idea also to create a soundscape of her family came to her immediately:

> At that time I don't think I had much else that was inspiring me other than my kids so I just felt like that was the way I would be able to show any sort of creativity. I didn't think it was going to work, but I went, 'No. I can do it. I could.' I knew I wanted it to be a day in my life kind of thing but trying to do it a bit more musically.

Jackie saw that her most fundamental musical creativity was tied up with her motherhood – that without her children, she would not be creative in this domain. The confidence that being a mother gave her enabled her to turn around her feelings of mortification in having to compose. She too was pleased with her work at the conclusion of the project, and she reported that her musician brother said, 'I can't believe you did that!'

Hannah's subjectivity as a student was also deeply entwined with her subjectivity as a mother: she explained that her children were her 'main inspiration for this whole journey' in returning to higher education. She too created a soundscape of a typical day in her family's life, but in contrast to Jackie and Karen, Hannah constructed this as being a way of creating something pleasurable for herself:

> I just wanted to sort of capture our day, not really just what we do but just the essence of the kids, like their giggles and stuff like that and the happy moments. I really wanted it to be something that if I was ever feeling quite negative or anything that I could listen to and really think about the good things. Yeah, so I wanted it to be positive and pretty to me, I guess. I liked

collecting the sounds; I liked that I only use the sounds that I collected, nothing just found off the internet or anything like that. Everything I recorded myself 'cause I wanted it to be authentic, just our sounds – it's supposed to be our essence, not someone else's.

Hannah's composition[3] used only sounds recorded on her mobile phone, which she edited on her home computer using free music editing software. Hannah did much more than document the sounds of a 'day in her family's life'. She purposely composed with these sounds using musical devices for an emotional affect. Hannah achieved this through a chronological sequence of sounds and music that symbolise events, rituals and interactions, such as the school gate drop-off and playtime with dad. She created a sense of time moving forward with the constant beat of her children's footsteps that run through the entire composition. Hannah included the music of Alanis Morissette, which she described as 'her music', to reconstruct an intimate exchange between herself and her six-year-old son. She sang a verse and chorus of 'Ironic' to him as a bedtime lullaby because 'that's the one that has been his lullaby since he was born ... probably 'cause it's one of my favourites that was always the first go-to song'. She draws the listener into a very personal intimate space through her musical performance, sung very softly and slowly. This song is used as a powerful symbol of her 'essence' as a musical mother, and the way she records her lullaby performance creates the sense for the listener, as does Karen and Jackie's music, that we are sharing in this loving space.

Converting emotional capital into creative capital

The stories of these pre-service teachers show the reach of musical mothering as something which goes beyond the development of the child. The intersection between mothering and music-making is something which capacitates the women themselves. Evidence of this is the way the pre-service teachers in this study have mobilised their experience of mothering – and being mothered, in Karen's case – as a means for musical creativity. Elsewhere I argue that musical mothering, like other forms of educational care for children, requires high degrees of emotional capital that middle-class mothers are typically more able than working-class mothers to convert into educational capital for their children (Hall, forthcoming). Nowotny (1981), inspired by the theories of Bourdieu (1986), was the first to coin the term 'emotional capital' as a subspecies of 'social capital'. Originally conceived as a capital of the private sphere, Nowotny (1981: 148) states that emotional capital is 'access to emotionally valued skills and assets, which hold within any social network characterised at least partly by affective ties'. Because the private sphere is historically dominated by women, emotional capital is conceptualised as a feminine capital (Reay, 2004).

The concept of emotional capital expands Bourdieu's economy of social action because it is a form of capital whose investment is not for the economic benefit of the self, but purely for the benefit of others. However, Savage's (2015) recent study of early years music classes shows that mothers' pedagogical commitments to their children – through participation in class and facilitation of musical experiences in the home – affords many social, emotional and symbolic benefits to the women personally. Musical mothering is clearly something women may engage in for the mutual benefit of their children and *themselves*; however, little research exists that examines the latter.

I expand this area of research by arguing that the women in this study use the emotional capital embedded in their experiences of musical mothering as a resource for music creation, and therefore, in this context, educational accomplishment. On the one hand, the women's emotional capital is very much outside the locus of the family, and on the other, these particular students' motivations towards higher qualifications are greatly bound up with their familial responsibilities and aspirations. This can be seen as an example of public/private blurring, and it is through these pre-service teachers' musical experiences that we gain a glimpse of the complicated intersubjectivity of mother–child–learner–teacher. They describe the affective ties of mother–child as a source of inspiration, motivation, pleasure and strength – capacities that they deploy as resources for the creation of music. In this sense, motherhood is more than merely a creative constraint used as a pathway into creativity (Burnard and Younker, 2002). I suggest that these pre-service teachers are highly effective in converting the emotional capital of their mother–child relations into cultural capital in the form of a musical product.

These students' music assignments were examined on their ability to explain the experimentation and reflexivity of their musical processes inspired by Amabile's (1982) consensual approach to creativity assessment. All the students in this study achieved high scores for this assignment, and in this sense were rewarded for acquiring high levels of 'creative capital'. One student exchanged these capitals for economic capital in the form of a scholarship the following year. Beyond the scope of this discussion are the range of other cultural, classed, gendered and generational dispositions these women also embody that act as resources in creating music, beyond music skills and knowledge. The key point is that to understand further how to educate for musical creativities, exploration of other sociocultural dimensions of musical experience in interaction with musical materiality is needed, and cultural sociology can play an important part in these discussions.

Being successful in composing music might have been unthinkable for these pre-service teachers had they not mobilised their emotional capital at the outset. I suggest that a significant aspect of this possibility was thinking in sounds rather than notes. These pre-service teachers' shift in thinking acted as a trigger for them to reposition their expertise as 'masters' of their domestic sphere. When constructing the soundworld of their families' home life, daily rituals and affective relationships as resources for music, these pre-service teachers tell a counter-narrative to the 'I can't compose' story. Hannah told this story about the release of her musical imagination by rehearing her sonic environment:

> After the first week here [in the course], it just changed the way I heard things. I think it was after the first workshop with you that I went home, and my husband scratched his head, and I heard a rhythm. I was like, 'Oh, God! Is everything gonna be musical now?' [laughs]. He scratched his head and

like for the next hour I'm sitting there going, 'Tssh tssh tssh,' because that's kind of the sound he made. So it was like this instant sort of realisation that anything could be music. So that was actually probably my first inspiration – you know, musical sounds within our little microcosm that is us.

Music composition as pedagogical imagining

The attraction to sound-based music for many of the students in this course was the freedom they felt as a result of wider and more accessible musical materials. For these women, sound is a portal into an intimate, personal space and a vehicle for the listener to travel with the composer through an emotion-scape. These performances of the self through music were indeed so personal for these students that few shared their compositions with anyone. For Hannah, the sounds of her everyday life were her way of performing her 'essence' – an authentic self. Her definition of creativity was to communicate her uniqueness, so in this way making sound-based music was *the* most 'creative' thing she could do. For many adult learners, experiences in sound-based music encourage a more playful approach to music, whereby students enact more child-like dispositions of 'what if' curiosity and experimentation, as opposed to being preoccupied with making music to sound 'as if' it matches accepted conventions (O'Toole, 2009). Becoming music composers and creating in sound has informed the way these students view themselves as future teachers. Their compositions can be viewed as performances not just of motherhood, but also of their emerging pedagogical identities. Karen explained what she had learned about herself from the process of analysing her music composing, how this had been inflected with her reading of O'Toole (2009), and how this was influencing the image she had of herself teaching, albeit still quite an anxious one:

> It especially came out that adult versus child thing and I could really see how much that was influencing me as an older person, how limiting of ourselves we are instead of just thinking 'Fantastic. This is my chance to be creative and let's just go for it and not be afraid.' It's amazing how afraid you are, yeah. So it was kind of eye opening to see that kids aren't necessarily like that. They're not as fearful, it's all about, 'Wow! Let's just give it a go.'

Karen's composition is a testament to her determination that she too should 'just give it a go'. Hannah and Jackie's compositions are also symbolic of their desire to push the boundaries of education as they see them in their future careers. Hannah said:

> My original plan was to just be the art teacher. I'm actually getting more and more excited to have a class, to do a bit of everything, you know, 'cause I don't just have to do Maths and English and all that. I can still do art and music and everything within my class. I want to incorporate all of it as a wholeness sort of thing. I think that would be really, really fun to just be *the*

arts teacher, to do all of it, 'cause I'm seeing my son bringing things home from school and, 'Oh, we did this in art,' and it's got nothing to do with what they've done in the normal classes, and I think that's really a shame, like they're missing out on making it fun or meaningful for them. I'm having everything I'm learning at uni making me so cynical of what my son is doing at school!

The creativity of these pre-service teachers' music is emblematic of how they imagine themselves as educators in the future, which is mediated by multiple dimensions of their subjectivities, and so they are contiguously performing motherhood and pedagogy through musical composition. The process of composing music has created a space to envision the dispositions they realise are central to their emerging pedagogical self – connectedness, courage, curiosity, caring – dispositions which are also central to their narratives of motherhood.

Concluding summary

Critical arts-based pedagogy has enabled this group of pre-service teachers to overcome negative self-identities and strong feelings of ineptitude in regard to music. Their orientation towards music may have otherwise limited their participation in music in their future teaching careers; however, as a result of this experience, they now imagine themselves teaching musically with their students. Becoming musical composers has helped them become more confident to teach music with children, but more importantly, it has released their imaginations in regard to their musical and pedagogical self. Not only has becoming composers deconstructed and challenged notions of musical talent, creativity and the 'good-enough' music teacher, it has given them a new means of articulating the deep significance of their mother–child relations that goes beyond words.

Changing dispositions and self-understandings towards musical creativities has been more than a theoretical project, it has been lived and felt *through* music. I suggest that the capacity to overcome feelings of ineptitude and creative paralysis described by these pre-service teachers requires emotional skill as much as musical know-how. This is demonstrated in the way these participants' high levels of self-reflexivity enable them to manage the anxieties, doubts and fears involved in the emotional work of creative learning, without which developing the musical skills and knowledge required for their goals might not be possible. Further research is needed to understand better the relationship between emotionality and teaching and learning musical creativities, particularly in regard to adult students.

Another of the most critical pedagogical triggers for these particular students seemed to be the inclusion of sound as music. The attraction to sound for these students was the opening up of sonic materials that previously were silenced as 'not music'. By rehearing what and where music is, the noise of their gender and emotions has not been silenced by this institutional framework. When sensitised to everyday creativities, these women realised that they had rich musical resources embedded in their family lives. To create sound-based music, they drew on the emotional capital in their mother–child relationships as material for their musical creativity. In becoming composers, these students were playing to their strengths and these particular students found great strength in motherhood.

The intersubjective assemblage of mother–artist–researcher–teacher enabled these pre-service teachers to construct soundscapes of motherhood that to them symbolised their most fundamental and creative selves. These musical processes and products are at once pedagogical in terms of learning music and learning about the self. Because of this, musical mothering is reconceptualised as a source of a range of affective dispositions that these students convert into creative capital that they recognise has value in their future careers in education. This recognition occurs because of the experiences with children and schooling that motherhood affords them, and in this way motherhood is reconstructed as a capacity rather than a deficit or liability to learning. The exchange of capitals is made possible by the creative space opened up by critical arts-based pedagogy. However, it is possible that the musical habitus of other pre-service teachers in this group did not enable them to rehear their environment and reconstruct their everyday creativities with the same degree of flexibility that these three pre-service teachers had. These women's creativity narratives show their high levels of self-reflexivity through the bridge they cross between the emotional work of musicking and mothering in higher studies. Examining individuals' experiences through the lens of competence and capital, rather than incompetence and deficit, reinforces the need to examine creative music learning as highly differentiated phenomena.

Intersections between sound-based music, gender, technology and creativity offer much to further explore, and I have argued that the potential connection between mothering and creativity in higher education is a fresh way to extend discussions about the ways we might analyse and advocate creative music teaching and learning.

Notes

1 'A/r/tography' is a term used to highlight the multiple roles of the artist-researcher-teacher in arts-based research expressed as creative practice and performative pedagogy.
2 See, for example, the work of Ros Bandt, Robert Davidson and Dale Gorfinkel.
3 Hannah's composition is available as a digital companion to this chapter accessible at https://soundcloud.com/sempreorguk/soundcollage (accessed March 28, 2016). Karen and Jackie's compositions cannot be reproduced because of copyright restrictions on the considerable music samples they incorporated.

References

Amabile, T.M. (1982). 'Social Psychology of Creativity: A Consensual Assessment Technique'. *Journal of Personality and Social Psychology*, 43(5), 997–1,013.
Bell, M.M. (2011). 'Strange Music: Notes Towards a Dialogic Sociology'. In: A. Goetting (ed.), *The Strange Music of Social Life: A Dialogue on Dialogic Sociology* (pp. 15–52). Philadelphia, PA: Temple University Press.

Bourdieu, P. (1986). 'The Forms of Capital'. In: L. Richardson (ed.), *Handbook of Theory and Research for the Sociology of Education* (pp. 241–58). New York: Greenwood Press.

Bresler, L. (2006). 'Embodied Narrative Inquiry: A Methodology of Connection'. *Research Studies in Music Education*, 27(1), 21–43.

Burnard, P. (2003). '"How Musical are You?" Examining the Discourse of Derision in Music Education'. In: S. Leong (ed.), *Musicianship in the 21st Century: Issues, Trends and Possibilities* (pp. 28–38). Grosvenor Place, New South Wales: Australian Music Centre.

——— (2012). *Musical Creativities in Practice*. Oxford: Oxford University Press.

——— and Younker, B.A. (2002). 'Mapping Pathways: Fostering Creativity in Composition'. *Music Education Research*, 4(2), 245–61.

Costantoura, P. (2001). *Australians and the Arts*. Sydney: Australia Council for the Arts.

DeNora, T. (2003). 'Music Sociology: Getting the Music into the Action'. *British Journal of Music Education*, 20(2), 165–77.

Denzin, N.K. (2003). *Performance Ethnography: Critical Pedagogy and the Politics of Culture*. Thousand Oaks, CA: Sage.

Hall, C. (2015). 'Doing Sociology with Musical Narratives'. *UNESCO Observatory Multi-Disciplinary Research in the Arts*, 4(2). Retrieved 20 October 2015 from http://www.unescomelb.org/volume-5-issue-1-1/2015/9/14/03-hall-doing-sociology-with-musical-narratives.

——— (forthcoming). *Masculinity, Class and Music Education*. London: Palgrave.

Hallam, S., Burnard, P., Robertson, A., Saleh, C., Davies, V., Rogers, L. and Kokotsaki, D. (2009). 'Trainee Primary-school Teachers' Perceptions of Their Effectiveness in Teaching Music'. *Music Education Research*, 11(2), 221–40.

Hennessy, S. (2000). 'Overcoming the Red-feeling: The Development of Confidence to Teach Music in Primary School amongst Student Teachers'. *British Journal of Music Education*, 17(2), 183–96.

Irwin, R.L. and Springgay, S. (2008). 'A/r/tography as Practice-based Research'. In: S. Springgay, R. Irwin, C. Leggo and P. Gouzouasis (eds), *Being with A/r/tography* (pp. xix–xxxiii). Rotterdam: Sense Publishers.

Lamont, A. (2002). 'Musical Identities and the School Environment'. In: R.A.R. MacDonald, D.J. Hargreaves and D.E. Miell (eds), *Musical Identities* (pp. 41–59). Oxford: Oxford University Press.

——— (2011). 'The Beat Goes On: Music Education, Identity and Lifelong Learning'. *Music Education Research*, 13(4), 369–88.

Landy, L. (2012). *Making Music with Sounds*. New York: Routledge.

McClary, S. (1989). 'Terminal Prestige: The Case of Avant-garde Music Composition'. *Cultural Critique*, 12, 57–81.

Moore, G. (2012). '"Tristan Chords and Random Scores": Exploring Undergraduate Students' Experiences of Music in Higher Education Through the Lens of Bourdieu'. *Music Education Research*, 14(1), 63–78.

Nowotny, H. (1981). 'Women in Public Life in Austria'. In: C. Epstein and R. Coser (eds), *Access to Power: Cross-national Studies of Women and Elites* (pp. 147–56). London: Allen & Unwin.

O'Toole, J. (2009). 'Art, Creativity and Motivation'. In: C. Sinclair, N. Jeanneret and J. O'Toole (eds), *Education in the Arts: Teaching and Learning in the Contemporary Curriculum* (pp. 4–12). Melbourne: Oxford University Press.

Partti, H. and Karlsen, S. (2010). 'Reconceptualising Musical Learning: New Media, Identity and Community in Music Education'. *Music Education Research*, 12(4), 369–82.

Prior, N. (2011). 'Critique and Renewal in the Sociology of Music: Bourdieu and Beyond'. *Cultural Sociology*, 5(1), 121–38.

Reay, D. (2004). 'Gendering Bourdieu's Concepts of Capitals? Emotional Capital, Women and Social Class'. *Sociological Review*, 52(2), 57–74.

Russell-Bowie, D. (2009). 'What Me? Teach Music to My Primary Class? Challenges to Teaching Music in Primary Schools in Five Countries'. *Music Education Research*, 11(1), 23–36.

Savage, S. (2015). 'Intensive Mothering Through Music in Early Childhood Education' (unpublished Master of Education thesis). Monash University, Australia.

10 Deconstructing and re-imagining repertoire in music teacher training

Tim Palmer

Our understanding of the professional artist's work may depend considerably on our ability to participate, even a little, in their activities.

Paynter and Aston (1970: 4)

Introduction

Over ten years, the author has led a number of creative projects with both secondary music PGCE[1] and undergraduate instrumental/vocal teaching (IVT) students, analysing simple children's piano pieces from Bartók's *Mikrokosmos* and creating semi-improvised and expanded cohort ensemble versions using Bartók's compositional building blocks as backbones (Walduck, 2005). The aim has been to develop teachers' skills in opening up repertoire to support pupils' simultaneous learning (Harris, 2006), creativity and retention in both IVT and classroom contexts, particularly in addressing set works. Creative activities have explored the relationships between notation and improvisation, and the use of fragmentary motifs and compositional tools to generate larger-scale structures. The re-imagining process has also been partly student-led to support the development of skills in creative direction, leadership and collaboration (Parker, 2010; Palmer, 2013).

This chapter will briefly explore some of the literature on the connections in music education between analysis, improvisation and collaborative composition. Student perceptions of the process and its ease of transfer into various contextual 'creative teaching' practices will be explored through research undertaken with two cohorts of a secondary music PGCE programme. The process's contribution to the development of creative teachers and as a model for creative learning in the classroom will be assessed. Finally, related concepts of enterprise pedagogy, mis-listening and nomadism in music education will be examined for the theoretical dimensions they shed on the practice.

Context

The lines between analysis, improvisation and composition are clearly drawn in conventional music education practices, and while there are texts that seek to make connections between theoretical knowledge, its contextual practice and the possibilities this gives for creative expression (for example, Summers, 2009; Brockmann, 2009), these often struggle to make their ways onto Initial Teacher Training (ITT) programme or IVT module reading lists. Meanwhile, classroom teachers can be castigated for music lessons that are not musical enough, although practitioners complain of an inability to innovate in the classroom and are too often caught in the cross-fire of the debate about the comparative value of skills and knowledge: 'Creative work in music has often been challenged as being of doubtful value in itself, having little bearing on conventional musical education. ... However, the first step must be the understanding of the medium and its potential. We can only discover this through creative experiment' (Paynter and Aston, 1970: 6).

We know that too much instrumental learning can reveal a 'copy-typist approach' (Priest, 1989: 174) where the visual decoding of notation supersedes aural awareness and musical aspiration. While excellent examples of the creative engagement of instrumental learners exist (for example, Animate Orchestra, Orchestra One, LPO Soundworks, the King's Cross Collective), it may take a generation for the groundbreaking results of research such as the Ear Playing Project (see, for example, Green, 2014; Baker, 2013) to filter through to everyday practice in instrumental teaching. Meanwhile, Ward (2004) has evidenced that spontaneity, personal choice, composition, music analysis and music theory were all rated among the least important aspects of performance teaching by a sample of instrumental teachers.

Higgins (2012) writes about the 'deterritorialisation' of the workshop environment as a primary aim of community music. The Bartók projects similarly have deterritorialisation as an aim – but of the musical object, the score itself, out of the 'canon', away from the technical and cognitive aspects of instrumental/vocal learning and into the liminal space of creative manipulation. The projects share some characteristics with informal learning, mostly through the self-directed small-group activities. While it is undoubtedly important that ITT 'programmes should explicitly live informal learning' (Finney and Philpott, 2010: 10), they should also explicitly live new relationships between notation, analysis, improvisation and composition that empower learners to demonstrate and articulate new skills and understanding *through* the music and through personal and collaboratively negotiated choices as to how that knowledge is worked out in any practical activity. By taking notation as a starting point, the argument is deliberately moved on from the 'first principles' approach adopted by John Stevens and others[2] into a world that inhabits the majority experience of instrumental learners and GCSE/A level students.

This chapter offers a case study of one teacher trainer's approach to these issues, although a model will also be presented for supporting the generalisation of the emergent learning. While some have found that ITT experiences have limited impact on teachers' perceptions of creativity in comparison to students' prior musical backgrounds and professional trajectories (Odena and Welch, 2009), Palmer and Bunting (2015) have evidenced lasting connections between significant training experiences and subsequent approaches to creative teaching.

Bearing in mind the double-layered approach that any exploration of teacher training needs – dealing with both student learning (in community) and these students' subsequent teaching practices (in institutions) – this research acknowledges Burnard's (2012: 17) 'social/realist' approach to the social production of musical creativity as its starting point, along with Jeffery's (2005: 3) description of creativity in the classroom as 'questioning, acting upon and reconstructing knowledge, rather than simply reproducing it'. Burnard (2012: 234) identifies a relevant spectrum of behaviour modalities in the manipulation of 'serious' composed musical works, including 'performance-composition', 're-composition', 'improvisation-performance' and 'rearrangement' that help identify creative acts within stages of these projects: 'By starting with activities that are not too far removed from the child's immediate experience, creativity becomes integrated within the child's existing musical experiences and skills' (Burnard, 2000: 21).

The projects

The second term of the PGCE music programme 'Musicians in Education' run by University of Greenwich in collaboration with Trinity Laban starts with a two-day creative project exploring and demonstrating principles that trainees are then expected to apply to their classroom, instrumental/vocal or alternative context placements. The two projects under examination here took Bartók's *Mikrokosmos* no. 61 'Pentatonic Melody' (see Example 10.1) as a starting point, although *Mikrokosmos* 70 and 74 have both also been used. All are for solo piano at the level of children who have been learning for three or four years.

In class, the group listened to the piece, performed it together as an ensemble, and analysed it, exploring the music from its smallest units to the formal architecture of the whole. It has, for example, a four-note pitch set (bar 1), a melody made up of two pentatonic scales, inversions, a retrograde, transposition, rhythmic displacement, and a diatonic mutation of the pitch set. The original tetrachord is made up of the first four notes of the Javanese *pelog barang* and Balinese *pelog sunaren* scales (notwithstanding the tuning differences), although the sense of exoticism is lost briefly in a diatonic A minor section, only to return in an ambiguous ending of open fifths. Throughout the piece, the numeric relationship of 2:1 is present in both phrase structures and intervals (for example, a minor third followed by a tone). Trainees then explored possible meanings behind the compositional choices, noting Swanwick's (1999) four-layered framework for analysis (materials, expression, form and value).

A new ensemble semi-improvised version of this piece was then created and recorded over two days, along with some shorter unrelated devised pieces. Trainees were given examples of ways to take individual concepts from the piece and collaboratively improvise them into extended structures, manipulating and reassembling them in an order to match Bartók's overall framework while maintaining an effective narrative and sequence. For example, improvised riffs on the opening pitch set were paired with improvised solos on the E minor pentatonic, then retrogrades of the riffs were followed with a shift by the soloist into A minor pentatonic, as in the first phrase of the piece.

Example 10.1 Bartók, *Mikrokosmos* 61 'Pentatonic Melody', with author's annotations.

Source: Reproduced by permission of Boosey & Hawkes Music Publishers Ltd.

On the basis of Borgo's (2006: 143) observation that 'relatively simple decentralized activities can produce dramatic, self-organising behaviors', much of the planning activity took place in small groups or was led by individual students given specific sections or concepts within the piece for the ensemble to amplify and work out. The freedoms offered by fragmentary motifs and concepts were set against the demands of a large-scale structural framework and the collaborative requirements of a cohort of up to 16 trainees. Genre was considered a fluid variable, and tasks had to be differentiated to cater for the varying degrees of improvisational fluency among the cohort. After setting out the possibilities of the task and leading the first section, the role of the project leader was principally to manage effective transitions from one section to the next and the timings of the workshop sessions. The project culminated with a recording session.

Project outcomes

Over ten years, resultant pieces have lasted between five and eight and a half minutes, although current copyright legislation means that these recordings unfortunately cannot be disseminated. It is not in the remit of this chapter to provide a detailed analysis of the musical outcomes of these projects, although they have variously exploited a variety of genres, including minimalism, gamelan, choral, aleatoric, and even a Spanish-infused funk soundworld, with each piece demonstrating a number of genre influences. Compositional techniques adopted in addition to those used by Bartók include canon, heterophony (of both accompaniment and melody), polyrhythms and hocket. The quality of outcome is, in the author's view, sufficient to evidence Fautley's (2013: 14) assertion that 'repertoire-based composition works'.

Methods

Four months after both the January 2013 and the January 2014 projects, questionnaires were issued to the PGCE cohorts to be returned anonymously with an incentive of a bottle of champagne to one respondent; 19 out of a possible 22 were returned (Q1–Q19). Questionnaires contained a mix of quantitative and qualitative data, with questions specifically on the experience of taking part in the project, initial responses to the tasks, learning about leadership skills developed, and the application of the project learning to a variety of contexts, both in experience and in expectation. Data has been analysed on a question-by-question basis, with themes extrapolated on the basis of prevalence and weight of argument. Example responses are included, identified by questionnaire number.

Contextual data

Trainees were asked to identify their principal instrument/voice, with some overlap permitted: 26 per cent identified as singers, 47 per cent as single-line melody instruments and 32 per cent as harmony instruments, with no choices for drums/percussion. One respondent failed to identify. Between the project and completing the questionnaire, 63 per cent had taught their instrument/voice in a one-to-one setting, 74 per cent had taught their instrument/voice in a group setting and 79 per cent had analysed a piece of notated music with a class.

Before the project, 58 per cent of trainees had taken part in an improvisation based on a notated piece, although only 11 per cent had led pupils in such an activity. The influence of the project can be seen in the next figure: in the four months between project and questionnaire, 63 per cent of trainees had led pupils in an improvisation based on a notated piece. While this figure is significant, the schedule of a PGCE programme may be influential, in that students have less opportunity to plan and teach their own lessons in the first term.

Responses to the task

> Our mission is to take music education into the twenty-first century. It is not enough to say that we are already living there when our practices are still firmly fashioned after nineteenth-century models. Twenty-first century teacher preparation must be bold. It must break free from its traditional conservatory strictures and be flexible, creative, and complex. It must stride the landscape of a rapidly changing world brimming with new challenges and opportunities as well as new possibilities.
>
> (Kaschub and Smith, 2013: 12)

Despite the plurality of approaches represented in Table 10.1, some broad themes can be drawn from the responses. There is evidence that for these trainees the connections between the varied modes of 'input' (aural and notation) and of 'output' (performance, improvisation, composition), theoretical understanding and devising/reviewing/appraising skills could be further developed, and that trainees welcomed this staged approach to supporting such connections as a key part of creative learning. In this sense, creative learning could here be defined as the increased connectivity between discrete areas and types of knowledge, thus 'developing our capacity for imaginative activity' (Spendlove and Wyse, 2008: 14). Trainees also find links to creative teaching, demonstrating the relevance of this multimodal strategy in challenging their approaches to drivers such as assessment, differentiation and collaborative working. There is some indication that creative learning practices do not fit easily into a culture where learning has to be regularly evidenced (Table 10.1(d), Q6).

Applications of the task

The task has a variety of possible contextual applications, and although it would need adapting, for example, for one-to-one instrumental lessons, the principle of improvisatory activity stemming from analysis can remain the same even if the outcome is very different to those in the projects under examination.

The student responses in Table 10.2 demonstrate different conceptions of creative teaching and learning, including the use of creativity for new knowledge, and new knowledge for creative outputs. They relate the project to the development of creative pedagogies, including the facilitation of self-directed learning; in assessing the obstacles to incorporating this type of work more readily into the school environment, they support the notion that one facet of creative teaching is responding obliquely to the pressures imposed by school parameters, maintaining pedagogy and professional practice in balance (Burnard, 2012: 261).

Table 10.1 Responses to the task

(a) Notation as a starting point for improvisation	(b) Improvisation to aid internalisation and memory	(c) Leadership skills	(d) Rehearsal and recording	(e) Teaching skills
Trainees were asked whether starting with notation made improvising an easier activity. While a few experienced improvisers expressed concern about the limitations notation imposed, most stated that notated ideas gave an approachable starting point. One student additionally commented on the support of structural principles as well.	Trainees were asked whether the project helped them to understand and remember Bartók's compositional choices. Responses were almost entirely affirmative:	Those trainees who had a specific leadership role were asked what they considered the most significant learning from that experience. Responses centred on developing a musical style and on the practical experience of leading an ensemble:	Trainees were asked what new challenges the rehearsal and recording of a collaboratively composed piece offered. One automatically related the question to the 'proof of outcome' ethos of their school placements; others focused on specific creative and practical musical challenges:	Trainees were asked which aspects of the exercise were most significant or challenging in their development as a teacher. Some related it to valued pedagogical principles. Others described the activity as equipping them with a toolkit for classroom music-making.
Q9: 'The notation gives the performer a starting point (notes to use, rhythms).'	Q3: 'By experiencing the music I felt that I could understand it better and therefore remember it.'	Q6: 'You have to be quite strong in your decision-making. This is both in terms of knowing what you want and communicating this to your musicians.'	Q6: 'The main challenge for me was assessing for myself what I had learnt; as a teacher it meant accepting that the aim for learning was experiential; as a musician it meant exploring the difference between understanding a piece from a technical point of view, and from a musical, more innate one, and accepting that it might be hard to prove the learning had taken place.'	Q1: 'Suggesting musical ideas that could be used as a scaffolding technique to get pupils to improvise. This is crucial to stretch pupils.'

Q12: 'Planning differentiated tasks while promoting pupil motivation.'

Q6: 'A chance to share your understanding of the piece with others and explore theirs … this is very important – unveiling what your students know already is as important as sharing your knowledge and views.'

Q2: 'To see that using a score as a starting point can open up improvising and making your own music to some pupils. It was important to be able to experience that to be able to use that in the future.'

Q14: 'Working collaboratively and developing initial ideas with confidence. As a teacher it has helped me recognise the problems and challenges that pupils may face.'

Q11: 'Putting together contrasting ideas in a cohesive manner.'

Q19: 'Communication without conductor, just knowing where we were.'

Q2: 'How to choose the best ideas.'

Q8: 'To create something with intention rather than something that fits.'

Q8: 'I think to move further away from something considered "safe". Incorporating your own music style actually worked better.'

Q3: 'How to take existing ideas and transform them drastically to create something new.'

Q13: 'Explaining devices clearly.'

Q2: 'You saw the ideas first and picturing your own melodies was easier then.'

Q6: 'Improvising gives you a chance to put some of those choices into a context. By improvising you experience them and make a more direct connection with their effect and function than by listening.'

Q7: 'Understanding how Bartók used small ideas to create a big piece.'

Q14: 'I am more confident when reading notated music; therefore I found the improvisation task more approachable.'

Q19: 'It was useful to experiment practically instead of just sit and stare at notes.'

Q1: 'Having the choice to analyse the music from the score gave me a better understanding of the structure and of the relationship between the notes/motifs used, which therefore meant that I could produce improvisation of better quality.'

Table 10.2 Contextual applications of the task

(a) Instrumental/vocal teaching	(b) Exploring a set work or other notated piece in a classroom environment	(c) Informal learning or community environments	(d) Obstacles to integrating task processes into professional practice
Responses particularly focused on the development of practical creative skills in IVT. Some also stressed the embedding of theoretical concepts.	There was a clear focus on the teaching of compositional devices here. There were also comments both on the possibilities for student-led group work and for moving the theoretical concepts from the page to the ear.	While most workshop leading and informal learning environments tend to underplay notation and 'knowledge about', trainees found value in the ways that tasks were differentiated by outcome, opened up theoretical constructs and offered opportunities for collaborative engagement by all, particularly through self-directed elements.	Most related this question to their secondary school placements. Concerns were about resources (time and instruments), restrictions on innovation, choosing the right piece, and the use of notation automatically distancing some pupils, no matter how carefully supported. Again, the pressure of assessment was cited.
Q1: 'Taking basic elements from an existing piece & improvising allows students to build on their creative skills.'	Q10: 'Looking at the compositional devices used could really help with improvisation in a classroom environment.'	Q13: 'Everyone can contribute in some way.'	Q1: 'Ensuring that the set work I choose can push pupils to be creative enough, but not be too complex at the same time!'
Q3: 'Spending little time on analysing through notes, and then exploring the ideas practically.'	Q6: 'Sharing ideas of ways to recontextualise ideas and compositional devices.'	Q14: 'The participants could be of any ability as they choose their own level of input.'	Q12: 'This type of work would not fit with my placement's current units of work.'

Q10: 'Definitely breaking down and analysing the score. This would be great with one-to-one piano lessons.'

Q3: 'Giving leadership to students, which could help stretch them & their compositional activities.'

Q19: 'Makes music accessible to those who may not be fluent note-readers.'

Q3: 'Size of groups, fear that some students may find notation an obstacle.'

Q6: 'The experiential aspect – particularly useful in explaining modes/harmonies.'

Q18: 'Analysing through performing and recognising things by ear rather than on the page.'

Q8: 'Demonstrating ideas and then leaving them for informal development.'

Q6: 'The need to prove learning has taken place, and that learning has been planned for. The demand for progress to be continually assessed on an individual level.'

Q19: 'Being able to demonstrate devices or sections of a piece practically to instil wider harmonic and stylistic understanding.'

Discussion

The project has a ten-year history of almost exactly the same process being explored each time, with only minor variations (three different Bartók pieces have been used, for example). The most significant variation has been the involvement of schoolchildren alongside trainees in the most recent (January 2015) project. The project emerged from the experience gained by the author from a career as an animateur leading work in schools and the community, often on behalf of orchestras and other 'guardians' of the classical tradition. There was throughout this time a frustration that the standard processes of devising music with learners did not adequately bridge the gaps between the aural-centred workshop environment – the notation-centred environment which most instrumental learners, for better or worse, were familiar with – and the quality of compositions that the orchestras were ostensibly introducing learners to. If composers were dramatically combining and shaping musical elements into dynamic forms, then no matter how skilfully created, riff-based or aleatoric process-driven responses in the workshop were often inadequate, and any large-scale harmonic, motivic or formal structuring devices tended to be superimposed by the workshop leader rather than understood and enacted by the participants.

By 'piggy-backing' on simple, tightly constructed works by highly established contemporary composers (other works that would be useful for this include, for example, the Associated Board of the Royal Schools of Music *Spectrum* series[3]), improvising ensembles can employ 'backbones' that are both sophisticated and approachable (Table 10.1(b), Q7). Stimuli can be straightforward enough to be approached by those with limited technical and reading skills (Table 10.2(c), Q19), but dynamic enough to permit the creation of music with a satisfying complexity and strong architecture. Simple instructions can generate complex outcomes, as evidenced by, for example, a PGCE trainee working hard to figure out a retrograde of an invented four-bar motif, or to transfer Bartók's pentatonic 2:1 interval proportion into a rhythmic event in $\frac{5}{4}$ time (equating to 3 plus 2 semitones).

Related concepts

Although the following related concepts have mostly emerged in music education literature since the project process was devised in 2005, they add a robust dimension to the debate about the practice and pedagogy of this work and articulate it with a depth of insight that illuminates possible avenues for the future of a music education that values and nurtures the classical tradition while permitting 'free play': 'Music education lingers on the edge of a significant rupture of practice and pedagogy, a turn from a closed-form concept of musical performance and score interpretation … to a reconfigured practice of composing, where creating, playing and sharing exists within and across open discursive fields' (Allsup, 2013: 57).

Enterprise pedagogy

Garnett (2013) has taken the existing concept of enterprise pedagogy and related it specifically to compulsory 11–14 music provision, describing a central feature as 'the use of a brief to set a musical task that would involve students in engaging with particular musical learning objectives' (ibid.: 15) and particularly valuing the possibilities for differentiation inherent in the task. Enterprise pedagogy is related to informal learning practices, but Garnett's research also depended significantly on the involvement of the teacher not only in promoting the ethos, but also in proactively setting up and managing student activity, focusing more on process learning than outcomes. Garnett states that in music enterprise pedagogy, the teacher:

*   sets a brief that requires students to create a real piece of music for a real purpose;
*   encourages students to be imaginative in creating their own response to the brief;
*   puts students in control of their own work;
*   allows students to make mistakes, accepting the risk that students will get things wrong rather than guiding them towards a preconceived solution;
*   facilitates learning, supporting students in working out what they need to learn;
*   guides students towards considering the different roles required to meet the brief and who in their group is best suited to each role.

The Bartók projects offer a clear connection to the principles of enterprise pedagogy. They ended, for example, with time for the cohort to have sessions in a professionally run recording studio. For some trainees, this was daunting, and the opportunity to create a product of significant value added a sense of urgency and reality to the project that inspired creative responses. The experience reinforces the value of a stimulating environment in supporting both process and product in composition pedagogy (Odena and Welch, 2009), and represents a 'real' purpose in Garnett's terms.

Trainees on the projects were given open tasks within defined parameters or a clearly explained brief; they sometimes worked in self-directed groups or with a pre-appointed trainee leader. The ensemble was expected to support these leaders by ameliorating their 'mistakes' and negotiating outcomes based on their intentions: in improvisation settings, both Sawyer (2008) and Borgo (2006) describe how musical mistakes may be 'manipulated into the context, thus creating new directions in dialogue' (Ward-Steinman, 2012: 82).

Garnett's last two bullet points are less straightforward to evidence, although the peer-to-peer learning that took place represented a process of collaboratively identifying problem areas and the skills or knowledge required to improve outcomes. While some roles were specifically allocated by the project leader, leadership often emerged as those more confident in collaborative composition guided fellow trainees into musically appropriate and satisfying contributions. Trainees often had a high degree of autonomy, operating without centralised control in a 'self-organising system' (Borgo, 2006).

Mis-listening

While enterprise pedagogy offers us some practical perspectives on classroom pedagogy, Schmidt's (2012) concept of 'mis-listening' offers a philosophical response to the deeply embedded divisions in music education between the traditionally dominant emphasis on 're-creation' of musical events through notated music, technical skill and the cognition of theoretical constructs on the one side, and the creative, expressive and communicative act of 'acquaintance-knowledge'-dominated 'play' (Swanwick, 1994) on the other. While this chapter gives one example of addressing these issues, Schmidt (2012: 13) articulates the problem much more profoundly, with a concern that educational systems today have led to 'the devaluing of musical reflective enquiry and creativity'. Mis-listening is described as: 'The capability to intentionally hear "wrong". That is, to understand that any interpretation, any practice, any text, any musical interaction produces a surplus and ramifications of meaning and sound, a multiplicity of on-looks and outlooks upon which one can and should enter, contribute, and extend' (ibid.: 13–14). Schmidt argues that conventional listening and understanding of musical artefacts are too dominated by recognition rather than by engagement, and lack '*potenza*' – the power to create. Instead, 'students have to *mis-listen* to the original in order to appropriate, adapt, and create something new' (ibid.: 14). Engagement on this level creates improvisatory products which are identified more by their sense of play than any artificially imposed notions of structural integrity or internal tension. Instead, Schmidt concludes that a notion of 'versioning', a sequence of temporary constructs that have an internal instability, assuming 'adaptability and provisionality as [their] premise and form … a constant remaking' (ibid.) is the most ethical response to this crisis. Ward-Steinman (2012: 82) goes on to argue that the aims of 'decentralized power and conflict, multiplicity and meaning, and mis-listening may be met in the improvising music ensemble'.

Nomadism in music education

While Schmidt offers a compelling philosophy for the viewpoint of the student, Gould (2004) and Johansson (2012) both evoke the idea of the nomad as a suitable descriptor for the contemporary music educator – Gould through a lens of postmodern feminism and the creation of political agency, Johansson (2012: 45) through notions of competence, skill sets and the tension between responsibilities as both 'carriers of tradition and innovative artists'. Both articulate a vision of the teacher-artist as rejecting orthodox interpretations and encultured systemic approaches, 'the subject that transgresses boundaries and subverts conventions … the nomad makes multiple connections while constantly moving in an aesthetic of open spaces' (Gould, 2004: 68). This echoes Becker's (1997: 22) description of the artist as 'the exile … spiritually, if not literally, removed from his or her land'. Gould imagines a music education where generative processes are the norm rather than the exception, and as Allsup (2013: 64) describes it, 'there is never only one way to know a piece of music, never only one way to interpret it, perform it, use it or cite it … the curiosity seeker [is] in charge, not the teacher, not the author-composer'.

The model set out in Figure 10.1 demonstrates the links these three related concepts have to the project processes: 'nomadism' in describing some attributes of trainees and practising teachers, and influencing the characteristics of the musical product of the project; 'mis-listening' in affecting how we relate and respond to the published work, and equipping our pedagogical practice with the imperative to own musical objects through play, and 'enterprise pedagogy' in informing the mechanisms of this specific project and subsequent trainee-led activities.

The twenty-first-century revolution in conceptions of ownership, editing rights and dissemination practices has profound implications for creative teaching and learning: 'the curiosity seeker can approach any kind of music and read the codes left behind as an open text or interpretive event' (Allsup, 2013: 65). In effect, ownership has become a playful '*wondership*' – those with most wonder about any musical text, who are prepared to invest most in the deconstruction and re-imagining of it become de facto the new owners of it. Musical objects are no longer a 'given', but rather give birth to new 'emergent objects' (Wright and Kanellopoulos, 2010: 82). In fact, Humphreys (2006: 355) goes as far as to argue that 'the concept of composition itself, as currently described in curricular materials and even the research literature, is … Western, elitist, and counter to our avowed goals

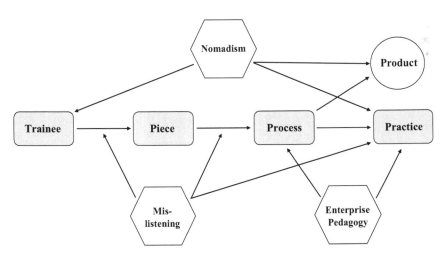

Figure 10.1 Diagram developed from the PEPP (Pupil, Environment, Process, Product) framework.

Source: Adapted from Odena and Welch (2009).

in multicultural education'. It should be pointed out that Bartók himself exhibits porous boundaries when it comes to the ownership of musical artefacts, as not only does *Mikrokosmos* 61 use a gamelan scale, but *Mikrokosmos* 70, also used for these projects, quotes and adapts Wagner.

Burnard (2012: 30) asserts musical creativity as '"an enacted freedom", that always goes beyond, and never simply derives from, that which already is'; creative teaching, especially in a conservatoire setting, demands that the representation of 'knowing' can never be simply the reproduction of a known artefact (Wells, 2002). The Bartók projects demonstrate the development of one specific tool for facilitating the connection of multimodal musical behaviours (Burnard, 2012) as a creative learning practice in higher music education, specifically in this case to support creative teaching in schools.

Conclusion

ITT should provide firm foundations on which new teachers can continue to build, forming the start of their professional journey.

(Carter, 2015: 23)

The Bartók projects were devised as a way of initiating trainee secondary school music teachers into ways of thinking that subvert standard practices, a means of 'unsettling dominant conceptions of music learning' (Wright and Kanellopoulos, 2010: 82), placing the 'transformative culture' of 'mashups and remixing' (Burnard, 2012: 13) into both the mainstream classroom and the mainstream repertoire. Enterprise pedagogy, mis-listening and nomadism all provide related approaches that reinforce this as an important aim. We often need reminding that the verb for making music is to 'play' and that musical training should be an induction into a world of play through organised sound. While many writers have placed play at the heart of the musical learning transaction in IVT, classroom and community contexts, too much classroom practice is still defined as not musical enough (Ofsted, 2012) – that is, with insufficient 'playing'.

In their teaching experiences before the project, only 11 per cent of trainees had led pupils in an improvisation based on a notated piece, but four months afterwards, the figure was 63 per cent, indicating that many of them were inspired to try out versions of the task with learners. The evidence from trainees is that, notwithstanding the difficulties in finding the right pieces and putting similar activities into practice within the confines of their school placements, they acknowledged the value of the processes they went through in terms of how they illuminated the possibilities for more meaningful musical encounters with published music across a range of contexts. Finding space within a packed PGCE programme for activities such as this is therefore essential in creating a generation of music educators who are skilled in working in any music learning environment, using the performance and manipulation of musical ideas 'in the moment' as their principal form of communication, and the creative exploration of published works as one important tool in their arsenal.

Notes

1 The Postgraduate Certificate of Education (PGCE) is the most common route to gaining Qualified Teacher Status in the UK. It is normally a one-year full-time programme in a university, with substantial active placements in schools. A professional training programme with rigorous government guidelines, it offers a practice-based education in a reflective and theory-centric frame.
2 Stevens's *Search and Reflect* (1985/2007) is an influential collection of generative community music activities that represented a period when both free improvisers like Stevens and pedagogues like John Paynter were inspired by contemporary art movements, encouraging teachers to remove cultural 'overlays' and to return to pure sound and rhythm as the starting point for musical experiment and learning.
3 A series of contemporary miniatures for instrumentalists.

References

Allsup, R.E. (2013). 'The Compositional Turn in Music Education: From Closed Forms to Open Texts'. In: M. Kaschub and J. Smith (eds), *Composing Our Future: Preparing Music Educators to Teach Composition* (pp. 57–74). New York: Oxford University Press.

Baker, D. (2013). 'Music, Informal Learning and the Instrumental Lesson: Teacher and Student Evaluations of the Ear Playing Project (EPP)'. In: M. Stakelum (ed.), *Developing the Musician: Contemporary Perspectives on Teaching and Learning* (pp. 291–309). Farnham: Ashgate.

Becker, C. (1997). 'The Artist as Public Intellectual'. In: H.A. Giroux and P. Shannon (eds), *Education and Cultural Studies: Towards a Performative Practice* (pp. 13–24). New York: Routledge.

Borgo, D. (2006). *Sync or Swarm: Improvising Music in a Complex Age*. New York: Bloomsbury.

Brockmann, N.M. (2009). *From Sight to Sound: Improvisational Games for Classical Musicians*. Bloomington, IN: Indiana University Press.

Burnard, P. (2000). 'How Children Ascribe Meaning to Improvisation and Composition: Rethinking Pedagogy in Music Education'. *Music Education Research*, 2(1), 7–23.

——— (2012). *Musical Creativities in Practice*. Oxford: Oxford University Press.

Carter, A. (2015). *Carter Review of Initial Teacher Training (ITT)*. London: Department for Education. Retrieved 30 January 2015 from https://www.gov.uk/government/publications/carter-review-of-initial-teacher-training.

Fautley, M. (2013). *Listen Imagine Compose: Research Report*. Esmée Fairburn Foundation. Retrieved 30 January 2015 from http://bcmg.s3.amazonaws.com/assets/File/1192.pdf.

Finney, J. and Philpott, C. (2010). 'Informal Learning and Meta-pedagogy in Initial Teacher Education in England'. *British Journal of Music Education*, 27(1), 7–19.

Garnett, J. (2013). 'Enterprise Pedagogy in Music: An Exploration of Multiple Pedagogies'. *Music Education Research*, 15(1), 1–18.

Gould, E. (2004). 'Feminist Theory in Music Education Research: Grrl-illa Games as Nomadic Practice (or How Music Education Fell from Grace)'. *Music Education Research*, 6(1), 67–79.

Green, L. (2014). *Hear, Listen, Play! How to Free Your Students' Aural, Improvisation, and Performance Skills*. New York: Oxford University Press.

Harris, P. (2006). *Improve Your Teaching! An Essential Handbook for Instrumental and Singing Teachers*. London: Faber Music.

Higgins, L. (2012). *Community Music: In Theory and in Practice*. New York: Oxford University Press.

Humphreys, J.T. (2006). 'Toward a Reconstruction of "Creativity" in Music Education'. *British Journal of Music Education*, 23(3), 351–61.

Jeffery, G. (2005). *The Creative College: Building a Successful Learning Culture in the Arts*. Stoke-on-Trent: Trentham Books.

Johansson, K. (2012). 'Experts, Entrepreneurs and Competence Nomads: The Skills Paradox in Higher Music Education'. *Music Education Research*, 14(1), 45–62.

Kaschub, M. and Smith, J. (eds) (2013). 'Introduction: Embracing Composition in Music Teacher Education'. In: M. Kaschub and J. Smith (eds), *Composing Our Future: Preparing Music Educators to Teach Composition* (pp. 3–18). New York: Oxford University Press.

Odena, O. and Welch, G. (2009). 'A Generative Model of Teachers' Thinking on Musical Creativity'. *Psychology of Music*, 37(4), 416–42.

Ofsted (2012). *Music in Schools: Wider Still, and Wider*. London: Ofsted.

Palmer, T. (2013). 'Assessing Leadership Skills in the Conservatoire'. In: M. Stakelum (ed.), *Developing the Musician: Contemporary Perspectives on Teaching and Learning* (pp. 265–90). Farnham: Ashgate.

——— and Bunting, P. (2015). 'Artist-teacher Identities: An Overview of Issues in Conservatoire Partnership Secondary Music PGCE Programmes'. Paper presented at *The Reflective Conservatoire Conference: Creativity and Changing Cultures*, 26 February–1 March 2015, Guildhall School of Music and Drama, London.

Parker, D. (2010). 'The Improvising Leader: Developing Leadership Capacity through Improvisation'. In: S. Kay and K. Venner with S. Burns and M. Schwarz (eds), *A Cultural Leadership Reader* (pp. 106–13). London: Cultural Leadership Programme.

Paynter, J. and Aston, P. (1970). *Sound and Silence: Classroom Projects in Creative Music*. Cambridge: Cambridge University Press.

Priest, P. (1989). 'Playing by Ear: Its Nature and Application to Instrumental Learning'. *British Journal of Music Education*, 6(2), 173–91.

Sawyer, R.K. (2008). *Group Genius: The Creative Power of Collaboration*. New York: Basic Books.

Schmidt, P. (2012). 'What We Hear is Meaning Too: Deconstruction, Dialogue, and Music'. *Philosophy of Music Education Review*, 20(1), 3–24.

Spendlove, D. and Wyse, D. (2008). 'Creative Learning: Definitions and Barriers'. In: A. Craft, T. Cremin and P. Burnard (eds), *Creative Learning 3–11 and How We Document It* (pp. 19–33). Stoke-on-Trent: Trentham Books.

Stevens, J. (1985/2007). *Search and Reflect: A Music Workshop Handbook*. Twickenham: Rockschool. First published 1985.

Summers, A. (2009). *Creative Music Manual*. Frome, UK: Luniver Press.

Swanwick, K. (1994). *Musical Knowledge: Intuition, Analysis and Music Education*. London: Routledge.

——— (1999). *Teaching Music Musically*. London: Routledge.

Walduck, J. (2005). 'Collaborative Arts Practice and Identity'. In: G. Odam and N. Bannan (eds), *The Reflective Conservatoire: Studies in Music Education* (pp. 301–32). Aldershot: Ashgate.

Ward, V. (2004). 'Good Performance, Music Analysis and Instrumental Teaching: Towards an Understanding of the Aims and Objectives of Instrumental Teachers'. *Music Education Research*, 6(2), 191–215.

Ward-Steinman, P.M. (2012). 'An Invitation to Play: A Response to Patrick Schmidt's "What We Hear is Meaning Too: Deconstruction, Dialogue, and Music"'. *Philosophy of Music Education Review*, 20(1), 82–6.

Wells, G. (2002). 'Inquiry as an Orientation for Learning, Teaching and Teacher Education'. In: G. Wells and G. Claxton (eds), *Learning for Life in the 21st Century: Sociocultural Perspectives on the Future of Education* (pp. 197–210). Oxford: Blackwell.

Wright, R. and Kanellopoulos, P. (2010). 'Informal Music Learning, Improvisation and Teacher Education'. *British Journal of Music Education*, 27(1), 71–87.

Part III

Philosophies, practices and pedagogies

Teaching for creative learning

11 Imagined structures

Creative approaches for musical analysis

Mark Hutchinson and Tim Howell

Music analysis can be quite a troublesome subject within university-level music teaching. Some students gravitate to it naturally and get a lot out of it from the very beginning; others struggle to engage with it, finding its technical challenges taxing, but also experiencing difficulties in relating it to the rest of their musical activities. Analysis is often seen as a kind of musical All-Bran – undoubtedly very worthwhile, and good for overall well-being, but often rather unpleasant and difficult to swallow (definitely an acquired taste). Indeed, sometimes it can seem well-nigh indigestible. We argue here that this difficulty arises above all from a problem of epistemology, the tendency to view analysis as distinct from other musical activities, a musical 'science' that requires a different set of skills. No rigid separation can be made between analytical practice and analytical teaching in this regard: teaching analysis creatively necessarily means teaching creative analysis – where 'creative' here is taken in its literal sense as 'involving an act of creation'. This is the basis of the viewpoint outlined here.

For Tim Howell, joining the academic staff of the Department of Music at the University of York, UK, in 1986, the strong emphasis on practical activities – especially performance and composition – presented a particular challenge: how to make analysis approachable and useful to students. For his part, Mark Hutchinson was naturally drawn towards this field as an undergraduate at York in 2005; yet he has also encountered, throughout his time as a PhD student as well as in his teaching thereafter, students who feel that their analytical skills are inadequate. What is striking is just how this sense of inadequacy is perceived. The most frequent comment about music analysis made by students is that they would really like to understand it better, and they feel it would benefit their overall musicianship, but they're 'just not very good at it'. And this is a feeling that has persisted for many, even though the UK A level courses and ABRSM theory exams that many students have taken will already have introduced them to the basics of analytical thought.[1]

This situation is a classic example of the way in which particular conceptions of knowledge can lead to very different kinds of teaching. Burnard (2012) notes that the concept of musical creativity has often been treated as if it were something monolithic, bound up with the ideal of the composer-hero, when in reality there is a vast field of different musical 'creativities', varied acts of creation and re-creation arising as social and cultural systems interact with individual preferences and talents. The same is true of the ideas underpinning the teaching of theory and analysis: these are often bound up with a monolithic concept of musical knowledge as an objective 'science', with little recognition of the mediated character of all music. As a result, students often measure their analytical abilities against a formulaic and unyielding standard, emphasising the absorption and regurgitation of prefabricated musical 'facts'. Yet, on the contrary, the academic field of music analysis is increasingly dominated by approaches that emphasise creativity and fresh connections above strict adherence to pre-established theoretical frameworks.[2] Encouraging students to think about music theory and analysis in new, more flexible ways thus not only helps help them to see the skills they already have and how they can develop them, it also prepares them for further academic study.

The vision: Creative musical analysis

The idea of 'creative' musical analysis may at first seem rather unlikely. Creativity in music is most often associated with the act of composition and the (arguably somewhat re-creative) activity of performance. But as soon as composers and performers begin to *think* about their artistic endeavours, they are, at a most fundamental level, starting to analyse. If musical analysis is to be appreciated and valued as a creative process within an active and practical community of musicians, it must, first and foremost, be seen to have relevance. The common denominator for performers, composers and (analytical) thinkers is the listening process: all musicians engage with the perception of sound. Analysis therefore must have direct connections with the listening process – it is a quest for understanding – and its starting point should be an instinctive and emotional reaction to hearing a piece of music. From this subjective, collective experience, trying to rationalise that response, outlining the compositional means that engender these effects, is what *musical* analysis aims to achieve. This of course implies a thought process that is essentially interpretative, rather than definitive; it offers a particular listening strategy which, despite gathering evidence to support its particular view, is merely one among many. Just as a single piece of music may be subject to a variety of interpretations in performance (indeed, that diversity is positively welcomed), so too is any open-minded analytical discussion. It also has a productively cyclic quality – analytical observations feed back into the listening process – as we may hear additional qualities upon re-listening.

'Creative musical analysis', as it is defined here, thus involves a reconfiguration of the relationships between the different elements of musical activity, as illustrated in Figure 11.1. In the 'closed' perspective shown in Figure 11.1(a), all forms of musical activity are seen in terms of a single, fixed musical work (or, in the case of music theory, a fixed set of musical patterns deriving from such works): behaviours such as composition, performance or analysis are seen as active, in that they involve some degree of conscious decision-making and/or interpretation, while the process of hearing a work (for an audience-member) or initially learning it (for a performer) is more about passive absorption.[3] Even putatively active behaviours are in this model subject to the limitations imposed by the view of the musical work as fixed, above all by the intention of the composer or a scientific conception of the 'rules' of a musical language. By contrast, Figure 11.1(b) shows an 'open' perspective: here, the focus is not on any fixed product, but rather on a collection of interacting *processes*, each of which is equally active and equally capable of creating something new. The arrows illustrate the cyclical relationships that connect each kind of musical activity: composers are informed in their work by their own listening and performance; performers use their listening and analytical reflections to generate fresh interpretations; listeners, responding to their own analytical or compositional work, are empowered to hear music in new ways.

Analysis is about asking questions. It transforms the potentially passive process of listening into something highly active. Students are asked to move beyond compositional details and relate them to a whole, to develop critical awareness, to engage with a process of understanding. Nicholas Cook (1987: 232) puts it as follows:

> It is at undergraduate and college level, not as an instrument of advanced research, that analysis seems to me to have its most vital role to play in today's musical culture. It has this role because the ability to set aside details and 'see' large-scale connections appropriate to the particular musical context, which is what analysis encourages, is an essential part of the musician's way of perceiving musical sound.

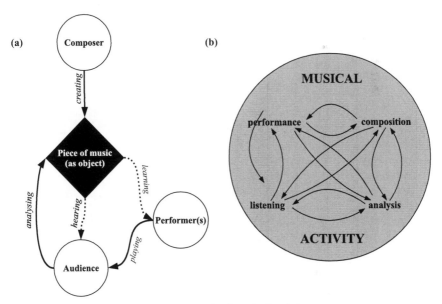

Figure 11.1 (a) Closed and (b) open models of musical activity.

Note: Dotted and solid connectors indicate passive and active engagement respectively.

Facing the indigestible: Student expectations

The model of 'creative musical analysis' outlined above is rather distant from the expectations of many undergraduate students. The perception of analytical topics as worthy but rather unpleasant remains remarkably persistent. Historically, there have been two main factors that account for the 'difficulty' some students experience when analysing music at university. (Interestingly, both factors persist, and have done so for some considerable time.) The first is a perception that 'analysis' is description: a detailed, painful, blow-by-blow inventory of the succession of events that make up a piece of music – nothing more than a running commentary. This is, and stubbornly remains, the most common experience that students have endured before starting a degree. They find this to be incredibly boring, for one simple reason: it *is* boring! At the other end of the spectrum is a rather dauntingly academic approach: the Schenkerians, set-theoreticians and semiologists (to select the most alliterative of their number). These adopt a quasi-scientific manner, publishing treatises of charts and tables in an overwhelming array of technical data; all this is painstakingly couched in language of alienating complexity. So you have a straight choice: analysis can be boring or bewildering. The teaching of creative musical analysis must address issues of tedium and alienation: it needs to be enlightening.

At the beginning of an introductory analysis course which has been running for several years at the University of York, students are asked how they would define analysis. A few representative examples give a flavour of their responses; for them, analysis means: 'to look into the different components of a piece to see how they fit together and make the piece work as a whole'; 'the study and critique of music from an objective point of view'; 'the breaking down of a piece of music and looking at the way it has been written, in order to gain a greater understanding of the music'.

Going through the record of responses from the last few years, there is a striking consistency about the definitions students come up with. They return overwhelmingly to a few central principles. First, analysis is all about *segmentation*. It involves taking pieces of music and 'splitting them up' into their constituent parts. This might mean marking out the main 'sections' of a piece, or it could mean taking individual musical elements such as harmony, rhythm, melody or instrumentation and describing each in isolation. Second, analysis is a kind of *second-hand composition*. It serves as a way of reconstructing the compositional process of a piece, possibly with the intent of understanding the composer better or of justifying the status of the resultant work within a canon of 'masterpieces' (by showing how it is innovative or ahead of its time). Third, and most tellingly, analysis is seen as offering the possibility of *rational, objective understanding* beyond any other kind of musical engagement: students repeatedly talk about explaining 'how the music works', gaining a 'deeper understanding', and almost always define analysis as 'detailed study' first and foremost.

These features, and especially the last, give us a hint of the kind of perspectives that might underpin these definitions. Underneath them all is the assumption that analysis is a kind of musical 'science', which offers clear-cut answers that go beyond the perceived subjectivity of normal performance and composition: it allows you to understand the basic building blocks of which pieces are made, and the processes by which these units interact and develop. There is an underlying idea that unless you can break up a piece into all its constituent elements and show how they work at an abstract level, you don't really understand it 'properly', even if you can play it beautifully or listen to it appreciatively and enthusiastically. And the flip side is the assumption that once you can trace all these internal relationships, then you *do* 'understand' the piece, and you don't really need to do anything else – perhaps not even listen to it any more.

Frameworks, classifications, recipe books?

These perceptions of analysis don't come from nowhere, of course – they often carry over very easily from students' study before university. A lot of early engagement with analysis – through theory grades and A level work – can be described as the acquisition of a framework of objective knowledge about 'the rules of music' in various eras. This might involve discussions of the 'grammar' of music – cadences, phrase structure and other ways of segmenting a piece; it might involve a kind of musical 'taxonomy' – using particular stylistic features to categorise pieces by period or genre; and it might even involve elements of composition such as pastiche, so long as these serve primarily to demonstrate and reinforce students' understanding of the analytical rules. All these facets of analysis are important and should not be denigrated; they are crucial elements in developing general musical awareness. But they are all at the level of technique – what we might call analytical 'craft'; although they are very useful tools for thinking about music, they carry with them a particular viewpoint of the purpose, method and limits of analytical thought. The implication is that 'being good at analysis' is above all about absorbing a large collection of musical 'facts' which we can then retrieve and apply on demand.

But by this definition, it is also quite clear why so many students might feel both that they 'ought to' be good at analysis, but also that they 'just aren't'. On the one hand, portraying music theory as a kind of science makes its mastery very desirable for a conscientious student: after all, who wouldn't want to feel that they 'really understand' the pieces they play in a verifiable, objective way? It is thus not surprising that students might feel that they are somehow 'inadequate' when they cannot produce a comprehensive harmonic analysis of a Chopin prelude, even though they can play it beautifully or listen to it with deep engagement. On the other hand, analytical skills can appear unattainable (or at least impractical to attain) because this viewpoint places them as something quite disconnected from day-to-day musical activity, requiring a completely different approach to learning.

It is perhaps this sense of separation between analysis and other kinds of musical activity that is the most problematic aspect of this viewpoint. If one of the primary intentions of the university experience is to encourage a more *integrated* and critical approach to knowledge, then this must have a knock-on effect here. In many ways, it would be easy to structure an introductory analysis course primarily as a kind of 'recipe book' of different techniques to be acquired – each of which could be listed clearly as SMART learning outcomes,[4] and explicitly assessed at the close of the course. There is certainly no shortage of different analytical techniques which could be seen as fodder for this, each with its own vocabulary, appropriate repertoire, collection of techniques and set of 'rules' to which we might expect pieces to conform. But taken by itself, this kind of 'recipe' approach leaves little room for creativity except in the narrowest possible sense – the kind of creativity required to make a piece fit neatly into a particular analytical framework.

A problem of epistemology

At root, it seems that that these problems are specifically related to the *kinds* of knowledge that students expect analysis to produce. As Nicholas Cook (2002: 78) has pointed out, any claim to present some kind of knowledge or truth about music is necessarily underpinned by a particular epistemology – a particular view of 'what sort of truth it aspires to'. The trouble is that the viewpoint of analysis held by many students, as primarily a repository of objective 'facts' about music, links it to a category of truth which is fundamentally about reproducing existing data rather than about creating new experiences or responses. This marks it out as something quite different from most other musical arenas, where 'hard' facts about performance technique or compositional methods are always counterbalanced by issues of expression, inspiration and instinct in ways that open up possibilities for fresh acts of artistic creation. In other words, it ignores the interpretative qualities of other musical activities. This problem is very aptly summed up by another student's rather wry (and very creative!) definition: 'Analysis is akin to performing an autopsy on a murder victim, and then reconstructing the corpse with complete precision.'

Finding fresh approaches to the teaching of music analysis means first expanding our conception of what it is that analysis can tell us, and how we might go about doing it. Where student views of analysis (as outlined below) tend to emphasise its status as a process of dissection, parasitic on other musical activities, a view of it as creative – that is, serving to create new experiences and artistic responses – allows it to be rehabilitated within the wider community of musical activity.

Analysis in practice: Listening, questioning, exploring

Two short analytical case studies will help explore how this might work out in practice. The first is based around a few bars of a short piece of recent classical music, a study entitled 'Arc-en-ciel' from the first book of piano études by the Hungarian composer György Ligeti (1923–2006) (see Ligeti, 1986). Contemporary music can be a very useful arena to explore some of these issues, because it often challenges existing analytical frameworks anyway, so there is perhaps less temptation to settle for rigidly factual models of musical knowledge – it can force us to rethink what we are actually trying to do when we 'do' analysis. It is useful to see what happens here when we take a rational, segmentation-based analytical approach to its logical extreme and look just at the opening of the score (Example 11.1).

Trying to get some straightforward analytical 'facts' from this piece is a bit like trying to nail jelly to the wall. We could begin by taking individual elements in turn. Starting with rhythm, we might try and establish the underlying metre and the basic unit of pulsation; but that doesn't work – the dotted bar-lines suggest that each hand has its own metre, and it's hard to tell whether the pulse is in semiquavers, quavers or crotchets (or even dotted crotchets). Or we could try and split it into melodic phrases: the slurs at the start help at first, but quite quickly it starts getting blurry again (and it's also difficult to tell what is melody and what is accompaniment). Or we could look at the harmony; but again, on sight, we can't even take the basic step of categorising this piece as tonal or atonal – it seems to be full of triadic material, but it's all piled together

Example 11.1 Ligeti, 'Arc-en-ciel', bars 1–6.

seemingly haphazardly, with no clear cadences or sense of harmonic syntax. (We could sidestep this by calling it 'non-functional harmony', but that's just putting a name to an absence – it merely makes us feel better about our inability to tell what's going on by giving us a word to describe the situation.) So essentially, we seem to be stuck.

If we take a step back, though, and rid ourselves of the necessity to begin by building up clear analytical 'facts', we find other ways of approaching this work, particularly those that focus on our experience of it as listeners. We could start by thinking about the title, which is 'Arc-en-ciel' – the French term for rainbow. Before even hearing the piece, this evokes a certain character. Rainbows are colourful but evanescent, and perhaps bittersweet (since they come from the combination of sun and rain). They are awe-inspiring, but in a very different way from vast or terrifying natural events such as thunderstorms or earthquakes. Their effect is much more delicate, but they are still miraculous in the way they seem to defy gravity and come from nowhere. So we now have a collection of expectations that might inform our experience of this piece. The next thing to do is to listen to the music, and see whether this gives any further clarity.[5]

Listening to this opening, it fits with several of these expectations – it does seem bittersweet, delicate and evanescent, shimmeringly coloured and somehow 'weightless'. So there are certain very distinctive expressive qualities it conjures up which invite further exploration. Analysis can help in this process. Returning to our previous observations, several that seemed frustratingly ambiguous at the time now fit very well. The difficulty of rhythmic segmentation actually demonstrates a carefully achieved sense of continuity here: the very slow tempo means that it is always unclear whether semiquavers or quavers constitute the basic pulse, and the different metres of the two hands mean that we are constantly caught in a kind of slow-motion cross-rhythm – this sense of suspended time is a large factor in the feeling of weightlessness that is present in this opening. The ambiguity of the harmonies produces a similar effect: each hand moves constantly between different triadic sonorities, so that we as listeners find ourselves constantly having to reorient our expectations of what's coming next. There is very rarely any clear sense of key, but equally, it never becomes so dissonant that we can only hear it in purely atonal terms (although listeners are likely to find that their experiences vary in this respect). Instead, it presents a constant shuffling between keys – as if we were traversing the harmonic spectrum in the same shimmering, unstable way that a rainbow traverses the colour spectrum.

This train of thought could be continued for some time, but hopefully the purpose of the example is clear by now. Once we shift our mindset from one which is focused upon fact-finding to one which is based upon questioning and reflecting upon our experience, details of the piece which were previously seen as obstacles become meaningful and important parts of its character, and there is a sense that the analytical work we do begins to relate more clearly to other aspects of our musical activity. Thinking in this way can actually help us enjoy this piece more, and it is clear too that performers could benefit from some of these insights as they think about what elements they might emphasise in playing the piece. It should be stressed, of course, that there is nothing 'certain' about this analysis:

there has been no definitive explanation of 'how this music works', and indeed, it is quite likely that some readers will find their own listening experience totally at odds (in one respect or another) with that just described, and may consequently disagree with some of the details that have been drawn out. But that is the point: we *cannot* build a conclusive 'explanation' for a piece like this, and there is no real reason why we should try to. But what analysis *is* really good at is helping us to ask meaningful questions about our own experience, and to connect that experience with the other things we do as musicians.

Rehabilitating analysis: Debussy and Brahms

A further case study of a short piano piece by Debussy (with reference to another by Brahms) illustrates ways in which this approach could be developed further, allowing more traditional analytical vocabulary – which has often been associated with 'indigestible' views of the subject – to be rehabilitated as an integral part of this fruitful questioning process. It also helps us clarify the sometimes problematic boundaries between description and analysis in university music teaching. Debussy's prelude 'La fille aux cheveux de lin' is a small-scale, self-contained musical structure – but typically not one that adheres to any traditional formal prototype. (Space only permits an overview here, but you are encouraged to track down a recording or score[6] and listen to or play through the piece at this point.) Segmenting naturally into phrases allows immediate observations of the extent to which this succession of elements stems from the compositional potential of its initial statement.

Example 11.2 shows that the opening gesture and the simple pentatonicism of its first four pitches offers harmonic ambiguity between possible G♭ major or E♭ minor triads, with the rhythmic shaping and metrical stress of this arpeggiation favouring G♭ as the prevailing centre. The plagal cadence is remarkably affirmative in this regard, begging the fundamental question of any analysis: why? By noting that its C♭ major sonority is merely an extension of the descending-thirds sequence so far, now presented simultaneously, with horizontal continuity manifest here as vertical colour, the cadence is merely a further stage in a process of intervallic unfolding. It also establishes a basic principle: harmony emerges from linear considerations, and is not governed by traditional functional logic.

Très calme et doucement expressif ($\downarrow$ = 66)

p sans rigueur

Example 11.2 Debussy, 'La fille aux cheveux de lin', opening.

By placing these observations alongside another piano work that derives its materials from chains of descending thirds – but in a totally different way – the value of analytical commentary in the service of historical and stylistic awareness is evident. Example 11.3 shows the opening four-bar phrase of Brahms' Intermezzo in B minor (op. 119, no. 1 of 1892; see Brahms, 1893). Despite the blurred sound world of overlapping chains of thirds, the underlying harmonic succession (shown in the reduction here) is a cycle of fifths: B–E–A–D–G–C♯–F♯. Indeed, given all the attendant ground-bass (*passacaglia*) associations that so interested Brahms at this time, this sequence has resonances with music from the Baroque era; thus, a range of historical and stylistic issues come into play. More immediately, though, the harmonic language is functional and goal-directed in its organisation.

Returning to the Debussy, we now have a greater appreciation of his novel harmonic construction – concepts of 'colour' rather than function and tonal/harmonic ambiguity – while understanding that it has a logic all its own. It is possible to follow through each phrase of the piece in turn (some 10 of them in total), demonstrating how each exploration builds upon features of its predecessor in a process of variation and growth that culminates in the climax (of bars 21–3), a moment identified in any instinctive response to the piece as significantly striking. Although there is insufficient space to follow through all the detail here, just a couple of larger points will help draw things together. The idea of harmonic divergence – the establishment of centres that stand in contrast to the prevailing G♭ major of the piece – is worth outlining: an emphasis on E♭ major in bar 6 (a return to G♭ by the end of phrase III perhaps confirming a point of formal articulation by way of recurrence). The next contrasting centre is that C♭ major (bar 16) with all its associations from the generative plagal cadence of the opening, setting up the notion of correspondences between local- and large-scale events. The climax point of the piece offers a (somewhat modal) cadential

Example 11.3 Brahms, Intermezzo in B minor, op. 119, no. 1, opening, with reduction of cycle of fifths harmonies.

assertion of A♭ major (bars 22–3), after a considerable degree of E♭ (dominant) preparation (over bars 19–21).

Enough description – though this is information gathering that any group can engage with when asked to outline the events of the piece as they unfold. For many students, of course, this kind of detailed observation is what they consider 'analysis' to be. Having collected that information through student input, ensuring some kind of engagement in the process, making sense of this activity is a crucial next step. It can be almost revelatory for students simply to stand back and take stock, not merely noting what has happened and how, but asking *why*? This full sequence of cadentially established centres is as follows: G♭ (bar 3)–E♭ (bar 6)–C♭ (bar 16)–A♭ (bars 22 and 23). By playing these tonal centres as a succession of notes on the keyboard (and you are encouraged to do this for yourself!), their origin is immediately (and aurally) apparent. As a transposed version of the opening melodic shape – a gesture shown to be the generator of successive events – we can see, hear, understand and imagine its large-scale, structural ramifications.

The idea that analytical discovery can generate a new perspective on the music in question emerges forcefully here. Engaging with creative analysis reveals 'the meaning of the obvious' by deriving it from what is hidden. An obvious, surface, melodic chain of thirds gains meaning when we realise that it is being subtly projected – hidden – in terms of a background sequence of harmonic centres. By understanding how one such pattern is derived from the other, our immediate and instinctive reactions, that 'La fille aux cheveux de lin' is a satisfying, coherent and well-constructed piano piece, and one that moves to a point of climax in a particularly effective and affecting manner – can be rationalised and understood. (For those who like to take things to a more theoretical level, that point of climax – in terms of the tonal resolution of the piece – is at the golden section of the work.)[7] The final stages of the piece, after its climactic focal point, retrace this sequence of thirds in order to return to the G♭ tonic.

What next? Strategies for creative teaching

In closing, it is useful to consider some of the more general implications this kind of attitude might have for developing students' understanding of music analysis as a fundamentally creative activity, and the ways in which this under-standing might feed fruitfully into other important topics within university music studies. There is no simple 'solution' to the issues discussed here, of course; nonetheless, there are important consequences from our suggestion that creative analytical teaching necessarily involves rethinking the role of creativity *within* analysis. Creative techniques for teaching are not enough; what is needed are approaches that help students to develop their own creative practices. A starting point for these approaches is provided by the numerous principles of creativity outlined by Sternberg and Williams in their book *How to Develop Student Creativity* (1996); four of their principles are particularly relevant in this context.

The first principle they give is to *model creativity*. This demonstrates the role that can still be played by quite traditional lecture formats in teaching of this kind. Since students beginning their university careers tend to have quite a constrained idea of the practice of analysis, if we just give them more techniques and then send them off to practise them, we are likely to find that they continue to apply these techniques in a narrow way, continuing and reinforcing their prior understanding of analysis as a kind of 'dissection' rather than a potential act of fresh artistic creation. It is not enough simply to tell them that they should try to be 'creative' in using methods; we need to show them how the cyclic creativity outlined above works in practice. One helpful approach is to demonstrate analytical techniques not only using pieces which 'work' very easily with them (as in the Debussy example above) – the kinds of archetypal set works one might come across in an A level textbook – but also deliberately choosing some problematic pieces to talk about, such as the Ligeti case study discussed earlier. This gives the opportunity for lecturers to model the ways that these pieces might force us to think beyond any specific analytical method.

Another important principle is to *tolerate ambiguity*. This is something that came across very clearly in the Ligeti case study; it seemed impossible to avoid ambiguous answers when approaching the piece analytically, and yet this ambiguity ended up telling us a lot about the aural effect of the piece, and how this might fit with some of the resonances of the title. One (perhaps somewhat cruel) way to help students think about this is to set them unanswerable questions. One session with university music undergraduates on 'Arc-en-ciel' involved students being split into groups to discuss different features of the piece; one group was asked to decide whether it was in 𝄴 or 𝄵, with the result a minor argument, because one student thought it was clearly in 𝄵 and another was adamant it wasn't. Further discussion of this situation, as a class, provided a good opportunity to talk about how this ambiguous feature of the piece might actually tell us something important in its own right.

Connected with this is the idea that creativity involves *questioning assumptions*. It is important for students to recognise as early as possible that any theoretical construct they learn is only a structured set of metaphors for understanding music in a particular way – if it doesn't fit well with a particular piece of music, it is open to being challenged, altered or rejected. One way of putting this into practice is to set up conflicts between selected pieces and particular analytical frameworks. For example, students might spend a session thinking about what it means to state that a piece is 'tonal' by looking at a work such as Howard Skempton's *Lento*, which is made entirely of triads, but contains no functional cadences and none of the other trappings we would associate with the 'syntax' of tonality. The result is that we are forced to question the assumption that something which sounds like it has triads in it must therefore be tonal (or, indeed, to question our assumption that 'tonality' is a single clearly defined phenomenon at all). Even the Debussy case study, despite the 'traditional'-sounding surface of this music – or indeed, maybe because of it – raises issues of ambiguity (of form, tonality, harmony and texture).

Sternberg and Williams also encourage us to *cross-fertilise ideas* in our teaching by making connections between different subjects and disciplines. Again, within music theory and analysis, the obvious application of this is to make connections with performance and with composition, and there are many ways we might do this. Ever since Berry (1989), there has been a recognised subdiscipline of 'analysis and performance' within music analytical/theoretical circles, and a burgeoning literature on the subject has followed on from this. A significant part of that trend is Cook's perceptive account of the whole analysis-performance area within a new-musicological agenda (see Cook, 1999), which summarises these issues well. In fact, he makes reference to a chapter by Tim Howell (1992), which drew on the direct experience of working in the Music Department at the University of York which specialises in practical music-making, and rather brings us back to where we started. Cook highlights the following:

> in Howell's words, 'The role of analysis in this context is one of raising possibilities rather than providing solutions' (1992: 709). Yet another way of saying the same thing is that analysis contributes as process not as product which is why, as Howell says, 'Reading someone else's analysis is almost the equivalent of asking them to practice on your behalf' (702).
>
> (Cook, 1999: 249)

The other growth area of creative musical analysis is that of composition and contemporary music, a field in which both authors are actively engaged.[8] In relation to repertoire where listener instinct does not always result in understanding – where the demands of a modernist idiom challenge our perceptions – the value of adopting a more imaginative approach seems especially relevant, as the Ligeti example earlier demonstrated. In a music department like that at the University of York, with its particular emphasis on new music (both in terms of composition and performance), students who are less than familiar with this musical language, which may lack the immediacy of impact associated with traditional repertoire, can find analytical enquiry to be really useful. In any case, within analytical teaching it is important to encourage students to think about how the things they are learning might *affect* their own performance, listening or composition. It is important to realise that this is a reciprocal relationship, of course: the visceral appeal of learning a new work for performance can often lead to a desire to get a better analytical grip upon it, to gain a broader perspective on instinctive engagement – and this often suggests extra possibilities for performance, in a kind of virtuous circle. And the same could be said of composition, or indeed, of the basic act of listening.

To conclude, then, analysis need not be perceived as musical All-Bran, even if that may have been students' experience of it before their time at university. In reality, it is something that can emerge naturally out of other kinds of musical engagement, and can interact with them very profitably too. By encouraging students to think through the mindset that underpins analytical work, rather than simply giving them a toolkit of 'techniques', we open the door for an approach that values analysis as a fresh act of creation that interacts cyclically with other disciplines such as performance and composition. In this way, analysis stops being an esoteric health food and becomes simply another part of a balanced musical diet.

Notes

1 A levels are the most common qualification in the UK (with the exception of Scotland) for students leaving education aged 18 or preparing to go to university. Although syllabuses vary by exam board, an A level in music generally includes an introduction to music theory and analysis. The Associated Board of the Royal Schools of Music (ABRSM), an international exam board offering a range of independent musical qualifications, administers a number of music theory examinations which form many pupils' first systematic experience of music theory and analysis.

2 See, for example, Guck (2006); Dubiel, (2004); Samson (1999).

3 A more extreme version of this viewpoint might consider even the composer to be a purely passive receptacle of inspiration, as in Stravinsky's famous claim that 'I am the vessel through which *Le Sacre* [*du printemps*] passed' (Stravinsky and Craft, 1962: 147–8).

4 SMART is an acronym used to enumerate aspects of successful objectives within management and education: they must be *specific, measurable, achievable, relevant* and *time-bound.* See, for example, Skrbic and Burrows (2015).

5 Those seeking a recommended recording are directed towards Pierre-Laurent Aimard's superlative performance on Sony Classics (SK 62308). A snippet of this recording was included in the original conference paper upon which this chapter is based; the awe-struck silence that followed the extract confirmed, for us, the importance of listening as the basis of all analysis.

6 See Debussy (1910).

7 The piece is 39 bars in length, so the point of golden section would be $39 \times 0.618 =$ bar 24.1 (the moment when the opening material makes a significant formal return); however, the tonal resolution of the piece – a final cadence into G♭ major – occurs at bar 36 (the last three bars merely decorate this gesture). The golden section of 36 (36×0.618) is bar 22.2 – the exact moment of the A♭ major climax, reaffirmed in bar 23.

8 See, for example, Hutchinson (2016); Howell (2011).

References

Berry, W. (1989). *Musical Structure and Performance*. New Haven, CT: Yale University Press.

Brahms, J. (1893). *Vier Klavierstücke*, op. 119. Berlin: N. Simrock. Retrieved 19 May 2015 from http://petrucci.mus.auth.gr/imglnks/usimg/8/8c/IMSLP138599-PMLP04666-JBrahms_4_Klavierst__cke__Op.119_fe_rsl.pdf.

Burnard, P. (2012). *Musical Creativities in Practice*. Oxford: Oxford University Press.

Cook, N. (1987). *A Guide to Musical Analysis*. Oxford: Oxford University Press.

———— (1999). 'Analysing Performance and Performing Analysis'. In: N. Cook and M. Everist (eds), *Rethinking Music* (pp. 239–61). Oxford: Oxford University Press.

———— (2002). 'Epistemologies of Music Theory'. In: T. Christensen (ed.), *The Cambridge History of Western Music Theory* (pp. 78–105). Cambridge: Cambridge University Press.

Debussy, C. (1910). *Préludes, Premier Livre*. Paris: Durand & Cie. Retrieved 19 May 2015 from http://petrucci.mus.auth.gr/imglnks/usimg/c/c0/IMSLP00509-Debussy__Preludes__Book_1.pdf.

Dubiel, J. (2004). 'Uncertainty, Disorientation, and Loss as Responses to Musical Structure'. In: A. Dell'Antonio (ed.), *Beyond Structural Listening? Postmodern Modes of Hearing* (pp. 173–200). Berkeley, CA: University of California Press.

Guck, M.A. (2006). 'Analysis as Interpretation: Interaction, Intentionality, Invention'. *Music Theory Spectrum*, 28(2): 191–209.

Howell, T. (1992). 'Analysis and Performance: The Search for a Middleground'. In: J. Paynter, T. Howell, R. Orton and P. Seymour (eds), *Companion to Contemporary Musical Thought, Volume 2* (pp. 692–714). London: Routledge.

———(2011). 'Dualities and Dialogues: Saariaho's Concertos'. In: T. Howell, J. Hargreaves and M. Rofe (eds), *Kaija Saariaho: Visions, Narratives, Dialogues* (pp. 133–58). Farnham: Ashgate.

Hutchinson, M. (2016). *Coherence in New Music: Experience, Aesthetics, Analysis*. Farnham: Ashgate.

Ligeti, G. (1986). *Etudes Pour Piano, Premier Livre*. Mainz: Schott.

Samson, J. (1999). 'Analysis in Context'. In: N. Cook and M. Everist (eds), *Rethinking Music* (pp. 35–54). Oxford: Oxford University Press.

Skrbic, N. and Burrows, J. (2015). 'Specifying Learning Objectives'. In: L. Ashmore and D. Robinson (eds), *Learning, Teaching and Development: Strategies for Action* (pp. 39–69). London: Sage.

Sternberg, R.J. and Williams, W.M. (1996). *How to Develop Student Creativity*. Alexandria, VA: ASCD.

Stravinsky, I. and Craft, R. (1962). *Stravinsky in Conversation*. Harmondsworth: Penguin.

12 Curiosity, apathy, creativity and deference in the musical subject–object relationship

Nicky Losseff

Students of Western art music in higher education are often urged to 'find their own space' in relation to the pieces they are studying – to be creative, and to have original ideas. But what can creativity mean in the context of response to a musical work? Works also place other, more knowledge-based demands on us – of historical, biographical, social contexts and of formal processes. They also tend already to be overladen with interpretation. What are the implications of these issues for creative teaching?

I begin this exploration with some observations on students' relationships with pieces, offering a graphic model and a discussion of how that can be used in teaching. I then propose a second model, conceptualising musical relationships between an interpreter and a piece. This is an adaptation of the Johari Window, a schematic representation used in counselling to show knowledge and self-knowledge in relationships. Third, I suggest how musical material becomes part of the internal world of an interpreter: that through the interpretative process, the subject is *already in a creative relationship* with a work. Here, I draw on psychoanalytic object relations theory. Finally, I offer a case study where the Musical Johari Window was used in the context of a mixed, general seminar of MA students: a class designed to illustrate to student composers that their music is subject to interpretation through the projection/introjection process, and to student interpreters that they may already be in a creative relationship with a piece of music through that process.

Observations on attitudes to the relationship

Pieces of music have attributes which exist independently of interpreters' fantasies and projections. They were composed at a time, in a place, by a person who may have had intentions[1] which we may or not get to know. The composition may have been worked through different versions. Aspects of form and structure, genre and style, further define the work's character.

Over twenty-odd years as a lecturer in higher music education, I have noticed that many students feel a sense of *deference* towards these attributes, often combined with *curiosity*. Those students want 'facts'. Others back away from

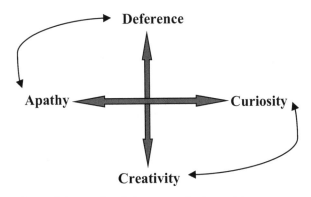

Figure 12.1 Basic creativity–apathy–deference–curiosity model.

'facts', but are interested in their own explorations of musical material: *creativity* combined with *apathy*. I have aligned these qualities along two axes – the *curious–apathetic* and the *creative–deferential* – in Figure 12.1.

Figure 12.2 shows the expanded implications of the axes. In the top right position, there is the *deferential-curious approach*, where the interpreter aspires towards understanding the piece as the composer did. They may believe the performance to be best served by diligent enquiry and by conceptualising the piece as external to the self. Here, musical study can seem emotionally safe. It is uncreative because it involves no investment of emotional energy.

In the bottom left corner is the *creative-apathetic* approach. Here, the student courts an interpretative position where the score is used as a point of departure. This type of reading is less about the piece and more about the projection of subjectivity – what Auslander (2006) terms the 'musical persona'. There is apathy in this position towards historical empathy – or perhaps more accurately, it just seems irrelevant, since the piece is first and foremost a vehicle for reflecting on, and performing, subjectivity. Other interpretative positions belong in this corner: those adopted by some schools of reader-response theory, where texts' meanings exist primarily within readers' experiences, and the position of Barthes (1977), who suggested that striving to understand authorial intention imposes limits on interpretation, denying interpreting subjects an actively and consciously creative role in relation to the text. These positions are united through the psychoanalytic concept of *projection*. In the relationship between interpreters and musical objects, interpreters' fantasies are projected into the piece of music; later, the interpreters are also likely to *introject* the music's properties, and the work will take on a life of its own inside the psychological material of the interpreter (see Losseff, 2011).

The top left corner presents the *deferential-apathetic* approach, lacking both emotional investment and information curiosity. The student wants to be told what to think and do. Though as teachers we sometimes despair of these situations, there is a safety in such a 'contained' position which the student might not be ready to abandon. Some students learn pieces in order to explore emotional content within

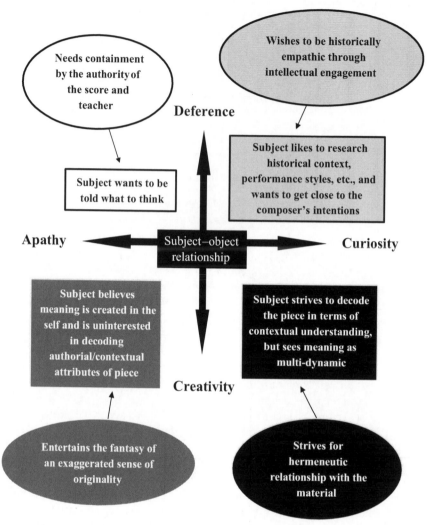

Figure 12.2 Expanded creativity–apathy–deference–curiosity model.

the safety of a work's musical resolutions. Music thus holds a very important therapeutic place in the student's emotional life.

Because Western arts and humanities value originality highly, there is a tendency to undervalue deferential approaches in comparison with creative ones. But deference may spring from a feeling that the inner life is not enough, on its own, to ensure continual emotional growth and understanding towards the music: it is limiting just to rely on what you already know. Creativity requires the ability to look deep into the self and to use what is found there to produce new 'readings' of music, but may also betoken laziness, narcissism, self-satisfaction and a failure to empathise. The creative-apathetic interpreter's projections also undermine any of the piece's attributes which denote its separate existence. Interpretative health will have aspects of both approaches to produce a real 'relationship', in that each party 'gives' to the other. It will involve the full recognition of the piece's external existence even as the relationship is invested with emotional energy. In this situation, the interpreting subject seeks knowledge leading towards historical empathy with the musical object, but also recognises that this kind of relationship requires creative energy; attention needs to be paid not only to the musical object's demands and the subject's inner life, but also to the well-being of the space between them: the relationship. We could call this position *creative-curious*, and it is represented in the bottom right position in Figure 12.2. As an interpretative approach, it offers the greatest possibilities for different forms of understanding, resulting in a richer, more layered set of views.

You may have guessed that I would place my own teaching agenda firmly in this square. At its base lie the values of hermeneutics: the exploration of the dynamic between individual and context and between past and present. Schleiermacher, the 'father' of the discipline, considered that an interpreter can make 'an analysis of his procedure which brings to consciousness what was unconscious to himself ...' (1998: 226). This is particularly interesting for the educational imperatives under discussion here: a 'deferential' student might be pushed towards realising that composers didn't see everything about their music and that others' readings will enrich possibilities for understanding while not threatening the authorial voice. Then again, Gadamer reflected on the constant process of projections which the striving for understanding involves, focusing on the 'intrapsychic' material – that which emerges from the internal psychological processes of the individual – in the process of interpretation:

> A person who is trying to understand a text is always projecting. He projects a meaning for the text as a whole as soon as some initial meaning emerges .... Every revision of the fore-projection is capable of projecting before itself a new projection of meaning; rival [projections] can emerge side by side .... This constant process of new projection constitutes the movement of understanding and interpretation.
>
> (Gadamer, 1989: 269)

Gadamer's concern is that however much we acknowledge the historic dimension, experiences take place in the present, and subjectively; but there is also something about the work of art that is Other: a 'fusing of horizons', which is the new set of meanings resulting from the discursive, interpretative process (ibid.: 301–3).

The projection-introjection process

The wealth of theoretical source material arguing these positions may be fascinating, but it does not always help students understand *where* there is space for creativity, or how creativity works in relation to the other aspects of academic work that are valued (knowledge of the field, well-constructed arguments and so on). It is one thing to theorise that all readers of a text are in a unique relationship to that text, but quite another to help a student to see *how to access* the intrapsychic material which characterises that unique relationship. I now explore this with recourse to object relations theory of psychoanalysis. My argument is that when a piece of music becomes the focus of an interpreting subject's emotional energy – an 'object cathexis', as Freud has it – a process occurs in which psychological material projected into the musical object alternates with psychological material introjected from the musical object. Subject/object and psychological/musical material fuse. This constitutes the 'interpretation': it is *ipso facto* a creative process.

In classic psychoanalytic terms, object relations theory (Klein, 1975) is a way of conceptualising interpersonal relationships. Klein saw all subjects as desiring to connect with another person (which she termed 'object'). Klein suggested that subjects *project* emotions into the object, and *introject* aspects of the external world. Because the interplay between projection and introjection of internal and external worlds is ceaseless, both are experienced in the light of the other.

But how can an object-*thing* (such as a piece of music) stand in for an object-*person*? Storr (1993) suggested that music possesses characteristics of the mind that created it, and is thus in some sense both human and alive. This seems plausible enough; where we know another human to have created something, it's difficult not to imagine that creation possessing some characteristics of its creator's mind. However, this doesn't explain how music can have so powerful and *active* a role in shaping our emotions and experiences. In polarised positions, music can nurture, comfort, be pleasurable; or it can disturb and even distress. Through our fantasies about its properties – nurturing or repelling – we start to have a relationship with it. Moreover, music's meanings and ways of existence are fluid; definitions of it slip out of reach very easily (see Goehr, 1992: 2–3).

Many commentators have offered perspectives on the possibility that when engaging with music, a 'virtual presence' or 'agency' can be felt. Dibben has reviewed these in relation to the construction of subjectivity through the music of Björk. She suggests that music:

> not only … represents or embodies a particular emotional experience, but also … contributes to the construction of the very idea of what emotion is and of how it is experienced. … The predominant Western conception of the subject in the modern era involves a unique, private, autonomous and bounded self, possessed of private feelings and emotions. *This self is therefore constituted by inwardness, and is maintained and produced with the assistance of Western culture.* (Dibben, 2006: 171; emphasis added)

Dibben writes from the perspective of a listener to popular song, but the theories on which she draws apply to other kinds of musical relationship whereby subjects perceive a musical object to interact with themselves. Because it has helped construct the subject's emotional world, it also mirrors that world. And – in object relations terms – it is through that dual process of projection and introjection that the piece of music, something separate and possessing its own attributes, takes on the status of an *internal object*: a 'mental and emotional image of an external object that has been taken inside the self, [and whose] character ... is coloured by aspects of the self that have been projected into it' (Melanie Klein Trust, 2015). As such, a piece of music can become an inseparable part of the subject; both take on characteristics of the other. It is at this point that creativity, in the form of intrapsychic material, enters the interpretative equation.

Conceptualising the relationship: The Johari Window

A musical object can become an internal object if a person engages emotionally with it and develops a deep knowledge of it. A subject may become able to conceptualise the processes involved in becoming an interpreting, creative subject by conscious awareness of the projection/introjection cycle. In this section, I turn to a graphic model widely known through the counselling literature – the Johari Window – in order to illustrate some of these issues of relationship involved in interpretation. Luft and Ingham (1955) developed the Johari Window to help people better understand themselves and their personalities in a social context. It has been widely used in personal and group therapy.

My aim in adapting the Johari Window is to place musical work and interpreting subject in a matrix where their relationships to each other can be explored: to facilitate an understanding of where 'creativity' is balanced by a view of the music as a separate object. The framework is useful for showing students how their work can be understood in the context of a relationship: where creativity is not only possible, but unavoidable – where they are doing it already, and why embracing that realisation is vital. This is the way in which this chapter offers implications for creative teaching. Here, 'creative' does not mean the production of something novel and extraneous to the self, but rather as *intrapsychic* material originating in response to a specific stimulus, and articulating something of the self – not something of the composer.

As Figure 12.3 shows, the Johari Window has four panes, created by the interaction of two axes: those of 'Self' and 'Other'. These are:

1. *Arena* – things known to the self and also known to others; the part of ourselves perceived by all;
2. *Façade* – things known to the self, but not to others; our private part;
3. *Blind Spot* – things other people can see about us, but to which we are blind;
4. *Unknown* – things unknown to ourselves and also to others; the unconscious part of ourselves which is also invisible to others.

An adapted version of the Johari Window can be used to symbolise four aspects of the relationship between musical work and interpreter: that the composer could not know everything about their work; where there is space for research and individual understanding; where one needs simply to find out what is known about a work, and that there might never be full knowledge about an aspect of piece or composer.

	Known to self	Unknown to self
Known to others	**ARENA** Known to both others and self	**BLIND SPOT** Known to others, but unknown by self
Unknown to others	**FAÇADE** Known to self, but not to others	**UNKNOWN** Not known by self or others

Figure 12.3 The Johari Window.

Figure 12.4 shows the adapted Musical Johari Window:

1. *Arena* – that which *composer and interpreters* know about the music; historical fact (historical practice, biography, other contexts) and all interpretative work. There is no space here for original research or creativity since the pane represents what is known. (Teachers can use this pane to point out that students are able to find out about what is already known, and that for most types of academic work, it is considered necessary to know your field.)
2. *Façade* – that of which *only the composer* had knowledge; 'secret knowledge' which may, however, have become known through biographical, historical or archival research and through intuitive, creative endeavour. We could only ever posit this 'hidden' knowledge as a possibility.
3. *Blind Spot* – that which *other people can see* about the work, but to which the composer was blind; this is potentially the most interesting, from the perspective of interpretation, because it suggests insights generated by the interpretative process which are hidden to a work's creator.
4. *Unknown* – that which is *unknown to all*; the unconscious part, reminding us that no single reading can ever be confused with closure. There are always insights to come.

	Known to composer	Unknown to composer
Known to interpreter	**ARENA** **Things about the music known to the composer and interpreters**	**BLIND SPOT** **Things about the music which the composer is blind to, but which interpreters can see**
Not known to interpreter	**FAÇADE** **Things about the music only known to the composer**	**UNKNOWN** **Things unknown to both composer and interpreter**

Figure 12.4 The Musical Johari Window.

Viewed thus, these dynamic interactions have interesting parallels with Butt's formulations of 'active' and 'passive' intentionality (2002: 89–91). Butt's 'active intentions' encompass a composer's specific decisions over instrumentation, tempo, dynamics, ornamentation and articulation, whether consciously notated or not. These fall into both 'Arena', where they concern what is already known, and 'Façade', where they concern anything which is discoverable. Butt's 'passive intentions' – factors over which the composer had little control, but which he consciously or unconsciously assumed – fall into 'Blind Spot' where unconscious, and 'Façade' where conscious. The implications are that 'passive intentions' have more to offer the interpreting subject with regard to creativity; 'active intentions' allow the interpreting subject space for research, both abstract and applied, and favour activity along the axis of curiosity–deference.

Case study

It was with these possibilities in mind that I approached the teaching of a class of mixed MA students at the University of York, UK, in Autumn 2013, using the Creativity–Apathy–Deference–Curiosity Model and Musical Johari Window, over two weeks. I wanted to test the models and to see whether they would help students understand creativity in the particular way articulated in this chapter. The class encompassed a jazz composer-saxophonist, two students of Baroque performance practice, five composers working in the contemporary Western art tradition, three pianists exploring the canonic tonal repertoire, five ensemble singers of renaissance vocal polyphony, four students of sound production, two conductors and a string player: students whose personal missions in embarking on an MA in music were very varied. The departmental rationale for teaching these students together is that individual musical quests can be contextualised more effectively in terms of the wider enterprise of musical endeavour by examining how each person's studies can be defined as a critical response to other material, and that for individuals to understand their responses to material in terms of knowledge and creativity, all aspects of the production and reception of music need to be examined. For these purposes, the more varied the body of students, the better.

I explained why I was developing these models, that I would be writing about them, and that I would like to use the students' responses as a case study. I sought and gained their consent in advance to audio record the sessions, and made it clear that responses would be anonymised. I then transcribed and analysed the audio files from both weeks. I decided to combine some of the responses thematically for the second class. The first was sufficiently focused not to require such manipulation.

My involvement as both researcher and lecturer gave me a dual role, made more complex by having taught many of the students before as undergraduates in a variety of modules. I aimed to be as person-centred as possible in the management of the discussion, but the counselling literature acknowledges that empathic reflection of comments can constitute active management of the dialogue (Mearns and Thorne, 2013: 55–77).

At the end of the two 90-minute sessions, I felt that the models had stimulated discussion, provoked insights into the learning process, tacitly reinforced some of our institutional values (such as the ability to contextualise knowledge and insight), and made most or all of the students more keenly aware that when looked upon from other perspectives, their individual endeavours were likely to take on quite different meanings.

However, I felt that the classes failed to provoke the radical shake-up of complacency that I had hoped for. As educators, we may be enthusiastic about promoting originality and creativity in various forms, but this is not why many students embark on their musical explorations. Those types of creative journey not only represent fear of the unknown, but also demand the good internal objects which are a prerequisite for secure departures towards something new. When I use these models again, I need to be protective of those fears.

Week 1: The Musical Johari Window

I asked the students to form groups each containing a mix of disciplines, and each to formulate a statement about how their current research/composition/performance project related to the axes. I presented the Window as a model which shows a piece of music on one plane and an interpreter on another, and began the discussion by introducing each pane. I then asked:

Arena – How do you find out what is already known about a piece?
Blind Spot – What might have formed blind spots in composers' knowledge of their music?
Façade – What sort of private thoughts about compositional process and 'intention' might fit here?
Unknown – What kinds of things can never be known about the music?

I stressed that the purpose of the Window was to help articulate *relationships*, not absolutes, and that each of us has a unique relationship to our texts because we take in material and embody it or process it creatively. I also stressed that in counselling, the purpose of the Johari Window was to show that mutual understanding can

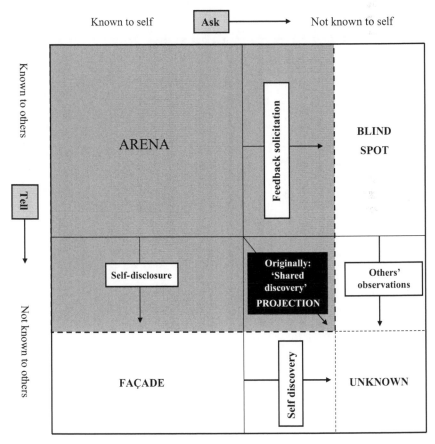

Figure 12.5 Johari Window with disclosure, discovery and projection.

be increased through disclosure by both parties (see Figure 12.5). However, the Window, in its original conception, does lack an important aspect of relationships: projection. Subjects displace psychological material into objects through forms of projection, but are blind to the origination of that material in themselves. Projection cannot be ignored in conceptualising relationships; unconscious processes operate in relationships, and perception is shaped by the subject with reference to an object. In human–object relations, subjects imagine parts of themselves to be properties of the object; similarly, musical interpreters, in forming relationships with music, cannot avoid conceptualising the music at least partially in terms of their own mental activity. The 'original' Johari Window's space for 'Shared Discovery' has therefore been replaced with 'Projection', since it is clear that no relationship is without this attribute.

Figure 12.6 is the adapted Musical Johari Window. Here, although nothing can be added to the Arena from the composer, knowledge and understanding can be increased by research and through empathy: by finding out, and through the

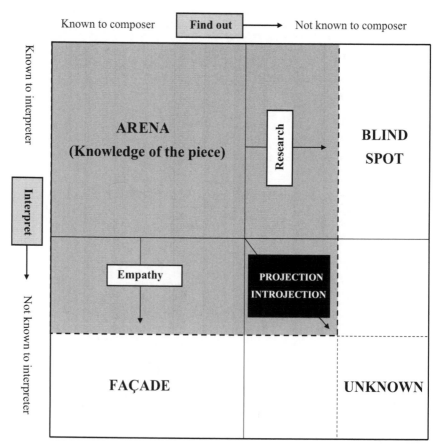

Figure 12.6 Musical Johari Window with empathy and projection.

process of interpretation. Hence, there is also a fundamental shift from the original Window's emphasis on a subject's *self*-knowledge to the interpreting subject's knowledge and understanding of the (musical) *object*.

The exercise began by eliciting examples for each pane of the Window.

Arena

Two main levels of information were identified for this category:

1. *traces of the past* – for example, a composer's holograph or an edition under their control; information the composer gave about the music in letters and documents;
2. *historiographical information* – that which is needed to 'complete' the score in historical terms. The recovery of this information lies within the remit of musicology, and includes all aspects of performance practice.

The students identified that Arena material is effectively accessed through musicology, and that a musicologically curious attitude helps in understanding these aspects of their 'quests'. Again, material fitting into this pane cuts across Butt's categorisations, since information about how composers expected their music to sound fits here, as well as what they imagined about the music's meanings.

Blind spot

We identified two main 'transparent' factors here:

1. *musical norms* – for example, the tone of the composer's piano, certain aspects of instrumental and vocal technique – aspects of the medium of the composition so familiar to the composer as to be more noticeable by their absence;
2. *psychological factors* – aspects of the psychological matter of the music of which the composer was unaware.

This pane engendered the most interesting discussion with regard to the tension between intentionality and interpretation. One composer suggested that if she looked back at earlier work, she saw previously unnoticed aspects. Another pointed out that we can't know that a composer didn't know something unless it's knowledge that has accrued since then. Students also identified that psychological factors are probably the aspect of subject–object interaction which most readily give permission for creativity and interpretation, but that in engaging with music creatively, the score can lose its authoritative position as a set of instructions or rules, and thus also lose its 'containing' function. It was only to be expected that some of the performance students clearly feared this type of interaction and preferred to stick to the 'orders' of material from the Arena.

One composer asked whether 'the veracity of the approach was subservient to its musical consequences' – was it considered a good thing to be historically informed even if the result sounded awful? A performer countered this by stating that it was 'selfish not to bother with historical empathic approaches; if you only focus on your own time and own subjectivity, it's like holding up a mirror'. There was some agreement that performance becomes 'merely' a narcissistic enterprise if the empathic dimension is altogether ignored.

Façade

In this category, the participants identified:

1. private, unshared thoughts;
2. unshared meaning-making intentions;
3. pre-compositional ideas now lost.

Discussion began by my asking how compositional process affects the way we engage in the piece. Many agreed that it is interesting because it tells you something about a piece's prehistory and creation, involving a series of decisions made by a human subject. We cannot know these 'intentions', but it is through our endeavours to do something with the space between us and the text that imaginative speculation is born: a reconstruction of 'plausible' intentions, as Levinson describes them (1996: 175–213). Moreover, there is no upper limit on how we imagine this space; and it still represents a position which is bound by an empathic dimension.

However, to some, the square had a harsh super-ego function. The absence of information did not represent a space of imaginative freedom, but rather placed *demands* to try to fill those gaps. This topic re-emerged in the discussion of the last pane.

Unknown

There was nothing to be identified in this square since it represents all that is unknown.

The overwhelming response to this pane was that it remains as an inspiration for interpretation and research, the part that *allows* you to be creative towards the music and gives you freedom. Here belong not only things you can't determine, but also things you can't over-determine. Most in the group decided that we have as much right as we wish to assume to probe into the secrets of the music, but that such probing belongs to the Façade box, where it was under tighter regulation.

This response was very telling to me, and caused me to radically revise my projections towards and aspirations for the group. It was clear that some had become anxious, and that as well as *allowing* creativity, this pane could seem to *compel* creativity. The class was rather hostile towards the idea of introjection and projection of material between self to musical object. As a result, the 'harsh super-ego' function of the Façade pane seemed to some horribly magnified in this Unknown pane, representing not permission, but a fearful journey into the new territory. Few were ready to embrace this. I decided that next time I used the model, I could present this pane as something to consider 'for the future'. It also became clear that my vocabulary influenced discussion; when applied to music, the Arena may become extended not by 'disclosure', with its connotations of 'over-sharing', but by empathic imagination – which might seem less threatening than the use of such words as 'creativity' and 'originality'.

To summarise these points:

1. Primary information, even if interesting, does not always need to be used. For instance, we tend not to slavishly re-create performances available in recorded form which were conducted or played by their twentieth-century composers. The issue here is with re-creating the superficial aspects of the performance: as one performer said, the issues are why it sounds like that and how it made sense to those people, which is different from copying surface features of their playing. This is why a person's understanding of musical meaning is so important – however that understanding has come to be formed and whatever it may be.
2. Many preferred a relationship with a musical object to which attributes were already ascribed. This can be a comforting source of authority, behind which issues of subjective engagement can be downplayed.
3. The position of composer-as-author/authority is not enough to delimit what the music means. But ignoring the fact that the musical object once had attributes – accretions connected with its composer, time and place – placing the *score alone* as a source of fantasies results in a narcissistic relationship.
4. It is possible, through imaginative and intellectual engagement, to push the boundaries between the panes: to extend what is 'known' by research and what is 'understood' by interpretation. However, there is a limit to how much this is desirable; push the boundaries into the unknown too far, and the enterprise becomes unsafe.

Week 2: The creativity–apathy–deference–curiosity model

The students again formed groups of mixed disciplines and were asked to discuss their initial reactions to the model. Their responses are themed here rather than linked to any particular section of the model. Many responses involved ways of moving around the model, but the discussion also circulated freely between ideas. I did not see all the implications of the remarks until transcribing the recording later. Some comments are paraphrased here where the original formulation was not clear.

Moving around the grid

Performers noted that you can begin as 'creative' and then become 'apathetic': work hard, do research, but then reap the fruits of your labour without further reflection. They also recognised that in different compartments of your life, you can fit into different categories. Things may wash over you as a casual listener; you can aim for a hermeneutic approach in your singing work, whereas your academic work might aim to be 'historically empathic'. Time constraints could influence your approach, and a teacher can nudge you into a different part of the grid – a realisation of how teaching can help in the creative process.

Another performer noted that certain boxes are prerequisites to be able to reach others, but also suggested that knowledge can be 'a restrictive burden'; you might need the flamboyance and confidence of the person who fantasises about their originality not to be bound by the accumulation of knowledge. A composer suggested that 'knowledge is ambiguous; you can move between the squares because it is possible to identify with all of them as they represent the shifting realities of thought'. The conclusion is that boundaries along the axes are fluid: one can occupy different parts of it as one's task progresses. For instance, you can begin learning a piece in 'deferential' mode, when it is not sufficiently embodied for any creative input. Later, engagement may be more critical and creative.

Delusional thinking

One composer said he realised that he could not depend on any shared expectations of a performance or 'get the listener to do anything', even though many composers might prefer deference from their performers. Another felt that 'deference' can masquerade as 'creativity', and vice versa. Different levels of self-awareness might mean not having sufficient insight into one's own learning process to be able to make correct judgements. A person might think they were being curious; but curiosity has a creative dimension beyond a facile search for information. Here, a critical/friendly other in this process (such as a teacher) can be valuable in flagging up where this input may come from.

The jazz composer/performer stated that he belonged entirely in the 'creative' domain. However, he had previously talked about the influence of a particular record label, so it was possible to point out that his endeavours could be seen more as a creative response to existing material.

Barriers to progression

One performer thought it was possible to get bogged down by trying to be correct, rather than understanding that the performance won't speak of any emotional realities unless the music has been processed through the performer. I suggested that we instinctively reject 'apathy' because it seems sloppy, but to some extent we have learned to hear things in particular ways because of our education. A composer noted that you can always reject aspects of knowledge, and in any case, knowledge does not actually tell you how to embody the emotional aspects of music. That path from score to embodiment is one way in which performers' endeavours lead to the kind of creativity I have been discussing here – another area in which the teacher's role is vital.

One group asked why you would want to subject your creative processes to unnecessary restrictions. Where music is some kind of discourse about psychological states, whatever those may be, *you can't be historically empathic to a psychological state.*

Many students believed it was impossible to be creative when playing musical works already overladen with interpretation. Although they wanted the enjoyment of playing familiar works, they realised they were more likely to 'say something original' in new or unrecorded repertoire. I feel in retrospect that playing works from the 'imaginary museum' (Goehr, 1992) allows performers the fantasy of entering a special community of musical 'owners'. For these people, originality is irrelevant. In future, I intend to stress this aspect more.

Interactions in the hermeneutic position

Interactions between general and specific learning processes were also mentioned. The string player said that one of his goals was to make his sound more nuanced; this could be enacted differently in each of his pieces, but also practised through exercises. Another performer argued that all his practice was creative because it was all connected with the search for particular sounds. However, other students were more realistic about what could constitute creativity, noting that this goal could not be divorced from knowledge-based aspects of the learning process.

The question of embodiment also arose for performers engaged in the quest to be historically informed: reading the correct treatises and adopting certain ornamentation does not in itself constitute a re-enactment in performance. Each different music-learning situation will inspire the subject to think about particular knowledge prerequisites; but these can become facile searches for knowledge for its own sake, and say nothing about the continued production of meaning through individual engagement.

The second week's discussion had clearly been informed by the previous week's class exploring the Musical Johari Window; the students readily engaged with the subject matter and were able to move around the model with ease. There was more ease with the idea of creativity. I felt that the Window had rendered creativity somewhat intimidating; but with the axes, creativity seemed more of an abstract concept. This is something to address in future classes.

Conclusion

The purpose of developing the Musical Johari Window and the Creativity–Apathy–Deference–Curiosity models was to demonstrate that knowledge and interpretation are in a mutable relationship, but that the relationship itself is paramount, and that it is through the production of this relationship that creativity could develop. In these initial classes, the models were helpful in understanding that mutability, and not so useful in demonstrating concrete, polarised positions.

It became clear that teachers could play a vital role in teasing out the two primary creative possibilities: emotional engagement and embodiment. In the first, discussing the possibilities of music as a discourse of psychological states is fundamental to the development of an interpretation. A 'good enough' teacher would be able to differentiate but also marry the 'knowledge' aspects of the learning process with those of intrapsychic engagement.

Few of the performance students were ready to engage with what it means to be responsible for instantiating a composition in real time such that there is no longer a separation from the music, and where subjectivity is not something *imposed onto* the music, but *performed through* it. In this position, the music becomes something you do rather than something *to which* you do something, and it is the interpreter who organises the music to be uniquely expressive of meaning, since only through an individual performer does a work become distinctively alive.

My own beliefs about the exploration of subjectivity through performance were checked. It might be technically impossible for a performing subject *not* to perform their subjectivity, but that isn't why some people do music. Many want the security of obeying a score's instructions, and that has an important containing function. For higher-level thinkers, this containing function can be enhanced by information supplementation (such as details of performance practice), and a curious-deferential approach provides this. Less intellectual students may derive mental benefit from the containment provided by deference and apathy. For those, there is safety in 'getting it right' and in the *rejection* of too much intrapsychic engagement. In all cases where creativity is emotionally threatening, the teacher's potential to play a role of containment is an essential feature – until such time as they can encourage students towards a safe (because contained) movement towards another pane. Here, the psychological journey can be taken together: the teacher verbalising where necessary, and through empathic attunement encouraging students to formulate their own ideas.

Note

1 For a long time, the literature on 'intentionality' suggested it to be a philosophically untenable position. Recently, Butt's (2002, Chapter 3) arguments for a real-life sound world against which the composer derived their own internal sound world and made a series of intentional decisions have given new life to the argument.

References

Auslander, P. (2006). 'Musical Personae'. *The Drama Review*, 50, 100–119.
Barthes, R. (1977). 'The Death of the Author'. In: R. Barthes, *Image, Music, Text*, translated by S. Heath (pp. 142–8). London: HarperCollins. Originally published in 1968.
Butt, J. (2002). *Playing with History*. Cambridge: Cambridge University Press.
Dibben, N. (2006). 'Subjectivity and the Construction of Emotion in the Music of Björk'. *Music Analysis*, 25, 171–97.
Gadamer, H.-G. (1989). *Truth and Method*. Translated by J. Weinsheimer and D.G. Marshall. London: Bloomsbury Academic.
Goehr, L. (1992). *The Imaginary Museum of Musical Works*. Oxford: Oxford University Press.

Klein, M. (1975). 'Our Adult World and its Roots in Infancy'. In: M.R. Khan (ed.), *Envy and Gratitude and Other Works* (pp. 247–63). London: Hogarth Press. Originally published in 1959.

Levinson, J. (1996). 'Intention and Interpretation in Literature'. In: J. Levinson, *Pleasures of Aesthetics* (pp. 175–213). Ithaca, NY: Cornell University Press.

Losseff, N. (2011). 'Projective Identification, Musical Interpretation and the Self'. *Music Performance Research*, 4, 49–59.

Luft, J. and Ingham, H. (1955). 'The Johari Window: A Graphic Model of Interpersonal Awareness'. *Proceedings of the Western Training Laboratory in Group Development*. Los Angeles: UCLA.

Mearns, D. and Thorne, B. (2013). *Person-centred Counselling in Action*. 4th edn. London: Sage.

Melanie Klein Trust (2015). 'Internal Objects'. Retrieved 30 January 2015 from http:// www.melanie-klein-trust.org.uk/theory.

Schleiermacher, F.D.E. (1998). *Hermeneutics and Criticism and Other Writings*. Translated and edited by A. Bowie. Cambridge: Cambridge University Press.

Storr, A. (1993). *Music and the Mind*. London: HarperCollins.

13 Recontextualised learning through embedded creativity

Developing a module that applies historically informed performance practice to Baroque music

Christina Guillaumier, Ruth Slater and Peter Argondizza

This chapter is concerned with how a specific module taught at the Royal Conservatoire of Scotland (RCS) both embeds and fosters musical creativity. Between 2008 and 2012, the conservatoire reassessed its undergraduate programmes, and one of the outcomes from the process of curriculum reform was an emphasis on the seamless integration of creative practice with contextual work.[1] The case study presented in this chapter is a module entitled 'Baroque Music and Ensemble: Before and Beyond' (BME). We will discuss how this module exemplifies the merger of creative, practical and academic teaching in the RCS, and how it demonstrates the usefulness and transferability of creative skills within an ever-changing and challenging performing arts landscape. Through this particular case study, we present a 'grass-roots' perspective on embedding creativity and engendering a cultural 'habitus' within music education. It is the contention of this chapter that this module provides a useful working platform to investigate the concept of creativity in the domain of historically informed performance practice (HIPP), which has – incorrectly in our opinion – often been perceived as an academic subject. Within this module, students are offered the opportunity to participate in the teaching, engage in debate, develop decision-making and leadership skills, engage with practice-based research and participate in collaborative learning. We seek to foster an environment similar to the working and performing practices of Baroque period musicians in order to create the 'habitus' to encourage an understanding and application of the creative performance practices of the period. We discuss our re-creation of the habitus of the historically informed performance space to teach and demonstrate the skills and techniques required to be a successful improviser and creative thinker in the context of Baroque music and beyond. We also describe the background to the module, detailing progression from its inception to its current form, and report on its working practices, the choices of topics covered and representative repertoire as well as the application of selected resources, the editions used, and its relevance to modern improvised styles and practitioners.

Baroque music and ensemble: Before and beyond

For a number of years, the RCS gave students the opportunity to engage with HIPP in two ways. One was a Baroque ensemble led by staff and consisting of both students and staff that met on a weekly basis and culminated in two public performances per year. The second opportunity came in the form of a module called 'Style in Performance' which provided a practical and performance-based experience. Now a 20-credit module, 'Baroque Music and Ensemble: Before and Beyond' began as a 10-credit elective offered to third- and fourth-year undergraduates as well as postgraduate students. This new elective module embodies the philosophies of the institution's curriculum reform process, which aimed to encourage creativity, ownership and decision-making. One of the main objectives of this module is to provide students with the skills to apply current research and practices from HIPP to their own learning and performing, and in doing so, to inform musical and career decisions that are both independent and creative. On a practical level, it inspires students to make decisions concerning repertoire, performance, leadership, directing and improvisation. Our revised syllabus combines academic and practical work that encourages students to develop informed performance skills from late Renaissance to early Classical on both period and modern instruments. We strongly believe that it is essential for students fully to comprehend both the evolution and the ensuing stylistic development of the Baroque period.

The module content was designed to equip students with the historical knowledge, practical skills and creative risk-taking to solve musical challenges relevant to the understanding and performance of earlier musical styles. Students are offered a combination of formal lectures, practical demonstrations, group work and discussions to develop and enhance a range of research, technical, musical and performance skills appropriate for Renaissance, Baroque and Classical period music within modern and period contexts. The module content includes workshops, rehearsals, chamber music, and vocal and solo performances that are directly related to the student's principal study and to the classroom lectures. Each two-hour class is typically divided into two sessions, with a lecture followed by practical work on the lecture topic. Students perform and experiment using their principal study instrument or voice. To immerse students in the relevant historical and social contexts for their musical performances, students are also taught the appropriate dances and courtly gestures of the period.

Course content is developed in three primary areas: historical/theoretical, performance and creative. Selected topics explore historical and theoretical perspectives, and provide the impetus and stimulus for the creative and practical components of each session. These topics include, but are not limited to, history, composers, genres, aesthetics, musical rhetoric, national styles, opera, motets and secular styles. We offer practical advice in the areas of embellishment, instruments/organology, equal-tension stringing, tuning systems, transcriptions, sources, editions and research. In preparation for each lecture, students are assigned reading and listening material aligned with each topic. Students apply the concepts to practical musical examples, using the second hour of each class as a workshop in which to experiment and apply the concepts in a rehearsal/performance setting. Workshops with students and teaching staff encourage repertoire choices ranging from the Western canon to South American music. Genres include cantatas and concertos and solo and chamber works, to name a few. Throughout the module, students experiment with improvisation and apply stylistic embellishments to their chosen repertoire. Furthermore, they participate in continuo for keyboards and plucked strings, learning alternative notation, including tablature and mensural notation.

In terms of admission requirements for the module, our minimum performance requirements are competency on a solo instrument commensurate with third-year British tertiary conservatoire standard as well as a pass in all first- and second-year contextual, historical and analytical modules. In addition, the module requires interest in early music and historical instruments (though not experience or comprehensive knowledge of them), some grounding in repertoire and style, practice in two-part counterpoint and some presentation skills. All these core competencies are developed in the first two years of the undergraduate degree.

More broadly, BME complements current conservatoire pedagogy. It offers an alternative to the standard practice in many music colleges where repertoire choices are guided by instrumental/vocal teachers and directed by course content. As an alternative, BME draws from the positive professional practices of HIPP: research, scholarship, collaboration, creativity, improvisation and entrepreneurship. The lecturers create an environment that encourages students to engage in practical tasks, creative risk-taking, improvisation and research. One application of this occurs when in-house specialists support students in editing and transcribing primary sources: a process which results in new editions of repertoire. These works are then brought to the community of practice for a group or individual to perform.

On reviewing the first year of the revised module, the tutors and institution recognised that the module had achieved its core goals. The student-led performances demonstrated creativity in repertoire, instrumentation and ensemble choices, and students participated maturely as collaborators and leaders. There was also a high achievement rate in the final assessed lecture recitals, which demonstrated applied scholarship, a good level of critical thinking and creative initiative. As a result, the tutors decided that credit should also be awarded for the crucial developmental and creative elements of the module experience: ongoing participation, improvisation, student contributions and engaging with the role of dance in its historical contexts. Previously, the module grade was awarded exclusively through one assessed lecture-recital. This was changed to enable students to choose one of three modes of assessment designed to demonstrate an understanding of current practices, scholarship and style through either a lecture-recital, an extended essay or a recital. The summative assessment seeks evidence of creativity and/or creative approaches, scholarship and research, effective planning and organisation. The formative component focuses on engagement, reflection, collaboration and participation, thus rewarding student creativity.

Creative processes, internalisation and acculturation

Traditional definitions of musical creativity tend to privilege composition as the ultimate example of creativity, with improvisation taking second place. However, our research and experience suggests that musical creativity is embedded in most of, if not all, musicians' activities. In this chapter, we will scrutinise the ways in which collaboration and ensemble work help students become both creative learners and innovative musicians. In essence, the students who participate in this module form a community of practice. Our understanding of creativity is encapsulated in pedagogical practice where emphasis is placed equally on process and on product. This module, both in its design and in its implementation, takes Csikszentmihalyi's thought-provoking question 'Where is creativity?' as a starting point to create opportunities for creative learning. Throughout BME, we interrogate our own pedagogical practices, our own understanding of creative teaching, while evaluating our students' experience. Through this process, we continuously aim to provide opportunities for creativity and help students search for the locus of their creativity. Burnard (2011: 141) notes that 'creative learning involves the learner shaping and being shaped by, as well as judging and being judged by "appropriate observers" within the community'.[2] Others have defined it as a 'significant imaginative achievement as evidenced in the creation of new knowledge' (Craft et al., 2006: 84). Creative learning steers students to take an active and participatory role in the learning process, bringing their own embodied and experiential knowledge to bear. Creative teaching is built on a willingness to experiment with approaches including those drawn from our own personal practices as well as those of our students. Team teaching, which is another aspect of creative teaching, plays a prominent role in demonstrating best practice in collaboration, in encouraging observation and participation. Creative learning and creative teaching thus result in a highly distinctive teacher–student relationship which challenges the culture of musical 'perfection'. Within this context, teachers may play alongside students, engage them in all performance-related (editions, arrangements, transcriptions) decision-making processes, and conduct practice- and process-based research encouraging creativity, experimentation and risk-taking.

There is no real agreement about what constitutes musical creativity, nor indeed how to research it. In this chapter, we offer a teaching-based perspective on the development and output of musical creativity as we observe it within our case study. Burnard (2012) argues that researching musical creativity is challenging because it is heavily dependent on the context of the output. Furthermore, she identifies that 'musical creativity is conceived differently and constructed differently within different historical practices' (ibid.: 11). Burnard notes that social perspectives of creativity 'are based on the conviction that creativity is vital to all societies, to all fields, domains and cultures' (ibid.). In our notion of creativity, we focus on its context, its application as well as its processes and products. We recognise that musical creativity manifests itself in ways that are crucial to our musical and cultural development.

Csikszentmihalyi's systems model of creativity is central to embedding creative practice in this module. Csikszentmihalyi (1997: 27–8) makes three distinctions, referring to domain, field and individual. Our process of acculturation, which we discuss below, provides a cultural context for students to operate in and a 'field' against which to benchmark their processes and products. Csikszentmihalyi (ibid.: 25–7) also identifies three common applications of the term 'creativity': (1) in widespread conversation when referring to an 'unusually bright' person, (2) in reference to people 'who experience the world in novel and original ways' (Csikszentmihalyi calls them 'personally creative') and (3) individuals who are creative 'without qualifications' because they have contributed to our culture in undisputed ways. It is the second group – the group of 'personally creative' people – that we are concerned with in our case study. The study is presented as a narrative inquiry supported by data sources which include observation of music-making practices, reflection on practice, written work samples, performances and analysis of final products.

Ambitious though it might be, one of the main aims of our module is to enable creativity to happen through internalisation and acculturation – that is, to encourage and enable students to fully immerse themselves in the cultural context of the works and to master the tools and techniques needed to be able to function creatively (for example, through improvising) within this area. Csikszentmihalyi (ibid.: 51) notes that to be creative, 'a person has to internalize the entire system that makes creativity possible'.

Drawing on the influential theories of the French philosopher Pierre Bourdieu, we aim from the outset to re-create the structures and systems of the cultural environment within which the students will function as creative musicians. We define musical creativity as the ability to engage in a specific cultural habitat or 'habitus' which Bourdieu (1977: 85) described as 'the product of the work of inculcation and appropriation'. We endeavour to create a habitus that is indispensable to students' assimilation of both the materials and the practices throughout this module. In positioning students within a specific cultural habitus, they will come to locate their own musical and creative identity. Through this process of acculturation, students become motivated participants 'possessed by their habitus', which becomes the 'organizing principle of their actions' (ibid.: 18). Students are thus immediately engaged in a community of practice. Within this habitus, they can actively participate in attaining knowledge and in practising that learning within a group setting, such as rehearsals. Students are able to explore and generate new ideas within this habitus, and further the ability to transfer that creative element into other areas of knowledge.

This module draws students away from their creative comfort zones, and they may initially find this environment challenging. The module was purposely designed to adopt interdisciplinary approaches – this facilitates students' recognition and assimilation of this cultural habitus and engenders what McWilliam (2009) calls 'creative capacity building'. One of the first topics introduced in the module is Renaissance and Baroque dance, which are fundamental to the repertoire of these periods. The module encourages the development of embodied creative learning through dance. Creation of habitus occurs in three phases: first, students listen to the music; they are then given a practical demonstration of a selection of steps from the set periods with a focus on the minuet; finally, students work in teams, alternating between playing and dancing. Student feedback has demonstrated that engagement in the physical activity of dancing enables body fluency, rhythm and movement and promotes both creativity and confidence. Learning the social dances of the period early on in the academic year accomplishes two goals: first, the physical assimilation and bodily internalisation of musical gestures to inform interpretation of chosen repertoire; second, a reduction in personal inhibition, which stimulates class participation, in turn facilitating communication and co-operation in rehearsals and decision-making. These skills are, to our minds, crucial to creative music-making.

To encourage the process of internalisation and construct the habitus, an example can be drawn from vocal music, where the specialist voice tutor provided another interdisciplinary approach for all participants. Initially, using Dido's well-known chaconne lament from Purcell's *Dido and Aeneas* as a 'case study', the students played the work while being coached in the appropriate style, exploring the relationship of the bass part to the harmonic structure. Rehearsals then focused on the first-study singers, coaching breathing, phrasing and applying the narrow vibrato appropriate to the period. Following the exploration of the chaconne form, students were introduced to examples of lesser-known vocal and instrumental works, such as Juan Arañés' *Chacona a la vida bona*. Participants worked from a four-part vocal score creating their own instrumental/vocal arrangement which was then given a public performance.

In time, students recognise that this is a safe environment in which for learning to happen and healthy practice to occur. Borrowing from McIntyre's (2006) assertion that 'products, processes and ideas are generated from antecedent conditions', we attempt to not only create the model (person, domain and field) of operation, but also to facilitate student participation within the wider community, enabling them to engage with the community with which they will continuously relate to as performing artists. The classes and workshops function as a community of practice where students can share ideas, try out performances and discuss work in progress with peers and staff. In introducing students to physical movement, and simultaneously creating a physical distance between them and their instrument (which can sometimes be a source of tension), we are providing an atmosphere that allows them to be free of strain and conflict while legitimising the concept of 'fun' in the practice room. This creates a gradual but sustained opportunity for students to assimilate the different aspects of the module and to start conceiving of problem-solving in teams. Indeed, as Csikszentmihalyi (1997: 95) notes: 'The creative process starts with a sense that there is a puzzle somewhere, or a task that needs to be accomplished.' Such problem-solving tasks provide the impetus for the creative impulse, stimulate the community of practice into action and encourage leadership within specific roles and settings.

An example of creative practice is a student's imaginative approach to the adagio from Bach's G Minor Sonata (BWV 1001) for unaccompanied violin. The participant applied his understanding of ornamentation and improvisation learnt on the course to his own reductive analysis of the harmony and counterpoint of this movement. The result was a live demonstration of his own version of this work.

This experience is both enabling and empowering – here, students have the comfort and security to interact with each other from the start. In doing so, barriers and potential inhibitions to the creation of an effective community of practice are broken down very early on in the course. Another major contribution of Csikszentmihalyi's to our notion of the creative process is his concept of flow. 'Flow' is the state of mind in which a person is equally challenged and successful when performing a specific task. The person loses both a sense of time and self-consciousness and is completely immersed in the activity, experiencing pure enjoyment. Csikszentmihalyi (ibid.) discusses each of the factors necessary to reach the state of flow during creative activity, most notably the clarity of one's goal, a good amount of self-judgement, the urge to face challenges and the ability to avoid distraction. Students are encouraged to engage with these factors through participation in the collaborative learning procedures during this module.

Creative teaching and learning through collaboration

Our pedagogical approaches entwine a number of styles, suited to both the content under discussion and the tasks. Within student-centred small group discussions, seminars and reflective periods, an approach akin to the 'guide-on-the-side' method is often used, as this enables us to facilitate discussions and highlight key areas of learning. This teaching style enables students to make informed performance decisions and to present and discuss varied viewpoints. Performance decisions are based on student-led repertoire selection, instrumentation choices and their own tempi preferences. A more active pedagogical approach, characterised by McWilliam (2009) as the 'meddler-in-the-middle', is also often used as we engage with students while they build a performance, which is essentially a cultural product. In this way, we participate in a learning partnership with the students, engage with their content directly, and negotiate the assessment of that output. This encourages a free-flowing dialogue between tutor and student.

Collaborative and peer learning is a core component of our degree. Particular topics are contextualised for students, and an active community of practice is promoted through debates based on the students' experiences as well as related to existing scholarship. One particularly valuable example concerns the subject of tuning systems: learning about equal and unequal temperament and their different applications on a harpsichord challenges students to listen in a very different way. This theoretical and mathematical subject has strong philosophical underpinnings, but also has a direct bearing on the students' practical instrumental work. Approaching this area from multiple angles, as well as beginning and ending the session with practical exercises, is particularly useful for relating theoretical understanding to practical experience. Group work where students need to present researched material to their peers also widens their notion of performance (which for a conservatoire student can at times be quite limited).

We reinforce the playing sessions of the Renaissance/Baroque/Classical repertoire by follow-up discussions of the historical and theoretical background of the music just played. These carefully planned yet open sessions often stimulate controversy and highlight the students' creative differences. Debates may concern issues ranging from the use of vibrato to pure sound versus more full-bodied tone and controversies over Romantic/non-Romantic styles of interpretation. The informal structure of the workshop sessions allows for creative thinking and encourages a collaborative critical approach to the repertoire. These tasks position students right at the centre of the 'action', thus empowering them to take control of their experience. Therefore, as student insight and creative decisions are integrated into each session, facilitated reflective activity draws together points that enable students to consider the processes and values of peer learning as well as of their academic and practical knowledge.

Peer learning on this module occurs through a variety of approaches and in different learning situations. During rehearsal sessions, learning often happens 'in the moment', and creativity is encouraged through specific in-the-moment problem-solving tasks. Group rehearsal is fundamental in facilitating collaboration as students make creative performing decisions, but also have to take on leadership roles to organise and lead the performances. Directing the ensemble also plays a major part in the learning process: students are given opportunities to direct practical sessions throughout the year, either from their instrument or through singing. Aligned with directing, this course encourages the development of leadership and organisational skills – key skills for a music graduate seeking to carve a professional career in a wider social context. We expect students to be proactive in researching and choosing varied, stimulating and appropriate repertoire for the ensemble. They also need to create and manage the environment and to plan the time-management of rehearsals. The rehearsal studio is therefore a vital space for peer learning and collaborative work.

The role of improvisation

Two particular areas that encourage, or indeed demand, creativity are the practices of improvisation and ornamentation. By the third year of their degree, students possess a set of skills including a basic level of both writing and hearing harmony. They also have some experience and practice in the writing and performing of two-, three- and four-part counterpoint, a basic level of composition skills that include writing in simple binary form, and a basic experience and competence in arranging and directing an ensemble of diverse instrumentation. In addition, students apply skills developed in music history classes, such as group work, organisation, critical thinking, extended writing and music editing. They must also have the desire to work both individually and within groups and be willing to organise and arrange ensembles for rehearsal and performance. Crucially, BME emphasises that improvisation is neither a type of musical thinking nor the practical application of prescribed rules to 'ornament' and embellish a given melody or harmonic progression. We see ornamentation and embellishment as the materials used to create the larger language of improvisation in a style; therefore, improvisation is also a type of creative thinking which is applicable to repertoire choices, instrumentation and research, and is considered in relation to concert settings.

The areas of stylistic embellishment and ornamentation are introduced early in the course. Improvisation is approached through a combination of guidance, scholarship and practice while also providing a safe and supportive environment for experimentation. The sooner the students start experimenting, the quicker they lose any possible inhibitions. The informal learning environment is essential for successful understanding and experimentation in this field of free expression, although an appropriate understanding of the basic principles is necessary. Initially, we give students specific material and examples for both ornamentation and embellishment. We acknowledge that there are numerous resources, facsimiles and methods available that can be used to create the larger language of improvisation within a particular style or period. Pedagogically, we select those that are similar to modern jazz methods, which provide a set of patterns and embellishments to set the music into the minds, ears and fingers of the students. Thus, we encourage improvisation first through carefully guided examples and then allow the students to experiment and extemporise freely in a non-judgemental environment much like the modern jam session.

Both embellishment and ornamentation are a subset of the larger area of improvisation. From the numerous early treatises on the subject, to get started we have selected Girolamo Dalla Casa's two-part treatise on ornamentation, *Il vero modo di diminuir, libri I et II* (1584/1970), and Giovanni Bassano's *Ricercate, passaggi et cadentie* (1585/1994). These volumes provide a historical foundation which is expanded through comparative work using facsimiles and modern editions while presenting clear and precise examples of ornamentation practice applied to French and Italian Renaissance vocal music. To set the historical and cultural context, the students learn that Della Casa's and Bassano's examples and methods contrast with earlier ornamentation treatises. Their methods use ornamental patterns that emphasise particular notes and heighten their emotional effect with angular rhythms, such as the *tremoli groppizati* and *groppi battute*. These divisions on wide intervallic skips, such as sixths and beyond, mark the end of the purely Renaissance style of ornamentation and the beginnings of Baroque practice. This approach of breaking down a longer note value into smaller durations that gradually become more florid is not unlike modern jazz pedagogy, and is an effective and comfortable way to initially approach improvisation.

We also encourage students to play by ear and to approach performance away from the score or part without dependency on notation; hence, performance becomes an act of listening rather than reading. Indeed, jazz and certain types of rock and folk music performance employ and encourage free improvisation not only to embellish and ornament current songs and structures, but also as a means of composition. For evidence, we need only reference iconoclastic jazz 'concept' records such as Miles Davis's *Kind of Blue* to see how musicians achieve structure and form through improvisation with nothing or little written down (see Kahn, 2001). Hence, within the environment of the BME class, we seek to enable and encourage composition simultaneous with its performance. The goal is to allow the musical ideas to emanate from the performers' concepts, experiments and imaginations. The habitus we have created allows for this freedom of expression and creativity. It is all about experimentation, not about the right or wrong way to ornament specific works and improvise. Our BME module considers the understanding of this technique to be at the core of creative learning. The module allows time and space for this free expression and experimentation as we start the initial process early on and then incorporate the technique into all our practical sessions. This mode of creative learning is spontaneous and unstructured to the extent that any possible inhibitions are dispelled. In a personal interview with Wesleyan University student Nathan Shane (2013), Robert Levin asserts that the ornaments and embellishments are in themselves less significant than the understanding of these processes and what the knowledge imparts to the performer. Levin stated that because improvisation is essential to certain musical ideologies, a musician's comprehension of a composition is more important than the creative expression itself. Therefore, understanding improvisation means understanding the composition itself.

There are further plans to embed more improvisation into the course that include utilising partimento to supplement continuo studies and expanding the scope of compositional improvisation through ear training and performance. Having students present merely literal performances of repertoire that was once originally fluid, embellished and spontaneous does nothing to capture the style of Baroque music. Indeed, if students are encouraged to improvise and compose new ornaments and to explore tempi and instrumentation, they will find themselves spontaneously compelled to consider aspects of the style and draw upon previous knowledge and stimulate creativity. Spontaneous composition encourages musicians to engage with the stylistic languages of the repertoire. Through experiencing styles, studying the past and encouraging risk-taking in this re-created habitus, musicians can set reasonable and informed boundaries for their musical creativity while claiming authenticity in performance.

Conclusion

To embed creativity within what is traditionally a more academic and historical study of music through creative teaching for creative learning, we have generated situations where students are out of their comfort zones, curious and open to solving problems. This task-based approach, where teachers adopt a meddler-in-the-middle method, underpins our conceptualisation, delivery and development of the module.

The multiple and interdisciplinary approaches adopted allow students to perform music both on period and on modern instruments. Although the module focuses on historically informed performance practice, we do not restrict students to performance solely on period instruments, which is normally the case in comparable courses. By allowing students to work on modern instruments if they choose to, we aim to provide a wider overall understanding of HIPP and how it can be used creatively in both the 'modern' and the 'early' instrument context. This unconstrained approach makes the course accessible and relevant to a larger student body.

This open approach enables students on the course to perform in a manner that is their own yet is informed by historical practice, and which includes appropriate application of improvisation and embellishments. Students can apply what they have learned about embellishment and other areas to mainstream repertoire. It encourages confident decision-making – from choosing their own repertoire to organising and directing their own ensemble. Students are empowered to engage with their sources, which can traditionally be alienating objects, and to make informed, creative and critical decisions. To succeed in today's performing profession, an understanding of historically informed performance practice is essential if students are to reach their full performing capacity. Many elements from this learning process are transferable and can be deployed effectively in other contexts. This course encourages students to unlock their creative potential by working collaboratively, by functioning within a community of practice and by assisting them to make connections where that possibility did not exist before.

Notes

1 For a detailed perspective on this curriculum reform process, see Duffy (2013).
2 'Creative learning' is not mainstream terminology outside the UK, but see Sefton-Green et al. (2011) for differing perspectives on this concept.

References

Bassano, G. (1585/1994). *Ricercate, passaggi et cadentie per potersi esercitar nel diminuir terminatamente con ogni sorte d'istrumento, & anco diversi passaggi per la semplice voce*. Facsimile edn. Münster: Mieroprint.

Bourdieu, P. (1977). *Outline of a Theory of Practice*. Translated by R. Nice. Cambridge: Cambridge University Press.

Burnard, P. (2011). 'Constructing Assessment for Creative Learning'. In: J. Sefton-Green, P. Thomson, K. Jones and L. Bresler (eds), *The Routledge International Handbook of Creative Learning* (pp. 140–49). Abingdon: Routledge.

——— (2012). 'Rethinking "Musical Creativity" and the Notion of Multiple Creativities in Music'. In: O. Odena (ed.), *Musical Creativity: Insights from music Education Research* (pp. 5–27). Farnham: Ashgate.

Craft, A., Grainger, T., Burnard, P. and Chappell, K. (2006). *Progression in Creative Learning (PICL Pilot): A Study Funded by Creative Partnerships*. Milton Keynes: Open University. Retrieved 16 June 2015 from http://www.creativitycultureeducation. org/wp-content/uploads/progression-in-creative-learning-106.pdf.

Csikszentmihalyi, M. (1997). *Creativity: Flow and the Psychology of Discovery and Invention*. New York: HarperPerennial.

Dalla Casa, G. (1584/1970). *Il vero modo di diminuir: con tutte le sorti di stromenti [di fiato, & corda, & di voce humana]*. Facsimile edn. Bologna: Arnaldo Forni editore.

Duffy, C. (2013). 'Negotiating with Tradition: Curriculum Reform and Institutional Transition in a Conservatoire'. *Arts and Humanities in Higher Education*, 12(2–3), 169–80.

Kahn, A. (2001). *Kind of Blue: The Making of the Miles Davis Masterpiece*. London: Granta.

McIntyre, P. (2006). 'Paul McCartney and the Creation of "Yesterday": The Systems Model in Operation'. *Popular Music*, 25(2), 201–19.

McWilliam, E. (2009). 'Teaching for Creativity: From Sage to Guide to Meddler'. *Asia Pacific Journal of Education*, 29(3), 281–93.

Sefton-Green, J., Thomson, P., Jones, K. and Bresler, L. (eds) (2011). *The Routledge International Handbook of Creative Learning*. Abingdon: Routledge.

Shane, N. (2013). 'Speaking Classical Music: An Argument for Improvisation in Classical Music Education' (unpublished BA dissertation). Wesleyan University. Retrieved 23 May 2015 from http://wesscholar.wesleyan.edu/cgi/viewcontent.cgi?article=2056& context=etd_hon_theses.

14 There and now

Creativity across cultures

Neil Sorrell

Introduction

In 1977, the Indonesian embassy in London acquired what was the first complete, playable Javanese gamelan in the UK.[1] As there were no other possibilities to play a Javanese gamelan at that time in the UK, I seized the chance to take a group of music students from the University of York for a weekend of workshops, generously hosted by the embassy staff. It was the culmination of a four-week intensive course on gamelan music, and one of the most abiding memories was of a student saying that he had spent those four weeks not understanding a word I had been saying, but just one afternoon actually playing a gamelan had made everything clear. My only (delighted) reaction was that this is exactly how things should be: music is understood by making it. (This simple truth was the basis on which Wilfrid Mellers had founded the Music Department at the University of York in the previous decade, surrounding himself with composers and performers, and then one ethnomusicologist – at that time, no less of a bold stroke.) While agitating for a gamelan of our own at York (which eventually came to fruition in 1981, thanks again in no small measure to the help and example of the Indonesian embassy), I happened to acquire a single instrument (a *saron*, or 'keyed metallophone') with two mallets. One instrument doth not a gamelan make, but it was still put to use for valuable exercises in the interlocking patterns that feature so much in gamelan music. The point emerging from this is that restriction led to creativity, and necessity was indeed the mother of invention.

Improvisation was famously described by Derek Bailey (1980: 1) as 'the most widely practised of all musical activities and the least acknowledged and understood'. We could say the same of creativity, and the two are inextricably linked: improvisation is inherently a creative act, perhaps in its purest and most direct form. It is tempting to go even further and say that all musical creativity involves improvisation. 'Fixed' performance (from a score) requires interpretation. If nothing else, this means additions to what is after all nothing more than an incomplete guide or blueprint, and we can expect at least some of them to be spontaneous. A composer refines ideas into a 'fixed' score, but the initial ideas and the preliminary ordering and reconfiguration of them involve a kind of improvisation, even if it is carried out entirely mentally and the listening public is not involved at that stage (as would happen in a performed improvisation).

At first sight, 'creativity' is a word that seems entirely positive and beneficial – as hard to criticise as motherhood or apple pie. While it is bandied about quite freely, its opposite lurks in the shadows, and we may even wonder what it is. 'Uncreative' (for want of a better term) suggests a lack of originality and something derivative. The more positive and complimentary adjective 'scholarly' has even been proposed to distinguish an activity that is somehow not creative, seemingly in an attempt to separate the rigorously academic from whimsical flights of fancy and courses of study viewed with suspicion by traditional academics, including 'creative writing', which nestles within departments of English literature. Were 'creative music' to exist as a similarly named subject within music departments, it would be rejected on the grounds that established titles like composition and performance already cover the ground, and if the creative element were to be excluded, the department should be renamed 'musicology'. (We see something like this happening with departments named 'history of art', in order to clarify that they do not exist to teach art. Contrast that with school lessons where art really means doing it, while in the UK music used to be taught more as music history or 'music appreciation' rather than focusing on doing it.)

In any rush to 'creativity' and unquestioning celebration of its benefits, we should warn that creativity for creativity's sake can be a double-edged sword. While it encourages flights of imagination and develops self-expression and confidence, it can also impose enormous pressure to be original, which can in turn lead to vacuous pretentiousness and fakery. Creativity is worshipped partly because it can be elevated to mystical heights where it does not need to be, as it can flourish from methodical teaching, assiduous practice and, above all, patience. All these virtues are earthly, devoid of mystery, and moreover, tend to be the ones most prized in non-Western cultures. Western culture loves to think of creativity as bringing something out of nothing, with possible links to creation myths. For that reason, it can ascribe to the creative individual divine, mystical talents, as 'the Creator' brought forth something out of nothing. Thus creativity can be turned into myth, explainable only as a gift direct from God, as happens all too often in the case of Mozart, where methodical training from an excellent and demanding teacher (his father Leopold) and sheer hard work from a very early age are downplayed in the interests of this more exciting explanation. Creativity does not, therefore, mysteriously descend from on high or necessarily have to be the preserve of an elite, but is something to be taught and learned (and of course, some may teach or learn it better than others). The purpose of this chapter is to show how both creative teaching and creative learning (as we cannot have one without the other) can function in two contrasting non-Western cultures.[2] In one of them (India), a creative ability is emphatically connected with the creative teaching received, as the *guru* is part of the student's very identity.

The attempt to separate the rigorously academic from flights of fancy noted above is paralleled by the separation of theory and practice, causing further room for misunderstanding, especially when we step outside the Western tradition, where any assumption that theory precedes practice and dictates it will give rise to serious misconceptions. This chicken-and-egg question not only situates performance as creative and theory as 'uncreative', but also becomes far more muddled when we investigate the intersection and teaching of theory and practice in other cultures. Best of all, the separation of the two can become irrelevant, as the two case studies later will show.

Along with the revolution in music education (around 40 years ago), which brought music closer to art and crafts by placing creativity above indirect traditional approaches, came a filtering down of the subdiscipline of ethnomusicology from higher to primary and secondary education. Although the majority of students (either at school or university level) have no expertise in the various branches of 'world music' on offer, a certain level of creativity is nevertheless encouraged, even expected. As we shall see later, the new enlightenment carries the danger of teaching, whether in schools or universities, only the more easily accessible features of the music, leading to errors comparable to syntactical and other grammatical flaws in language – and that is without even considering how the fundamental principle of ethnomusicology (the study of music in its cultural context) has been flouted. The problem with teaching only superficial facts about the music is that it can revert to teaching *about* music, rather than how the music actually operates and how it is driven by the creative thinking behind it. Dynamic tools are more important than inert facts, and the passive absorption of knowledge is not only inherently uncreative, but also conflicts with the ways that non-Western music tends to be taught and learned in its natural habitats: not as verbal data, but as sonic processes, as the following case studies will exemplify.[3]

Indian music

To return to the attempt to define creativity by defining its opposite, a simple antithesis to 'create' might be 'copy'. In pedagogic terms, this would be rote learning: the student merely repeats what the teacher has sung or played, adding or subtracting nothing. While this is clearly not creative, it can be the solid basis of creativity, providing the knowledge and technique just cited as essential foundations. This is how the learning process of Indian music traditionally works, and we should add another quality to knowledge and technique: patience. The novice over-eager to flex creative muscles is unlikely to fare well in the lengthy rituals of the *guru-shishya parampara* (master–pupil tradition), and all kinds of stories bear this out. Some singers were made to practise holding one note as long as possible, extending this minimal repertoire over a year; another was given a couple more exercises, also to last for the first year of training; several lost patience and gave up. One such delinquent complained that his *guru* had hardly taught him anything for a full year. When the complaint was relayed to the *guru*, he replied that the student was unsuitable as he lacked the patience and dedication (not forgetting another tenet of the *guru-shishya parampara*, namely an unquestioning obedience and acceptance of everything uttered in word or music by the *guru*) to become a musician. In all these examples, the basis of Indian music – the *rāga* system – was omitted, delayed until the basic skills described had been mastered.[4] Once the *rāga*s were approached, it would most likely be through a rote learning method. The student would be expected to repeat exactly what the *guru* had sung or played, repeating as often as necessary to obtain the *guru*'s satisfaction. One could say that at this stage neither the teaching nor the learning is creative, but the teacher is already established as a creative musician and the point of the exchange is to ensure that, in time, the student will *become* one.

This may all seem paradoxical – even the very antithesis of creative teaching and learning – in a tradition noted for its emphasis on improvisation, yet it underlines the importance of the foundations on which improvisation is built. Without verbal explanation, the student is able to grasp the workings of a particular *rāga* intuitively, but only as a gradual process. And it may remain a single *rāga*. A *guru* will typically focus on one *rāga*, as mastery of that one unlocks other *rāga*s, whereas a few superficial explanations of several *rāga*s without a deep understanding of any of them will equip the student with no more than the abilities of a passive listener. Through the honing of technical skills and the development of intuitive understanding, the pupil gains their wings and can start improvisation. Is this where creativity begins? Separating creativity from learning is a mistake, and the whole process should be viewed holistically – an indivisible continuum. This is also why the Indian tradition (and so many others) recoils from the familiar notion of improvisation as 'making it up as you go along'. Total freedom is no freedom at all, and the improvisation only assumes structure and meaning when it follows the principles of the *rāga* tradition or whatever tradition applies to the particular musical culture. It is thus a way of finding new paths through familiar landscapes.

Indian *rāga*s are nothing until they are created. This may seem a paradoxical, even nonsensical statement. The point is that a *rāga* does not exist as a piece of music, but rather as a set of procedures (often rather forbiddingly called rules) from which the musician fashions a performance. While it is always stressed that mastery of *rāga*s takes years of assiduous practice – and intensive teaching – and cannot be acquired from books or brief and diluted (group) teaching (violating the traditional *guru-shishya* one-to-one method), even the most distinguished Indian artists are prepared to impart sufficient information in single workshops or short series of (group) classes to get people started, and at least some of the basic principles of *rāga* can be understood. More importantly, it becomes possible to apply them creatively. It might be easiest to liken a *rāga* to a kind of map, perhaps of a huge field with many paths, some of which can only be travelled in one direction and connect only to certain other ones. So the traveller is free to choose an itinerary, but is constrained by these special features. Any *rāga* has a particular selection of notes (a minimum of five) evenly distributed within the octave. Many *rāga*s share the same basic notes, but each one has a different way of treating them, for example by omitting one or two in ascending melodic sequences, emphasising certain notes and avoiding stress on others. A basic scheme could thus be made for a *rāga*, showing the notes it uses and characteristic melodic movements. Using the Indian note names (corresponding to our sol-fa system) as well as a staff notation equivalent, we could have the ascending and descending lines shown in Example 14.1.

Sa Ga Ma Pa Ni Sa   Sa Ni Dha Pa Ma Ga Re Sa

Example 14.1 Rāga ascending and descending line.

Thus all seven notes are used in a straight sequence in the descending line, but two of them (corresponding to D and A) are omitted in the ascending one. Merely singing or playing up and down the scale observing these features would convey a *rāga*. To turn a very basic idea (where the student could become stuck in unimaginative repetition) into creative performance (which here also means composition), we can turn to an Indian concept at the heart of improvisation: extension. An added advantage of this approach is that it also chimes with a great deal of musical thinking in Western music (in such things as theme and variation, symphonic development and so on) and encourages the notion that much can be made of little. If, for example, we take a simple motif (Example 14.2(a)) we can vary it simply and methodically by a gradual unfolding (Example 14.2(b)) or extend it by incorporating the Re (used in descending phrases) (Example 14.2(c)), while further variations can be drawn out by a kind of permutational reordering (Example 14.2(d)).

If these seem like five-finger exercises, it should be pointed out that they are used as such by Indian musicians not only to exercise the muscles, but also to exercise the mind and serve as a stimulus for improvisation. The variation devices just illustrated are thoroughly assimilated by Indian musicians, and one can hear them being applied in actual performances (albeit in a more expressive manner, which is likely to involve a variety of note lengths and dynamics, ornamentation and so on). Apart from that, the point to make from these brief examples is that the novice can be equipped with something on which to build, and creativity can develop within clearly defined parameters that involve the guidelines first laid out by the teacher and the rules that apply to specific *rāga*s.[5] The key point here is

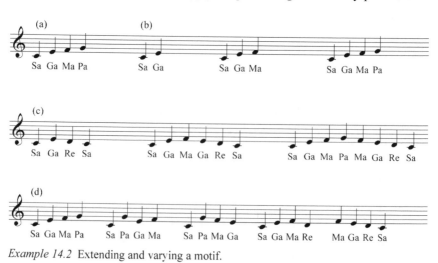

Example 14.2 Extending and varying a motif.

that much can be made from very little: just a few notes can be endlessly varied and treated in methodical ways that give the student the technique and confidence to begin improvisation.

Javanese gamelan music

A similar principle lies at the heart of the other case study: Javanese gamelan music. This is, of course, a very different tradition, and relies on the interaction of a large group, whereas Indian music is essentially a solo tradition. Here the focus will be on what may be termed analysis-in-action. That may sound dry and academic, but it challenges any supposition that creativity and analysis must be in any kind of opposition as it is what drives the music and gives the performers scope for creativity. Better than that, the players are expected to apply it there and then, and do not expect to be given parts as in Western orchestral music. They therefore become analysts, composers and performers in a simultaneous act, known in Javanese as *garapan* ('working out'). To illustrate some simple ways in which this happens, we can use the notation system every gamelan player knows, by which the notes are given numbers. One group of instruments plays a fixed melody, in which other instruments mark the subdivisions into phrases. These two roles of main melody and 'punctuation' frankly offer little scope for creativity, but another advantage of the gamelan it that it encourages – even expects – roles to be exchanged so that the musicians gradually learn to play a large number of the instruments within the gamelan orchestra and understand their specific roles. This case study relies on some of those instruments that must create their parts from the fixed, material provided by the central melody and its 'colotomic' (punctuating) support: these are the foundational points of reference when learning a new piece. The process of *garapan* going on in the ensemble creates what is often referred to as heterophony, which is a kind of polyphony based on the simultaneous combination of modified versions of the same melody. So it is not the same as our Western idea of counterpoint, where a tune is added to another one and the two may be unrelated except harmonically.

Gamelan music uses a simple notation in which each note of the two tuning systems – the pentatonic *sléndro* and the heptatonic *pélog* – is given a number. Although neither tuning conforms to Western concepts (in Example 14.3, the five pitches of *sléndro* are more equally spaced than the Western 'black note' pentatonic set), and also because there is no standard for the exact pitches and one gamelan will be tuned slightly differently from another, it is misleading to give the Javanese tunings in staff notation. A *very* approximate attempt might look like the passage in Example 14.3.

Example 14.3 Approximate pitches for the Javanese *sléndro* and *pélog* tunings.

The following examples are conceived in *sléndro* (though they could equally be in *pélog*), and are shown without a clef to give a more graphic approximation for the numbers, without precise pitches. The melodies tend to be organised in four-note melodic cells, so taking one as an example (Example 14.4(a)), one instrument can respond with a variant so simple it can hardly be called creative, by simply doubling each note (Example 14.4(b)), but the same instrument will be more adventurous if the tempo of the main melody is slowed sufficiently to fit four notes to each one; the *garapan* then divides the four notes into two pairs (2 3 and 2 1) (Example 14.4(c)).

Notice how the two lines go in and out of 'focus': when the main melody is the first of each pair, the *garapan* is the other note, the two parts agreeing on the second of the pair. Notice too how the *garapan* supplies the next note before it has been reached in the main melody. This process of anticipation lies at the heart of *garapan*, and compels the musician playing this particular instrument, the *peking*, to analyse not just 'vertically' – in the moment – but also 'diagonally' – by thinking ahead to what has not yet been heard. For those playing the basic melody, the *balungan*, hearing the *peking* anticipating their melody in a higher octave can also provide a useful auditory cue. Yet creative teaching and learning function in a fluid and very different way from, say, the one-to-one training in Indian music. The gamelan player, deciding on a particular *garapan*, does not listen just to one other player or melodic line, but to the totality of what is being played. In fact, Javanese musicians tend to create a kind of composite melody in their heads which may not actually be sounded. This is why they tend to resist the division of the ensemble into strictly defined functions, such as 'main melody', 'embellishments' and so on, preferring to hear the sum of the parts. A gamelan is indeed as much one instrument played by many as an ensemble which is divided and specialised like an orchestra. This account is therefore a simplification, focusing on one of the many relationships that flourish within the ensemble.[6]

The principle of dividing the basic melody into pairs of notes applies to certain other *garapan* instruments, for example, as in Example 14.5(a), or, in a slower tempo (ratio 4:1) as in Example 14.5(b). What the player will actually prefer, if only to avoid muscular and aural strain, is a version that leaves out some of the notes, so the above line could be played, more stylishly, as in Example 14.5(c).

Example 14.4 A simple *garapan*.

Example 14.5 Another *garapan.*

While all these examples seem to fix the procedures (*garapan*) and discourage further creativity, the point is that they demand creativity in the first place, as the musician is only given the main melody and expected to know how to derive the part by these processes, which also involve the crucial ability to think ahead. The part is therefore created on the spot. It should also be added that much more complex principles of *garapan* occur in the gamelan, and these enhance its special position, as well as educational potential, as a mixed-ability ensemble. At the front of the ensemble is a collection of soft-sounding instruments – including metallophones and a xylophone, all played with two mallets, a two-stringed fiddle, a bamboo flute, and a solo female singer – that provide the rich filigree of countermelodies and which require longer training and deeper understanding, as well as a greater degree of creativity. In Thai classical music too, which is usually performed on a percussion ensemble not unlike a small gamelan, the process of deriving a *thang* ('path') is comparable to *garapan* in Javanese music. While the actual procedures and resultant sounds are in sharp contrast, and the experience of learning and playing Thai music is quite different from that relating to the gamelan, the principle of deriving a complex part from a simpler melodic strand, aiming at focal points with that melody, is the same.

Producing something genuinely new has different connotations and priorities in different cultures. Although new *rāga*s are being composed all the time, the fundamental principles of the classical *rāga*s are maintained. The Javanese often use the word *kreasi* to describe a new composition that nevertheless adheres to traditional models. The word is obviously derived from 'creation', but actually describes a process we might almost be tempted to call pastiche. This could be the key to understanding how creativity can work in other cultures and why there is less pressure to be original at all costs. Pastiche is equated with copying, which, as we saw earlier, can be regarded as an antithesis to creativity, with its pressure to be original. Yet in music education, pastiche brings unique benefits and is a more direct and creative response to music than writing essays about it. The armchair may be good for watching sports, but is not a suitable place in which to do them. In other words, any practical musical procedure based on the application of principles, such as those given above as examples, is bound to stimulate creativity, be it based on existing models ('pastiche') or producing something new ('original').

The Department for Education, in its *National Curriculum in England: Music Programmes of Study: Key Stages 1 and 2*, applying to children aged 5–7 and 7–11, respectively, thus covering the period of primary education, published in September 2013, appeared to place 'creativity' at the centre of the curriculum: 'Music is a universal language that embodies one of the highest forms of creativity' (DfE, 2013).

On the surface, this looks plausible and very beguiling; we are back in the realms of motherhood and apple pie. Yet music, while being a universal activity, is not a language, and this affects our perception of creativity and how it changes according to cultural context. In a rush towards creativity, teachers (who could not be expected to have had any training in diverse cultures from around the world) were encouraged in turn to encourage their students to compose, for example, short gamelan pieces. Again, on the surface this looks like a positive move, and it is certainly much better than merely reading about the music, but it also encourages the application of a few principles to larger structures that require a deeper knowledge of *gendhing* (traditional gamelan form, analogous to formal, structured composition). Both Indian and Javanese music operate within clearly defined limits that focus the creativity, and both lay emphasis on balance and careful phrasing. Put like that, one might say that Western music does exactly the same things, albeit in different ways. Yet such simple guidelines can easily be ignored, so while some superficial musical features are employed, the aesthetic basis of the music is eliminated. This problem can be described as a variation on the saying that a little knowledge is a dangerous thing. Care has been taken in this chapter to show principles and creative procedures, without any ambition to compose entire pieces. It would be rather like showing some principles of functional harmony without expecting a symphony to come of it. Rather, it is hoped that creativity, even in a limited way, will be stimulated, and with further study and listening, eventually produce larger structures.

A favourite example for attempts at composing actual gamelan pieces is the Javanese *lancaran* form, usually regarded as the shortest and simplest in the traditional repertoire. It is constructed from 16-beat melodic phases (often eight notes alternating with eight rests, shown as dots in the ensuing examples), punctuated by gongs at specific points. This much can be learned in a matter of minutes, but then the mistake is to assume that pouring notes into this mould will produce a genuine *lancaran*, rather than an imitation of some of its features, but not others. To give an extreme example, in Example 14.6(a) the attempt is to produce an adventurous melody using all seven notes of the *pélog* scale (and one must be repeated to give the eight notes required). Even if readers unfamiliar with the gamelan and its special tuning cannot hear the effect, it should be obvious that this melody leaps about in a shapeless manner. Compare that with the very well-known *lancaran* in Example 14.6(b), which may be less interesting, but is more conjunct (a virtue in Javanese music) and better balanced (even more prized).

(a)

(b)

Example 14.6 Bad (a) and good (b) *lancarans*.

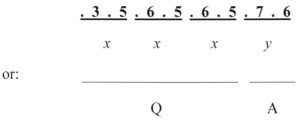

Example 14.7 Structural balance in *lancaran* form.

Analysis is easy, as the structure is abundantly clear, even just from the numbers notation (Example 14.7).

The first three groups of four beats (two rests and two notes) all end on note 5, while the last group ends on note 6. It could even be claimed that 6 is like the tonic, making 5, approximately a semitone below it (without needing to add a flat to note 6, given these are approximate pitches and no clef is given), sound like a leading note; to Western ears, this could resemble a drawn-out perfect cadence, even a 'question–answer' structure. The point is not whether it is any such thing, but that it has a pleasing shape and sense of balance both to Western and Javanese ears. There are at least some universals in music after all!

Applying the same principles to the first example would reveal its fundamental randomness and incoherence. Note also how the tonal palette is more restricted – 'focused' would be a better word – in the second example. In the traditional Javanese repertoire, the use of all seven notes (in *pélog*) is rare, and even if it happens, a clear hierarchy will be established and either 1 or 7 will be strong and the other very weak. This touches on one of the fundamental principles of both Indian and Javanese music: a set of notes does not in itself make a *rāga* or *gendhing*. We have seen how the mistake can be applied to Javanese music, while in Indian music, the commonest error is to describe a *rāga* simply as a scale. Without the modal organisation of the scale according to hierarchies of notes, typical melodic phrases, even time of performance, we would still have only the raw materials, but not the finished product. Ideally, the novice attempts at gamelan composition in the context of school music education alluded to above would have been followed by a critical examination and comparison with models from the Javanese repertoire to determine why they did not work and to try ways to improve them, thereby adding critical evaluation to the process of creative teaching and learning.

Conclusion

Both Indian and Javanese culture can be described as inherently conservative. Innovation is valued, and indeed occurs in every good performance, albeit in subtle ways that may not be apparent to all, and there are even some outrageously experimental new gamelan pieces, but iconoclasm based on ignorance is unlikely to gain the same respect. This is why I warn against pale pastiche, which may not only be based on insufficient knowledge, but also have limited potential to survive alongside the existing repertoire.

In the same way, after innumerable gamelan workshops spent teaching a *lancaran*, it was a breath of fresh air when another workshop leader asked the participants to improvise an accompaniment (with no priming in Javanese formal principles) to a story. To paraphrase Wagner: do not just try to imitate; make something new. Adapt traditional processes not to replicate existing products, but to create new ones. Creativity and self-expression are, after all, nearly always inextricably linked. Just as asking GCSE[7] candidates, let alone university music students, to compose a complete Javanese *gendhing* can be problematic, an Indian musician would be similarly concerned if the student were expected to give a typical exposition of a *rāga* after a couple of lessons. It would be far better for students to demonstrate an awareness of the procedures discussed here and apply them to their own music than try to mimic the 'real thing', and in any case, can the 'real thing' be mimicked without the real instruments?

The question is often asked: what if we don't have a gamelan (or any Indian instruments)? The point is that what has been offered here are sets of principles that can be applied imaginatively (and creatively) in other contexts, so one does not need a gamelan (or a *sitār* or to try to sing like an Indian). In fact, the element of rethinking in different contexts itself becomes creative. If such liberties are taken, it must be admitted that the resultant music will most probably not be recognised as Javanese by a Javanese or Indian by an Indian. To the former, if gamelan music is adapted to other instruments (or voices) that do not reflect the special tuning systems of the gamelan, then it ceases to be gamelan music.[8] To the latter, a *rāga* needs far more subtle nuances than have been given here. The principles can be 'imported' into the Western context, and while some of them fit well with Western ways of thinking about and organising music, others open up new possibilities, which can therefore be a springboard to further creativity. To quote Steve Reich's apt summary (a composer who most certainly used gamelan music, as well as African and other sources, creatively to help formulate his new musical language):

> one can create a music with one's own sound that is constructed in the light of one's knowledge of non-Western *structures*. ... This brings about the interesting situation of the non-Western influence being there in the thinking, but not in the sound ... [which] is likely to produce something genuinely new.
>
> (Reich, 1974: 40)

The assumption throughout this chapter has been that creativity can be taught, but a better way of describing it would be to invoke the literal meaning of education as leading or bringing out. Music can be taught by example rather than by verbal explanation, which is how Indian musicians (and probably the majority of other practitioners around the world) will teach. If practising musicians have no other way of expressing themselves than through creative acts such as performance, should the learning process not follow the same model? Children make up little songs quite readily, just as they draw, paint and make models. Art classes were never art appreciation or history of art lessons, so why were music lessons so often based on passive listening and ingestion of theoretical and historical facts? The aim is to learn music, rather than about music. In the Department for Education's curriculum statement quoted earlier, overlooking the tired fallacy of music as a universal language and the aesthetic problems discussed above, we are left with this key word (creativity), and if it is forefronted thus at the very beginning of a child's education – not forgetting that it actually pre-dates schooling itself – can there be any excuse for lowering the priority in later school and higher education? Another mistake is to separate creativity from other approaches to what Christopher Small (1998) dubbed 'musicking', rather than viewing it as an integral part of them. The conclusion is that music without creativity is both oxymoronic and unsustainable. We cannot therefore treat creativity as optional, especially by the time music has become an advanced and specialist study (in higher education) where the danger is a narrowing of focus and a potential avoidance of risk and trying new things (in order to obtain the best grades). I have sought to show that the study of non-Western music is not a frivolous exoticism, but may actually reinforce aspects of musicality that a more conservative curriculum might underplay or ignore. I have also argued that such study is inherently creative, and that is how it is conceived and taught within its own culture. In the end, it teaches not only creativity and how that unlocks the secrets of the musical system, but also how to think for oneself and learn to relate meaningfully to others – both transferable skills without which education would fail the student.

Notes

1 Earlier sets, dating back to the early nineteenth century and the collections of Sir Thomas Stamford Raffles (1781–1826), notably those at Claydon House in Buckinghamshire, UK, and the Museum of Mankind in London, had fallen into disrepair and disorganisation and were not in playable condition.

2 Further examples are outlined in Vulliamy and Lee (1982).

3 An important perspective on improvisation in non-Western music is offered by David Hughes (2004).

4 For general introductions to (North) Indian music, see Ruckert (2004) and Sorrell and Narayan (1980).

5 Similar procedures are exemplified by Farrell (1990: 51).

6 For more detail on *garapan* and Javanese gamelan music in general, see Brinner (2008); Pickvance (2005); Sorrell (1990).

7 General Certificate of Secondary Education examinations taken in the UK, except Scotland, by students aged around 14–16.

8 Which is why a work like Debussy's piano piece 'Pagodes', so often cited as a shining example of gamelan-inspired composition, cannot even begin adequately to imitate a gamelan at all. As a creative response to the gamelan, as well as a heavily stylised and complete rethinking of it in purely Western terms, however, it is beyond reproach, though there is no evidence that Debussy actually intended it as such.

References

Bailey, D. (1980). *Improvisation: Its Nature and Practice in Music*. Ashbourne: Moorland Publishing.

Brinner, B. (2008). *Music in Central Java: Experiencing Music, Expressing Culture*. New York: Oxford University Press.

DfE (2013). *National Curriculum in England: Music Programmes of Study: Key Stages 1 and 2*. London: Department for Education, Qualifications and Curriculum Authority.

Farrell, G. (1990). *Indian Music in Education*. Cambridge: Cambridge University Press.

Hughes, D.W. (2004). '"When Can We Improvise?": The Place of Creativity in Academic World Music Performance'. In: T. Solís (ed.), *Performing Ethnomusicology: Teaching and Representation in World Music Ensembles* (pp. 261–82). Berkeley, CA: University of California Press.

Pickvance, R. (2005). *A Gamelan Manual: A Player's Guide to the Central Javanese Gamelan*. London: Jaman Mas Books.

Reich, S. (1974). *Writings About Music*. London: Universal Edition.

Ruckert, G.E. (2004). *Music in North India: Experiencing Music, Expressing Culture*. New York: Oxford University Press.

Small, C. (1998). *Musicking: The Meanings of Performing and Listening*. Middletown, CT: Wesleyan University Press.

Sorrell, N. (1990). *A Guide to the Gamelan*. London: Faber and Faber. 2nd edn, M. Hatch (ed.). Ithaca, NY: Society for Asian Music, 2000.

——— and Narayan, R. (1980). *Indian Music in Performance: A Practical Introduction*. Manchester: Manchester University Press.

Vulliamy, G. and Lee, E. (eds) (1982). *Pop, Rock and Ethnic Music in School*. Cambridge: Cambridge University Press.

15 Dalcroze Eurhythmics

Bridging the gap between the academic and the practical through creative teaching and learning

Karin Greenhead, John Habron and Louise Mathieu

A musical work is not a scientific thesis that one can peruse at leisure and analyse coolly. Music acts on the entire organism like a magic force that suppresses the understanding, and with an irresistible grasp, lays hold of one's being. The attempt to analyse this force, before having felt the impact of it, is to kill its very essence.

(Jaques-Dalcroze, 1942: 176)[1]

Introduction

Pulse, movement, breath, gesture, rhythm, action and cadence, phrase and form, speech and song – these musical signs of our living being are part of our daily lives. Since infancy we have engaged in dialogue, listening, improvising, creating and responding (Malloch and Trevarthen, 2009). These pleasurable and essentially musical behaviours form the basis of our creative communication with one another. We bring the experience and knowledge of the dynamic activities of our senses, nerves and muscles to the practice of singing and playing an instrument, to improvising, performing, composing and listening to music. Music is not only something we do, it is part of what we are. The sounds around us and those we make set sound waves in motion that, striking both eardrum and skin, pass through to the bone and vibrate in the whole body. When we imagine music we recall sounds and rhythms we have experienced bodily. That musical perception, understanding and performance are rooted in the body and need to be taught through active bodily participation was asserted by Jaques-Dalcroze from the earliest years of the twentieth century (Jaques-Dalcroze, 1921/1967). He believed problems in music teaching, learning and performance arose owing to a dualistic view of mind and body and an over-intellectual approach, and so anticipated the anti-Cartesian critique that gathered strength during the twentieth century (Greenhead and Habron, 2015; Jaques-Dalcroze, 1921/1967; Juntunen and Westerlund, 2001; Mathieu, 2010, 2013). Through observation, experimentation and dialogue with students and colleagues, Dalcroze developed a method of teaching and learning that became known as Dalcroze Eurhythmics (DE).[2]

For neuroscientists, philosophers and psychologists alike the body-mind – as an entity – is the locus of all perception, experience and knowledge (Damasio, 2000; Dewey, 1934; Seitz, 2005; Sheets-Johnstone, 2011). The indissoluble interpenetration of mind and body and their essential co-involvement is reflected in the corporeal and social nature of music-making (Bowman, 2004). The cross-modal and multi-sensory nature of music is underpinned by a functional connection between the brain's auditory and sensorimotor areas (Chen, Penhune and Zatorre, 2009). Herholz and Zatorre's (2012) observation that neural changes result from the social interaction that usually accompanies musical activity suggests that motor experience and the kinaesthetic sense are closely linked to other senses, to time-based aspects of cognition such as sequencing and memory, and to emotion.

This chapter makes use of teaching materials, research on DE and the knowledge of experienced practitioners to show how the principles and techniques used in this practice address the needs of higher education music students in ways that are active, rigorous and creative and so bridge the gap between the academic curriculum and the making of music. We start by reviewing the role of the 'mindful body' (Sheets-Johnstone, 2011: 501) in music learning and cognition, then provide an overview of how we conceptualise creativity in teaching and learning, showing examples of this in DE practice. We consider the usefulness of DE within higher education and, finally, we share findings from three research projects in this context.

Learning through the mindful body: Overcoming the Cartesian divide

The Cartesian split between mind and body, subject and object, thinking and action, intellect and emotion, theory and practice is deeply engrained in Western thought and practice and affects our lives detrimentally. As a result, connecting the theoretical and performative in teaching and learning often presents seemingly intractable problems. Learning, attention, memory, decision-making and social functioning are all considered important in schools and are sub-sumed within and affected by emotion; 'we feel therefore we learn' (Immordi-no-Yang and Damasio, 2011: 115). The emotional and social aspects of cognition are also important to adults in tertiary education and are prized in certain traditional cultures. Commentators on the African notion of *Ubuntu* emphasise its participatory ethics (Swanson, 2007) and how this fosters an understanding of what makes us human: not 'I think therefore I am' but 'I am human because I belong, I participate, I share' (Tutu, 1999: 31).[3] *Ubuntu* resonates with Bowman's (2004: 38) observations on hearing: 'To hear is always to participate, to be corporeally involved, engaged, positioned.' The notion of learning through the body is also fundamental to teaching traditional Japanese arts. Here, verbal instruction and the use of concepts are avoided as they are thought to distract the student from a whole-body grasp of artistry. 'The best learning relies on *taiken*, an experience gained through the body, and *karada de oboeru* – to remember through one's body' (Matsunobu, 2007: 1107). Such active engagement with the world suggests the need for an ongoing responsive relationship with the objects of our experience – in short a 'mindful body' (Sheets-Johnstone, 2011: 501) that is dynamically alive.

Bodily participation in music-making and learning are considered exceptionally effective ways of engaging creatively with the world, developing a sense of both agency and belonging, and constructing meaning and self-identity (Malloch and Trevarthen, 2009; Stubley, 1998). Bowman and Powell (2007: 1101) assert that 'all musical experience is embodied' while Rabinowitch, Cross and Burnard (2012: 113) hold music to be a 'profoundly kinaesthetic activity' that is both personal and social. All this suggests that to be effective, musical learning must address the whole person in a social context.

These ideas are commonplace in general education and in music education for children. The UK Office for Standards in Education's report (Ofsted, 2012) declares the development of musical skills and understanding and the quality of musical response to be fundamental.[4] Engaging with music through movement, improvisation and rhythmic games is considered good practice for pupils in primary schools, where some of the best teaching includes 'music-specific techniques such as Dalcroze Eurhythmics' (Ofsted, 2012: 19). However, this type of teaching is less present in secondary or higher education. The reluctance to embrace body movement, sensation and emotional feeling as fundamental to musical participation is ascribed by Bowman (2004) to a deep-rooted mistrust, even suspicion, of the body. This originates with Plato and results in an exaltation of the reasoning intellect and a failure to accept the embodied and 'feelingful' nature of human beings and the way we relate to the world.

Tochon (2011) addresses the role of academic education in tackling the political and social effects of Cartesianism. Starting from Aristotle's philosophy of knowledge that leads to both practical and theoretical wisdom, he suggests a reconceptualisation of education across all disciplines and in particular of academic study. Tochon's views echo those of Jaques-Dalcroze who proposed that teaching should address the person holistically and that learning begin with experience rather than abstraction: 'theory should *follow* practice' (Jaques-Dalcroze, 1921/1967: 63, emphasis in original). Jaques-Dalcroze's principles and method, properly understood and applied, could provide a paradigm of the reconceptualised role of academic study that Tochon proposes and so act as a bridge between the academic and the practical. Dewey observed the wide-ranging negative effects of using the mind without participation of the body as long ago as 1934 (Dewey, 1934: pp. 20–23).

While some researchers consider gesture an effective way of bridging the Cartesian split (Leman, 2010), and Peters (2004: 25) suggests that an 'embodied curriculum' heals it, Stern (2010: 15) proposes a 'domain of vitality dynamics' dependent on arousal systems, bodily movement in time and space, intention, and force or energy. He suggests that all engagement with the world depends on a dialogical and circular flow 'from movement at the local level to mental operations at the abstracted level, then back down to instantiation in movement at the local level' (Stern, 2010: 136–7). The notion of dynamic motion (physical, mental, emotional, intentional) is supported not only by neuroscience (Damasio, 2000; Hodges and Gruhn, 2012) and philosophy (Sheets-Johnstone, 2011), but also by researchers into learning theory who note that bodily being-in-the-world is indissociable from social relatedness, emotional responsiveness and the capacity to imagine and think creatively (Boden, 2010; Jarvis, 2006).

All in all, research from many diverse fields supports to a remarkable degree the centrality of the body to all knowing and artistic engagement. This suggests that the arts, and in particular music, throw a compelling light on our understanding of what it means to be human. Our participation in them engages us in a process of becoming ourselves (Stubley, 1998) and this process is essentially creative. Situating the body at the centre of learning creates a shift from 'I think, therefore I am' (Descartes) to 'I know and I think because I feel and experience' (Jaques-Dalcroze, 1924: 7). Through action, knowing begins in the body and informs the intellect. The learning process is no longer fragmented when the gap is bridged through addressing bodily ways of knowing, since intellectual understanding emerges *with* bodily knowledge in the here and now.

Dalcroze Eurhythmics: Creative teaching and learning through dialogue, embodiment, improvisation and problem-solving

DE invites students and teachers to engage creatively in activities that develop musical understanding and communication; these activities include movement, singing, aural training, improvisation and musical analysis. It consists of a vast body of largely orally transmitted facilitation skills, developed experimentally and refined during more than a century of practice. DE is found at all levels of music education, from early years to higher education as well as in community and therapeutic settings.[5] Regardless of the context, several means and strategies are used creatively and dialogically in Dalcroze teaching and learning: engaging with music's motional qualities and embodying them, exploring, improvising, question-asking, problem-solving, performing, reflection-in-action, and indirect teaching and composing. Figure 15.1 shows how these elements of creative teaching and learning in DE coalesce around three major areas all of which rely on dialogue.

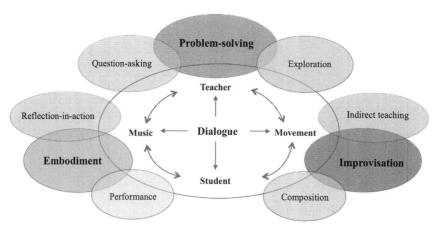

Figure 15.1 The means of creative teaching and learning in Dalcroze Eurhythmics.

Dialogue

DE is characterised by several simultaneous dialogues: between the student and the teacher, between students, between music and movement, and between all these participants and elements. Dialogues are often non-verbal and mediated through music, sound, movement, sight and touch. They are aesthetic experiences that rely on and develop interpersonal relationships. Developmentally, the capacity for dialogue is deeply rooted in our musical biology (Malloch and Trevarthen, 2009; Stern, 2010) and the musical ecologies of which we are part afford such engagement (DeNora, 2000). The learning approach in DE relies on and develops these potentialities. Dialogical interaction is therefore highly prized by DE practitioners as it helps foster the creative potential of the students and the teacher. It also leads to and requires cooperation and ensemble skills and enables students to work on joint projects.

Embodiment

In DE, all the parameters of music are worked on, in and through movement, which is used to deepen the sensory experience of music and its expression and is 'designed to lead to active listening, forming a link between what is experienced through movement and what is understood about music' (CIJD, 2011: 11). The learning is 'situated in action' and demands 'practical involvement', two notions considered essential to fostering creativity (Webster, 2002: 17; Lowe, 2002: 96). For example, the student may be asked to interpret a rhythm pattern along with its dynamics and articulation. In responding to the music, in movement, the students are asked for a personal response to what they hear *as they experience it*. This 'tuning in' to the music, responding and expressing one's own feeling, provides the occasion for many different possible responses and the students can see what other class members do and try it out for themselves, or look for new solutions of their own. Engaging with the music in this way is approached not by following a set of instructions or set steps but by improvising responsively in movement to what is experienced. Following this, the students may be asked to interpret the pattern with different tempi and dynamics, or to transform it metrically or by augmentation or diminution (Figure 15.2).

The pattern could also be used as a theme in improvisation or as one of two patterns in a two-voice context. This way of dwelling on a specific musical element fosters internalisation and creative thinking, since it relies on repetition of the same rhythmic pattern in varied ways (tempi, dynamics) rather than on drill.

Reflection-in-action

In the interpretative or 'follow the music' type of exercise exemplified above, the students' initial improvised movement response is often pre-reflective. As the exercise continues students become aware of discrepancies between the qualities of the music they hear and their own movement and try to find a fit that feels more satisfying. In experimenting with different responses in an iterative and reflexive process and reflecting in action (Schön, 1987), students test their ideas on the ground.

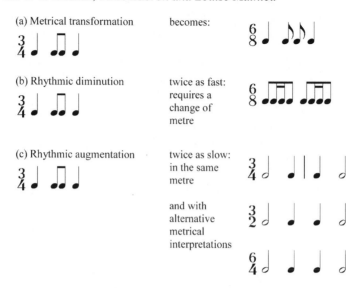

Figure 15.2 (a) Metrical transformation, (b) rhythmic diminution and augmentation, and (c) rhythmic augmentation with alternative metrical interpretations.

Performance

When students embody the music and reflect in action, they perform their understanding of the music and project their feelings and ideas in movement and space. Working in this way develops the communicative aspect of performance. By 'reading' the students' movement, the teacher gathers impressions of how the students are engaging with the music and as a result modifies the exercises given. Students will also perform their own music, composed or improvised, and the techniques used in class can be applied to the rehearsal and performance of repertoire. Performance as both a process and product of creative thinking (Webster, 2002) is central to Dalcroze teaching.

Improvisation

The Dalcroze method could not exist without improvisation as it is the first and principal teaching tool and the first learning response. Through improvisation the teacher converses with the class, makes and modifies musical proposals for students to respond to and creates musical puzzles for them to solve in action (CIJD, 2011: 6). In fact, the teacher is continually modelling the creative process of improvisation to learners. Students also learn to improvise vocally and instrumentally, alone, in pairs and groups, exploring and using the vocabulary they are studying. Their improvisation takes them away from dependence on the score. They take ownership of their own music-making and become primary creators, not only interpreters. In addition, they learn to improvise for and in response to movement, drawing on their own experience of what movement looks and feels like. Engaging students in collective improvisation in which learning experiences are guided and orchestrated by a responsive teacher is identified as effective teaching by Sawyer (2011: 2–3) who observes that 'Balancing structure and improvisation is the essence of the art of teaching.' In DE, sound is encoded somatically, kinaesthetically and mentally. In this cross-modal work students partake in one another's creativity as they observe, respond to and incite movement in one another. This quick transfer of learning from one modality to another is typical of Dalcroze pedagogy, requiring and developing flexibility.

Indirect teaching

The teacher's musical conversation with the students is a form of 'indirect teaching' (Alperson 1995) that invites them to be fully engaged with the music. This indirect teaching through improvisation creates distance between the teacher and the students. In a study by Alperson (1995: 238), the 'students perceived the teacher's distancing as an act which empowered them, gave them freedom, let them be independent'. Such a shift of power, from teacher to student, is considered essential for students to realise their creative potential (Csikszentmihalyi and Custodero, 2002; Willingham, 2002).

Composing original music and devising original exercises

Like improvisation, composition is an important part of the culture of DE teaching and learning, and teachers create both music and exercises for their lessons as Jaques-Dalcroze did himself (Dénes, 1965). Students also compose pieces that address the various topics covered in the classes as part of their coursework. Although Jaques-Dalcroze wrote music, books and collections of exercises, he never published a manual of specific and sequenced lesson plans. Rather, he encouraged personal development and creative thinking in teachers, to whom he wrote:

> It is for you to discover for yourselves ... how to make [these exercises] your own; how to use them according to your own temperament. In this way the worker forges the tools he needs for his profession and uses them according to the conformation of his own hand and arm, with the intensity of his breath and the aptitudes of his entire organism.
>
> (Jaques-Dalcroze, 1916a: 2)[6]

For Jaques-Dalcroze, the aim of education was to help individuals know themselves and develop their personalities, to act and think for themselves. Instead of the written word, it is the student's body itself that becomes the primary repository of knowledge. As Bachmann (1991: 137) states, 'all these exercises will eventually turn each pupil's body into a sort of "manual", a source of reference'. The experiences and mental representations that result from creatively engaging with music and movement in a Dalcroze class can be transferred to and accessed in other contexts, such as composing (Habron, Jesuthasan and Bourne, 2012), conducting (Bowtell, 2012; Daley, 2013), performing (Greenhead, 2016), musicianship (Van der Merwe, 2015), music analysis (Mathieu, 2016) and music theory (Moore, 1992).

Over a long engagement with DE, students come to realise that the same topic can be approached from multiple angles and so understand that crafting a Dalcroze class is a business of combining in novel ways Dalcroze principles, practices and repertoire and the teacher's personality. In one sense, practitioners are improvising over the Dalcroze tradition itself, as they renew it through their own style of teaching and learning.

Problem-solving

Creating musical challenges to acquire and develop skills is central to teaching in DE. The exercises in interpretation and expression mentioned above are complemented with other kinds of exercise such as quick reaction exercises in response to a signal. These are designed to tune up the body, develop flexibility and adaptability and bring the student to a state of readiness. Other exercises may emphasise metrical analysis. These exercises are preparatory to the creative work because 'to be creative you have to have something to be creative with' (Spurgeon, 2002: 147).

For example, the class might have to solve the problem of interpreting a rhythm pattern in movement and analysing it metrically by beating time while stepping it. Using full-arm beating gestures (Jaques-Dalcroze, 1921/1967) permits the student to experience the given pattern in the dynamic context of a metrical shape. Students experience metrical identity for themselves and are better able to appreciate the way composers play with the combination of pattern and metre. This activity is prerequisite to another in which students would be invited to improvise or compose a piece in movement and music exploring various metres or the notion of changing metres. Relying on convergent and divergent modes of thinking, such activities are essential in developing creative thinking (Webster, 2002).

The teacher's role in the creative use of these exercises is to pitch them at the right level and pace the increase in complexity, so that students have the satisfaction of knowing that they are fulfilling a task and meeting the challenge, which is personally empowering. The Collège de l'Institut Jaques-Dalcroze describes this process as follows:

> It is a student centred approach: the teacher guides and assists students in discovery and problem-solving. By keying into previous experience, adding new experiences, creating bridges between the student's inner and outer worlds, fostering cooperation between people, teaching through music itself … the teacher cultivates, nurtures and creates an environment in which

students can take risks and develop both as individuals and as members of a group.

(CIJD, 2011: 6)

The element of risk-taking is related to exploration and challenge, and is part of creative activity. 'Creative people take sensible risks ... Thus, teachers need not only to encourage sensible risk-taking, but also to reward it' (Sternberg, 2003: 123). The students in the DE class are encouraged to take risks within scaffolded activities. Alperson (1995: 216) noted this element in her observations of Dalcroze teaching and learning: 'The eurhythmics lessons seemed to engender a kind of risk-taking by the teachers – as well as the students – who could not know what was going to happen from one moment to the next.' In group improvisational activities that require spontaneity, imagination and expression, students challenge themselves and each other. They learn from the teacher how to consider and respect each other in terms of judging one another's limitations, asking 'How far can you go?' and 'How fun can the challenge be?'

Question-asking

Creative thinkers habitually pose questions. Such questions – whether verbal or musical, scripted or spontaneous – and the responses that are offered are central to the creativity of teaching and learning in DE. Thus, a Socratic or question-asking approach is another *sine qua non* of the method. The fundamental verbal questions to which the students will respond in movement include: Can you show me how the music moves? Can you show the relationship between the melody and the bass in this two-part piece? How can you show the structure of this music (for example, a fugue)? In addition, as we have seen, questions may also be non-verbal and posed by means of movement or musical improvisation.

Exploration

This question-asking leads to the exploration of music and its dynamic, motional, spatial and structural dimensions. In Dalcroze classes, students may ask themselves: How does this melodic phrase move through the space? How do I show its changes of intensity and articulation? How do harmony and cadence affect my feeling about the melody? How do I dose my energy according to the qualities of the music? How can I own and take command of the space and share it with others?

These explorations take place in carefully constructed activities, in which the parameters of the task are clear, but open enough for students to use their freedom to explore options and propose solutions. This is fundamental to teaching for creativity and yet, as Sawyer et al. (2003) point out, the notion of structure can meet with resistance. Jaques-Dalcroze was at pains to stress the importance of both elements with a creative education, speaking of the need 'to create mentalities, clearer, more in conformity with instinct, and, at the same time, more disciplined'

(1921/1967: 109). Teaching and learning in these lessons is not only dialogical but also dialectical as the relationship between structure and exploration is continually reframed. These are lived experiences of experimentation, play and gradual sense-making.

Creativity in higher music education

It is widely recognised that 'creativity is required to succeed in the modern world' (Sawyer, 2011: 10). Important in this context is the notion of 'thinking skills' or 'twenty-first century skills', identified as 'creativity and innovation … critical thinking and problem solving … and communication and collaboration' (ibid.: 10–11). All these are present in Dalcroze teaching and learning, to which DE adds an additional dimension, that of the 'mindful body' (Sheets-Johnstone, 2011). The Dalcroze approach is grounded in the notion that thinking skills arise from bodily experience, in particular movement and emotional and social engagement. What follows are brief reports on three research projects that show how DE helps to bridge the gap between the academic and the practical through creative teaching and learning in higher education.

In music body and soul

This project explores the creative practice of *Plastique Animée* and examines its contribution to the students' musical, artistic and personal development. *Plastique Animée* is the summary of the Dalcroze method 'as applied in practice to the analysis of musical compositions and the place where creative interpretation is the focus of the work' (CIJD, 2011: 20). It offers a way to discover how music from any style or period moves and to explore its composition: 'It is a kind of living analysis in real time' (CIJD, 2011: 19; see also Greenhead, 2009: 39). *Plastique Animée* begins with listening and exploring the piece through movement improvisation and working on the rapport between the intensity of sound and muscular energy, silence and stillness, thematic development and gestural transformation, musical form and the structuring of movement in space and orchestration and various ways of combining and placing body shapes. Decisions about performance follow, and the resulting choreography may be shown to an audience.[7] As they move between divergent and convergent modes of thinking, reflection enables students to articulate their understanding of their experiences and embed their learning. When several groups choreograph the same piece, different interpretations can be discussed. Embodying a piece in this way requires and develops the deep knowledge and understanding necessary for musical interpretation and performance; making the music visible transforms it into something new, the fruit of kinaesthetic, auditory and visual sensations (Mathieu, 2016).

During the *In Music Body and Soul* project (ibid.) students reported a wide range of personal, artistic and musical benefits from studying music through the practice of *Plastique Animée*. Personally, they reported an increase in openness, self-knowledge and self-trust through working in body-movement within a group.

Artistically, they felt that improvisation of all kinds was essential to creation and interpretation, and also developed personal qualities necessary to undertake this work: the ability to attend in the present moment, to respond spontaneously, to be open to the impulses of the music and the expression of feeling and emotion, to be 'at the service of the music' (ibid.) while remaining creative. Musically, the students said that responding in movement developed their ability to listen and their acuity of aural perception. In addition, studying melodic and rhythmic motifs, harmonic progressions and phrasing through movement enhanced their understanding of musical structures and the feelings evoked by music. Improvisation in movement was essential for them to grasp the energy of the sound, musical impulses and momentum in relation to orchestration, instrumentation, structure and harmony. All in all, they confirmed that embodying the music contributed to the development of their musicianship and creativity.

Moving into composition

This project (Habron, Jesuthasan and Bourne, 2012) explored the experiences of student composers during a short course of DE. Creative learning experiences were designed to develop aural acuity and deepen understanding of the elements of composition. Participants composed pieces in response to their movement-based learning. The students enjoyed the project and most noted positive influences on their compositional work, speed of learning, aural awareness and musical knowledge, especially with regard to metre and duration. Generally, using the body as the primary tool of learning was valued. Though some participants found it challenging, they recommended DE to other students. Burnard (1999: 171) discusses the important role of embodied knowledge when teaching children composition: 'It can be argued that the compositional process is manifested through the "knowing body."' This articulation of musical creativity is clearly applicable to composition pedagogy in higher education, as *Moving into Composition* successfully combined procedural knowledge and motor skills in a new composition teaching and learning model. A century ago Jaques-Dalcroze himself intuited this possibility, writing that his method 'could lead composers into entirely novel forms of expression' (Jaques-Dalcroze, 1916b: 11). In these ways, the project cultivated the mindful body, to afford students a radically embodied and social experience of an often over-intellectualised and sometimes solitary artistic skill.

Dynamic Rehearsal

A particular form of musical 'handling' occurs in Dynamic Rehearsal (DR), the application of DE to rehearsing and performing musical repertoire developed by Karin Greenhead since 1992 (Bowtell, 2012; Mayo, 2005). In DR, performers enact their thoughts, feelings, perceptions and sensations about their repertoire using materials and silent rehearsal in movement. They do this in response to specific questions regarding how they feel the piece deploys itself in time and space; they must make creative decisions relating to the way they hear the music and their intentions regarding it. Following this, rehearsal and performance focus on imagined movement and the memory of the sensation of moving in the space. The teacher consults the score to raise new questions relating to interpretation and the audience contributes feedback. This way of rehearsing achieves rapid changes in performance and in communication between players and the audience that generally include improvements in the engagingness of the performance, tone-quality, rhythm and the communication of musical structure and, on the part of the performer(s), greater confidence and security (Greenhead, 2016). Participants reported long-term changes in musical perception, practice and performance.

Conclusion

As can be seen from the practice of Dalcroze Eurhythmics, the elements of creativeness synthesised from Webster's (2002) overview of publications on creativity as a problem-solving context – convergent and divergent thinking and thinking processes, newness and usefulness – are all present. Other authors consider the role of the teacher, practical engagement (Lowe, 2002; Spurgeon, 2002) and the importance of challenges and skilfulness that permit exploration at a higher level essential to the development of creativity (Csikszentmihalyi and Custodero, 2002). Practice of this kind involves risk and is inherently empowering for students (Willingham, 2002). It reinforces the student's sense of ownership and agency – both distinct elements of creative learning – and so is highly rewarding (Wiggins, 2002). In DE, these elements are achieved through the full sensory presence of teacher and students engaged in a dialogical relationship by means of music.

Through improvisation, teacher and student 'converse', solicit responses and engage in dialogue. In keying into the somatically ingrained knowledge of musical elements in motion that forms every person's experience of aliveness and combining them in ever-shifting, dynamic patterns, the Dalcroze teacher brings memory into the active present and invites students to 're-cognise' prior knowledge, and apply it creatively. Into this matrix of experiences, new knowledge can be woven to create a springboard for further explorations. Galvanised by music to improvised self-movement in ongoing moment-to-moment realisations, the student unites conation, cognition and imagination in purposeful action (Greenhead and Habron, 2015) and simultaneously receives confirmation of his or her knowledge; the student feels he or she is right (Alperson, 1995) and gains confidence in engaging with and acquiring new knowledge and skill. Through moving here and now in time and space, participants create their own experience (Dewey, 1934) of aliveness, 'consciousness … "in constant motion" as a whole body, tactile-kinesthetically-grounded phenomenon' (Sheets-Johnstone, 2014: 266). In DE, teachers and students alike experience their own mindful bodies keenly and kinaesthetically and are dynamically engaged with music through the process of doing, creating and being. We suggest that such an experience of the symbiotic working together of thinking and action, intellect and emotion, theory and practice bridges the gap between the academic and the practical in music education.

Notes

1 Translation Karin Greenhead.
2 La rythmique Jaques-Dalcroze is called Dalcroze Eurhythmics in the UK. We refer to Emile Jaques-Dalcroze by his full surname and to the method as DE.
3 'Ubuntu is short for an isiXhosa proverb in Southern Africa. It comes from Umuntu ngumuntu ngabantu; a person is a person through their relationship to others. Ubuntu is recognised as the African philosophy of humanism, linking the individual to the collective through "brotherhood" or "sisterhood". It makes a fundamental contribution to indigenous "ways of knowing and being"' (Swanson, 2007: 53).
4 Ofsted (Office for Standards in Education, Children's Services and Skills) is a non-ministerial agency that regulates and inspects services providing education and skills in England; see https://www.gov.uk/government/organisations/ofsted (accessed March 28, 2016).
5 See www.fier.com for more information (accessed March 28, 2016).
6 Translation Karin Greenhead.
7 Those who watch performances of *Plastique Animée* often find the performances highly engaging and report having new insights into the music when it is performed in this way (Greenhead, 2009). For examples, see Meerkat Films (2014).

References

Alperson, R. (1995). *A Qualitative Study of Dalcroze Eurhythmics Classes for Adults* (Unpublished PhD thesis). New York University, USA.

Bachmann, M.-L. (1991). *Dalcroze Today: An Education Through and into Music*. Oxford: Oxford University Press.

Boden, M.A. (2010). *Creativity and Art: Three Roads to Surprise*. Oxford: Oxford University Press.

Bowman, W. (2004). Cognition and the Body: Perspectives from Music Education. In: L. Bresler (Ed.), *Knowing Bodies, Moving Minds: Towards Embodied Teaching and Learning* (pp. 29–50). Dordrecht: Kluwer Academic Publishers.

Bowman, W. and Powell, K. (2007). The Body in a State of Music. In: L. Bresler (Ed.), *International Handbook of Research in Arts Education, Part 2* (pp. 1087–106). Dordrecht: Springer.

Bowtell, K. (2012). *The Embodied Score: A Conductor's Application of the Dalcroze Approach to Interpretive Decision-making* (Unpublished MMus dissertation). University of Glamorgan, UK.

Burnard, P. (1999). Bodily Intention in Children's Improvisation and Composition. *Psychology of Music*, 27(2), 159–74.

Chen, J.L., Penhune, V.B. and Zatorre, R.J. (2009). The Role of Auditory and Premotor Cortex in Sensorimotor Transformations. *Proceedings of the New York Academy of Sciences*, 1169, 15–34.

CIJD [Collège de l'Institut Jaques-Dalcroze] (2011). *L'identité Dalcrozienne: Théorie et pratique de la rythmique Jaques-Dalcroze/The Dalcroze Identity: Theory and Practice of Dalcroze Eurhythmics*. Geneva: Institut Jaques-Dalcroze.

Csikszentmihalyi, M. and Custodero, L.A. (2002). Forward. In: T. Sullivan and L. Willingham (Eds), *Creativity and Music Education* (pp. xiv–xvi). Edmonton: Canadian Music Educators' Association.

Daley, C. (2013). *Moved to Learn: Dalcroze Applications to Choral Pedagogy and Practice* (Unpublished DMA dissertation). University of Toronto, USA.

Damasio, A. (2000). *The Feeling of What Happens: Body, Emotion and the Making of Consciousness*. London: Vintage.

Dénes, T. (1965). Catalogue Complet. In: F. Martin, T. Dénes, A. Berchtold, H. Gagnebin, B. Reichel, C.-L. Dutoit and E. Stadler (Eds), *Emile Jaques-Dalcroze: L'homme, le compositeur, le créateur de la rythmique* (pp. 461–572). Neuchâtel: Editions de la Baconnière.

DeNora, T. (2000). *Music in Everyday Life*. Cambridge: Cambridge University Press.

Dewey, J. (1934). *Art as Experience*. New York: Penguin.

Greenhead, K. (2009). Plastique Animée: Yesterday, Today and Tomorrow … ? *Le Rythme*, 2009, 37–40. Retrieved 24 May 2015 from http://www.fier.com/wordpress/documents/le-rythme-archives/#leRythme2009.

Greenhead, K. (2016). Becoming Music: Transformative Experience and the Development of Agency Through Dynamic Rehearsal. *Arts and Humanities in Higher Education*, special issue, H. Gaunt (Ed.).

Greenhead, K. and Habron, J. (2015). The Touch of Sound: Dalcroze Eurhythmics as a Somatic Practice. *Journal of Dance and Somatic Practices*, 7(1), 93–112.

Habron, J., Jesuthasan, J. and Bourne, C. (2012). *Moving into Composition – the Experiences of Student Composers During a Short Course of Dalcroze Eurhythmics*. Higher Education Academy. Retrieved 24 May 2015 from http://scotland.heacademy.ac.uk/assets/documents/seminars/disciplines/Moving_into_Composition_report.pdf.

Herholz, S.C. and Zatorre, R.J. (2012). Musical Training as Framework for Brain Plasticity: Behavior, Function and Structure. *Neuron*, 76(3), 486–502.

Hodges, D. and Gruhn, W. (2012). Implications of Neurosciences and Brain Research for Music Teaching and Learning. In: G.E. McPherson and G.F. Welch (Eds), *The Oxford Handbook of Music Education, vol. 1* (pp. 206–23). Oxford: Oxford University Press.

Immordino-Yang, M.H. and Damasio, A. (2011). We Feel Therefore We Learn: The relevance of Affective and Social Neuroscience to Education. *LEARNing Landscapes*, 5(1), 115–32.

Jaques-Dalcroze, E. (1916a). *Méthode Jaques-Dalcroze: La Rythmique*. Lausanne: Jobin et Cie.

Jaques-Dalcroze, E. (1916b). A bâtons rompus. *Le Rythme*, 1, 3–17.

Jaques-Dalcroze, E. (1921/1967). *Rhythm, Music and Education*. 2nd ed. Translated by H.F. Rubenstein. Woking: Dalcroze Society.

Jaques-Dalcroze, E. (1924). Lettre aux rythmiciens. *Le Rythme*, 13, 1–8.

Jaques-Dalcroze, E. (1942). *Souvenirs: Notes et critiques*. Neuchâtel: Editions Victor Attinger.

Jarvis, P. (2006). *Towards a Comprehensive Theory of Human Learning*. Oxford: Routledge.

Juntunen, M.-L. and Westerlund, H. (2001). Digging Dalcroze, or, Dissolving the Mind-body Dualism: Philosophical and Practical Remarks on the Musical Body in Action. *Music Education Research*, 3(2), 203–14.

Leman, M. (2010). Music, Gesture, and the Formation of Embodied Meaning. In: R.I. Godøy and M. Leman (Eds), *Musical Gestures: Sound, Movement, and Meaning* (pp. 126–53). Oxford: Routledge.

Lowe, G. (2002). Creativity and Motivation. In: T. Sullivan and L. Willingham (Eds), *Creativity and Music Education* (pp. 89–99). Edmonton: Canadian Music Educators' Association.

Malloch, S. and Trevarthen, C. (Eds) (2009). *Communicative Musicality: Exploring the Basis of Human Companionship*. Oxford: Oxford University Press.

Mathieu, L. (2010). Un regard actuel sur la rythmique Jaques-Dalcroze. *Recherche en éducation musicale*, 28, 17–27.

Mathieu, L. (2013). Dalcroze Eurhythmics in the 21st Century: Issues, Trends and Perspectives. Keynote address presented at *Movements in Music Education: First International Conference of Dalcroze Studies*, 24–26 July 2013, Coventry, UK.

Mathieu, L. (2016). De la formation auditive et corporelle à l'expression musicale: Une démarche de création et de formation artistique. In: F. Chaîné et al. (Eds), *Réfléchir à la formation artistique*. Québec: Les Presses de l'Université Laval.

Matsunobu, K. (2007). Japanese Perspectives and Research on the Body. In: L. Bresler (Ed.), *International Handbook of Research in Arts Education, Part 1* (pp. 1107–8). Dordrecht: Springer.

Mayo, S. (2005). *The Movement of Music: A Study of Karin Greenhead's 'Dynamic Rehearsal'* (Unpublished MMus dissertation). Royal Northern College of Music, Manchester, UK.

Meerkat Films (2014). *Dalcroze – Plastique Animée* [DVD]. Newcastle: Meerkat Film Productions.

Moore, S.F. (1992). *The Writings of Emile Jaques-Dalcroze: Towards a Theory for the Performance of Musical Rhythm* (Unpublished PhD thesis). Indiana University, USA.

Ofsted (2012). *Music in Schools: Wider Still, and Wider*. Retrieved 24 May 2015 from http://webarchive.nationalarchives.gov.uk/20141124154759/http://www.ofsted.gov.uk/resources/music-schools-wider-still-and-wider.

Peters, M. (2004). Education and the Philosophy of the Body: Bodies of Knowledge and Knowledges of the Body. In: L. Bresler (Ed.), *Knowing Bodies, Moving Minds: Towards Embodied Teaching and Learning* (pp. 13–27). Dordrecht: Kluwer Academic Publishers.

Rabinowitch, T.-C., Cross, I. and Burnard, P. (2012). Musical Group Interaction, Intersubjectivity and Merged Subjectivity. In: D. Reynolds and M. Reason (Eds), *Kinesthetic Empathy in Creative and Cultural Practices* (pp. 109–120). Bristol: Intellect.

Sawyer, R.K. (2011). *Structure and Improvisation in Creative Teaching*. Cambridge: Cambridge University Press.

Sawyer, R.K., John-Steiner, V., Moran, S., Sternberg, R.J., Feldman, D.H., Nakamura, J. and Csikszentmihalyi, M. (2003). *Creativity and Development*. New York: Oxford University Press.

Schön, D.A. (1987). *Educating the Reflective Practitioner*. San Francisco, CA: Jossey-Bass Publishers.

Seitz, J.A. (2005). Dalcroze, the Body, Movement and Musicality. *Psychology of Music*, (3)4, 419–35.

Sheets-Johnstone, M., (2011). *The Primacy of Movement*. 2nd ed. Amsterdam: John Benjamins Publishing Company.

Sheets-Johnstone, M. (2014). Animation: Analyses, Elaborations, and Implications. *Husserl Studies*, 30(3), 247–68.

Spurgeon, D. (2002). Fostering Creativity in Dance Students. In: T. Sullivan and L. Willingham (Eds), *Creativity and Music Education* (pp. 140–50). Edmonton: Canadian Music Educators' Association.

Stern, D.N. (2010). *Forms of Vitality: Exploring Dynamic Experience in Psychology, the Arts, Psychotherapy, and Development*. Oxford: Oxford University Press.

Sternberg, R.J. (2003). The Development of Creativity as a Decision-making Process. In: R.K. Sawyer, V. John-Steiner, S. Moran, R.J. Sternberg, D.H. Feldman, J. Nakamura and M. Csikszentmihalyi, *Creativity and Development* (pp. 91–138). New York: Oxford University Press.

Stubley, E.V. (1998). Being in the Body, Being in the Sound: A Tale of Modulating Identities and Lost Potential. *Journal of Aesthetic Education,* 32(4), 93–105.

Swanson, D.M. (2007). Ubuntu: An African Contribution to (Re)Search for/with a 'Humble Togetherness'. *Journal of Contemporary Issues in Education,* 2(2), 53–67.

Tochon, F.V. (2011). Deep Education: Assigning a Moral Role to Academic Work. *Educação Sociedade & Culturas*, 33, 17–35.

Tutu, D. (1999). *No Future Without Forgiveness*. New York: Doubleday.

Van der Merwe, L. (2015). The First Experiences of Music Students with Dalcroze-inspired Activities: A Phenomenological Study. *Psychology of Music*, 43(3), 390–406.

Webster, P. (2002). Creative Thinking in Music: Advancing a Model. In: T. Sullivan and L. Willingham (Eds), *Creativity and Music Education* (pp. 16–34). Edmonton: Canadian Music Educators' Association.

Wiggins, J. (2002). Creative Process as Meaningful Music Thinking. In: T. Sullivan and L. Willingham (Eds), *Creativity and Music Education* (pp. 78–88). Edmonton: Canadian Music Educators' Association.

Willingham, L. (2002). Creativity and the Problem with Music. In: T. Sullivan and L. Willingham (Eds), *Creativity and Music Education* (pp. xvii–xxi). Edmonton: Canadian Music Educators' Association.

16 Creativity and community in an entrepreneurial undergraduate music module

Fay Hield and Stephanie Pitts

Higher education institutions (HEIs) have been awash with buzzwords in the last decade or so, as teaching has become 'entrepreneurial', 'enquiry-based', 'reflective', 'collaborative' and 'creative' (for example, see Gaunt and Westerlund, 2013; Burnard and Haddon, 2015). While the words may change with sometimes alarming rapidity, these approaches share an underlying encouragement to academics to think creatively about educational practice, and to consider the impact of students' learning experiences on their broader development and future destinations. The 'Music in the Community' module that forms a case study for this chapter came about through one such University of Sheffield initiative around 'enterprise' education – a term used (often interchangeably with 'entrepreneurial' education) to capture the interplay of thinking and doing through cycles of reflexive and experiential learning.

First popularised in school curricula with an increasing focus on preparation for work and citizenship, enterprise learning involves students having 'the freedom to come up with ideas for creating and maintaining a project, take responsibility for it and experience first-hand learning which offers a real sense of utility and audience' (Deuchar, 2004: 224). The approach has relevance for university-level musicians who need to be responsive and flexible thinkers in their learning and their future careers, and worked well as a framework for our shared research and teaching interests in community music. Our new undergraduate module put students in touch with community groups in Sheffield and engaged them in commissioned pieces of research and planning around potential musical activities. These community-based projects were intended to support and enrich the organisations while developing the students' skills in managing group work, applying their musical skills to new contexts, and articulating and evaluating the benefits of music in community settings.

Authors more experienced than us in the teaching of community music have pointed out the risks of the 'marriage of convenience' (Cole, 2011) which links formal sites of learning (HEIs) with the activist roots of many community groups, risking a clash of cultures that might be unhelpful for both parties – and particularly for the students who traverse the two. While Moran and Loening (2011) write in positive terms about their experience of 'knowledge exchange' as a motivation for research connections between academics and community musicians, Williamson, Cloonan and Frith (2011) have pointed to the 'knowledge resistance' that can inhibit the sharing of mutually valuable perspectives across institutional boundaries. Despite these cautionary notes, the value of learning within community contexts has also been affirmed in previous case studies (Mellor, 2011), and the potential for benefit to both universities and community partners has been highlighted through the development of communities of practice (Hart and Wolff, 2006). We therefore embarked on the module with a naïve enthusiasm for broadening our students' (and our own) experiences, learning from and with local community partners, and hopefully contributing something to the valuable musical work that was taking place in the city.

Having now taught the module twice, with different partners and students involved, this chapter offers us the opportunity to reflect on how a module which aimed to be 'enterprising' brought with it many creative and educational challenges – for us, the students and the community partners. These challenges came at all levels, from module planning through the design of the research briefs with the partners to facilitating the students' group work and deciding on the fairest ways to assess their learning.

Priorities and possibilities in module design

Our 'Music in the Community' module was offered to second- and third-year music undergraduates at the University of Sheffield in Spring 2013 and Autumn 2014. We recognised from the outset that we had insufficient time (and indeed expertise) during the course of a twelve-week module to train our students as 'community musicians' as defined by Higgins (2012) – namely, musicians with the skills to design and deliver semi-professionalised politically motivated music educational interventions. Instead, we focused on building their understanding of the practical effects and theoretical positioning of community music in its various forms, through interdisciplinary weekly lectures, discussions and reading, and applying and further developing this understanding through a reflective journal and a group research project. Following Kolb's (1984) 'experiential learning cycle', we designed the module to combine traditional lecture formats with practical engagement and to encourage connections between group and individual learning. Within the enterprise framework of the module, this diversity of approaches enabled us to explore and emphasise creativity in multiple forms. Alongside building individual creativity, students worked to develop collaborative creativity in their groups, communal and intercultural creativity with their community partners, and empathetic creativity as they navigated the experiences and needs of the wider community (Burnard and Haddon, 2015). Following Csikszentmihalyi's (1999) assertion that creativity is 'the ability to add something new', we focused on advancing our students' skills in identifying opportunities for the development of new approaches rather than specific skill-set transfer.

Our partner organisations were drawn from the diverse musical provision in the Sheffield area: in 2013, the students were commissioned to produce feasibility studies for musical projects to support mental health service users (Sheffield NHS

Trust) and refugees and asylum seekers (Learn for Life), and in 2014 we worked with an urban regeneration group (Heeley Development Trust). In each case, the partner organisations were already engaged in some musical provision, but were looking for ways to evaluate and expand this, or to demonstrate its effects to external funders. The students' task was to review existing provision and spot the gaps and potential in the organisations' activities: while a few students engaged in practical workshop delivery as a way of demonstrating and developing their ideas, their main creative input was in the design and justification of their plans. All partners expressed awareness that there might be costs in staff time and potential inconvenience to the organisation, but also a clear hope that the projects might yield valuable insights and information.

In the first lecture of the module, the partners came to meet the students, who then worked in groups of six to eight to develop a strategy for fulfilling the research brief, which had been written by us in consultation with the partners, but with sufficient flexibility for the students to find their own focus and interests for their project. Heeley Development Trust, for example, were already putting on concerts, but wanted to know how to reach more of the local audience, to extend their provision to children and young people, and to gather evidence to demonstrate the value of their activities.

Alongside their group work, we wanted the students to develop their individual understanding of music and/in communities, so we asked them to write a weekly reflective journal, which they submitted online for feedback before selecting three entries for assessment. This too was a creative challenge for the students, as they were required to think and write in new ways and to engage in personal analyses and interpretation rather than drawing solely upon established theories. We provided guidelines that encouraged them to move beyond description of their learning experiences into genuine reflection on their changing thinking (Department of Education and Training, 2007). Finally, the students also submitted an essay – the most 'traditional' element of our multifaceted assessment approach, but one which still allowed the students freedom in their choice of essay topic and led several of them into new areas of community music not explored in the lectures and set readings.

The requirement to assess generated a sometimes uncomfortable tension between the encouragement of risk and exploration that was central to our understanding of developing creativity and entrepreneurial skills, and the provision of criteria, word limits and deadlines. We recognised the barriers to creative teaching identified by Spendlove and Wyse (2008: 16) of 'playing safe' and being constrained by accountability – in this case, to our partner organisations as well as to our students. Of particular concern to us and the students was the assessment of group work, which is notoriously problematic (Burdett, 2003) despite its increasing presence in higher education (Hillyard, Gillespie and Littig, 2010). We made a deliberate choice to avoid the further pitfalls of peer assessment and self-assessment (McLaughlin and Simpson, 2004), choosing instead to weight the assessed components more heavily towards the individual essay (50 per cent) and the reflective journal (20 per cent). While this alleviated the students' fears, expressed at the point of module enrolment, about the negative impact that undertaking group work might have on their marks, it resulted later in complaints that the high level of work involved in the group report (30 per cent) should have been recognised through a more substantial weighting. However, the implicit link between the weekly reflections and the group work did have the advantage of focusing the students' attention on their own learning over time, which previous studies have shown to be a critical dimension of effective group work (Goodman and Dabbish, 2011), and one which focuses evaluations of student creative practices by measuring success as *process* rather than *product* or *output* (see Bennett, Reid and Petocz, 2015).

Research methods

To reflect more closely for this chapter on the students' experiences of the module, we sent them a short research questionnaire after the assessment process had been completed. In this, we asked a series of multiple-choice and open-ended questions about their learning in the module and the ways in which this might connect with their other experiences as music students. We explored how their experience of the module fitted with our conception of it as enterprising and creative by asking them 'What should we call this kind of learning?' and offering a selection of possible descriptors drawn from the higher education pedagogy literature (see Table 16.1 in the discussion below). We also sought students' permission to use the reflective journals they submitted weekly during the module, as these had proved to be rich with examples of the creative application of academic knowledge derived from lectures and reading to the practical community contexts in which the student groups found themselves. These data collection methods were approved through the University of Sheffield research ethics processes, and students were assured of their anonymity and their freedom to participate or not as they chose, without any consequence for their assessment or future learning.

Relatively small numbers of responses were received, perhaps due to the unusual nature of the request and its timing around the assessment period. From the 2013 cohort of 17 students, five questionnaires and journals were submitted, while from the 2014 cohort of 26 students, we received only two responses. While the data collected cannot therefore be considered as representative of the two cohorts, the responses did add useful perspectives to our own reflections on the modules, providing illustrative case studies that helped to question and develop our own observations as module tutors. In the discussion that follows, students have been allocated pseudonyms and any personally identifying details have been removed. We also consulted the partner organisations about anonymity, and all agreed to be named in our chapter, allowing us to acknowledge here their substantial contribution to the students' learning.

Creativity in student learning and experience

With its enquiry-driven and entrepreneurial approaches (Craft, Cremin and Burnard, 2008), the 'Music in the Community' module aimed to engage the students in crea-tive learning both at the individual level, as they reflected on their learning in their weekly journals and carried out independent reading for their essays, and collaboratively, as they worked on their group project and liaised with the external partners. The students' responses to these challenges were evident in the enthusiasm and anxieties they expressed at different points in the module; in the discussion that follows, we explore how their individual and group experiences contributed to creative learning, allowing them to take risks, generate new knowledge and communicate their understanding to new audiences (Spendlove and Wyse, 2008).

Individual creativity and reflection

The impact of the module upon the students was demonstrated in their reflective journals, in which we had asked them to make connections between their deliberate learning through lectures and wider reading, the progress of their group work, and their more informal encounters with music. This style of writing was quite unfamiliar to the students, and some took to it with greater ease than others, capturing moments of understanding that might otherwise not have been revealed in essays or class discussions: 'I don't class myself as a musician, as for me, I never knew there was another way – I just assumed everyone's parents got their guitars out before breakfast – and so I never made the choice to be musical, it just happened' (Anna's journal, April 2013). Other students found the journal writing more challenging, sometimes missing weeks or making a very formal entry that resisted the invitation to be reflective: 'Having decided on our group aims and objectives last week we split the workload into more manageable tasks for individuals of the group to carry out. I think this will work well as everyone now [has] a specific task in relation to the larger project' (Jo's journal, February 2013).

Students occasionally used the journal as a 'cry for help', commenting on group dynamics that were becoming hard to manage, or personal difficulties with workload or anxiety in this or other modules. Responses of this nature raised questions over who the students perceived their audience to be: writing at once for feedback, future assessment and their own reflective learning clearly presented some challenges in finding an authentic 'voice' with which each student felt comfortable. Other authors have noted similarly that obligatory reflection brings with it some paradoxes that not all students will readily resolve (Conway et al., 2012). Few students commented on this in our survey, but among the broader responses were some acknowledgements that keeping a journal had been a useful learning tool that might be taken forward into future modules (see also Absalom and De Saint Léger, 2011).

There was agreement among our survey respondents that the module had been 'reflective', although this was set in the context of general agreement with most of the words we had offered to describe the module. While some students made selections from the list provided, most retained nearly all the 12 suggested descriptions, as shown in Table 16.1.

The only surprise here is the low rating for 'individual' experience, given that the majority of the assessment was for individual work. The group work and collaborative nature of the module appear to have dominated these respondents'

Table 16.1 Words chosen to describe the student experience (with responses out of 7)

Enterprising (5)	Problem-solving (5)	Outward-looking (5)	Individual (2)
Challenging (6)	Creative (5)	Engaging (5)	Difficult (4)
Reflective (6)	Group-focused (6)	Problematic (4)	Collaborative (7)

overall experiences, and our attempts to include individual and collective learning in the module had perhaps resulted more in an overloading of experience and assessment rather than the balance we had hoped for. Claire's survey response confirmed this with the comment that there were 'quite a lot of different tasks going on at the same time'. However, individual learning and self-discovery were evident in the students' journals and survey responses, where they expressed new realisations about themselves, their possible careers or their intentions to partic-ipate in community music in the future: 'I feel that I have learnt not to worry about a situation before it has even happened. I have also become more aware of my own anxieties and feel I can now be prepared in managing my own enthusi-asm and opinions within a group context' (Beth's journal, February 2013); 'The first lecture was actually quite emotional for me as it was the first time I realised that I could have a future doing something that heavily involved both people and music in such a positive way' (Fiona's survey response, February 2015).

The students' multiple descriptions of the kind of learning they had experienced (see Table 16.1) were confirmed in their comments about how the connection between the module and the wider community had made their learning feel more 'real' or significant – described by Fiona as coming out of the 'book bubble' of student life: 'Felt more empowered in learning, the responsibility of a project and contact with professionals motivates me more because it feels more geared towards a professional application of learning and it makes my contributions feel more valuable' (Claire's survey response, May 2013); 'The Music in the Community module has definitely got me thinking more about my academic work, how different points relate to each other and how actually everything studied can help out somewhere else in the degree' (Jo's survey response, May 2013).

Liz Mellor has reported similar blurring of boundaries between academic and applied learning in her teaching of community music modules, as students 'acknowledge their developing skills of social and musical flexibility across a variety of settings' (2011: 271). These reflections on finding relationships between and beyond modules are a reminder that learning in HEIs can be a disjointed experience, for which reflective learning provides a partial solution:

> Higher education socializes individuals to view time and process in the same way that it socializes them to view and understand knowledge – as cumulative or linear bricks in a wall rather than as nesting and interacting frameworks coexisting in creative interaction. ... Altering one's approach to incorporate an awareness of the present moment radically changes the lens through which one views the world.
>
> (Rogers, 2001: 53)

Students in university music departments are expected to make connections between their instrumental lessons and their academic learning and their degree studies and their wider identities as musicians and young adults (Pitts, 2003). The reflective journals – and indeed, the post-module survey – appear to have heightened students' awareness of those connections, offering them a tool for assessing their own learning and considering its relevance for their current and future lives.

Group creativity and collaboration

Working in groups brought particular challenges to the students, and we engaged with these through sessions dedicated to exploring theoretically how groups function and mapping individuals' roles within their specific group. In week two, we used Belbin Team Roles theory[1] to discuss how teams are made up of different people adopting different roles: following use of Belbin's chart demonstrating contribution and allowable weaknesses for each role, we asked students to individually identify themselves as one of the nine 'roles' (plant, resource investigator, coordinator, shaper, monitor evaluator, teamworker, implementer, completer finisher, specialist), and plotted these on a wheel grouped under 'social', 'thinking' and 'action'. The group could then identify any potential gaps in their natural collective leaning and work constructively and consciously to address these. This had the additional effect of encouraging students to assign leaders and set task responsibilities at the start of the project. For some, this was a useful managerial device that led to further reflection on their own learning and behaviour: 'I learnt new skills regarding ways to work around naturally domineering people' (Anna's survey response, May 2013); 'I have learnt about myself as a part of a group and what my strengths and weaknesses are. I have learnt not to try and control a group work situation – to take a step back and trust others' (Beth's survey response, May 2013).

Group work analysis was revisited halfway through the module, with a conflict-resolution and team-building exercise, the 'four word build' – an exercise supplied by the University of Sheffield Enterprise Centre. This involved each member of the group choosing four words they felt best defined their project. In pairs, these were discussed and the total of eight words reduced to an agreed selection of four. This process occurred twice more, until each group had a set of four words that were then read out to the whole class as the distillation of each group's thinking about its project work. While this was useful for focusing the attention of the group on each contributor's understandings and the necessity to have a group consensus, the more powerful impact came when we asked everyone to reflect silently on the process of the exercise. How many of their words made it to the final cut? Was this because they were the best words, or because they argued loudest? How well did they consider other people's ideas? If their ideas did not make the cut, why did they not speak up more? This was a powerful moment, as the students were being asked to consider specific behaviour rather than a preconceived idea of how they thought they worked – a challenge beyond classifying themselves in a Belbin team role.

Communicating creativity

In addition to the challenges of group dynamics and function, communication between the students and the community partners was another area of potential tension. This communication occurred as a three-stage process, shifting the information transfer power from partner to student as the projects developed. In the first instance, the partners visited the university to introduce their organisations and the briefs. At stage two, the students met with the partners in the community contexts to answer student-generated enquiries. In the third stage, the students reported their findings to the partners on university premises, but away from the weekly classroom, through a presentation given in the University of Sheffield Enterprise Centre.

Reaching out beyond their group of peers, the students also connected with communities in Sheffield, in several cases approaching the client brief by investigating existing musical provision in the city, and finding a world of community choirs, active amateur musicians and resourceful musical projects that often remains hidden to students: 'Being able to work with and being given a serious project with organisations outside the uni ... the module felt like it made a real impact rather than just being theoretical' (Beth's survey response, May 2013). Awareness of the impact of their research shifted the students' focus from the generic to the targeted: 'We need to ensure that we tailor our work towards Learn for Life's specific needs and not just come up with a generic idea that will not be feasible. ... We need to ensure that the information we have gathered is useful' (Beth's journal, April 2013).

The students' concern that their research should be targeted on the partners' needs meant that each group wanted to speak with the partners to clarify their projects and gather data about the organisations. In all cases, this took longer to come to fruition than the students wished, and in one instance there was no mid-point communication between the students and the partner. This was a source of stress for the students: 'This week has been quite trying, not in terms of group work, just in terms of the logistics of working with a charity. We have found that ... we may need to factor in a lengthy period for them to reply to us' (Beth's journal, February 2013); 'I would have liked the partners to have collaborated with us, as we were not sure whether we were heading in the right direction a lot of the time, and it would have been great to be able to contact them more easily' (Anna's survey response, May 2013).

While many students found this frustrating, it gave them a very real experience of interacting with professionals conducting varied types of work within the community, and helped them place their own projects within the workscape of our partners' wider obligations. It also gave them the experience of taking ownership of their ideas, working independently, translating the brief in their own ways and having to make autonomous judgements on whether their ideas 'fit the brief'. This differs considerably from the majority of their other modules, where assignment guidelines and marking rubrics are focused inward, on the learning objectives and criteria of the degree, rather than outward towards the wider application of newly generated knowledge. However, for one dissatisfied student, this emphasis on the needs of the community partners did not meet his expectations of the module: 'I presumed we would be actively taking part in a community project, or at least gaining first-hand experience. It kind of felt like we were just evaluating work that had already been done' (Edward's survey response, February 2015). Edward's response shows an expectation that practical, musical creativity would be at the heart of the module, and suggests that we had not made our focus on developing the impact of pre-existing musical skills sufficiently clear (at least to him). Further explicit theorising of the creative applications of musical knowledge could have helped to address this more directly – as indeed would a longer-term connection with the community partners in which students voluntarily implemented some of their ideas beyond the scope of the module.

In the final stages of the module, the students presented their findings to the community partners. While they were universally met with enthusiasm and gratitude – thereby fulfilling the definition of creative learning which emphasises 'outcomes which are judged by appropriate observers to be original and of value' (Spendlove and Wyse, 2008: 14) – there were also instances where criticisms of existing practices were presented. It was interesting to us as tutors to see the students alter their appreciation of the anonymity of academic study: while they typically write their thoughts in essays only accessed by a supportive tutor, here they were openly criticising the working practice of people they had been working closely with for the previous three months. The desire to achieve a good module mark meant they sought creative and dramatic recommendations; however, these were not always realistic to the circumstances, and some reports were a hybrid mix of community-based research and rather more speculative ideas, intended to meet the perceived assessment aims of the module.

Our chosen forms of assessment differed from those of other modules that the students had previously experienced. This caused anxieties for some students, and was a potential barrier to participation for Anna – she chose to persevere, but this could have influenced other students' decisions not to engage: 'Not being heavily essay based did put me off initially, as I know that is where my strengths lie (and I HATE GROUP WORK), and in addition to this, not having done any presentations before I was unsure of how well I could do in the assessment' (Anna's survey response, May 2013).

Anna was not alone in her insecurities about how the group work and presentation would affect her assessment, and students appeared to feel a lack of clear measurement of their progress, despite our provision of ongoing feedback through mentoring of the group work and commenting on individual reflective journals and draft essays. Previous studies have shown that students favour con-tinual assessment of their development through a module (Rees, 2007), with this approach making little difference to the final marks, but providing a stronger sense of progress. In future versions of this module, we might need to think further about how to balance the genuine uncertainties of the community partnerships with the students' anxieties about their learning and assessment. Tackling this dilemma more directly would allow us – and the students – to embrace the riskiness of the module activities more wholeheartedly, avoiding the danger of limiting creative learning by 'the safe production of predictable rather than creative outcomes' (Spendlove and Wyse, 2008: 15).

The students' work was warmly received by the community partners, with great value placed upon the students' contributions, while remaining sensitive towards the limitations of their expertise and available time. For Beth, identifying as a student had a profound impact as she more deeply considered her place in the world as others might see her:

> Jill (from Learn for Life) had pointed out that whilst we were using labels [to describe mental health service users], people also label students with negative connotations. ... This experience made me more aware of how we describe and discuss people who are not the same as ourselves for whatever reason. I have become more aware of how I come across to people and how the student population as a whole is perceived by the outer world.
>
> (Beth's journal, May 2013)

Conclusions

The opportunity to reflect in this chapter on the enterprising and creative processes of this module has highlighted some features of learning music in higher education that have potentially wider implications. The combination of group work and individual reflection, for example, has illustrated how personal, social and musical development are intertwined in meaningful musical learning, as our students applied their skills in new contexts and reflected on those processes in their journals. Working as a group and representing their group in communication with the community partners required the students to situate their own learning in a broader context, through processes that to them seemed valuable, if sometimes challenging or frustrating. Some made discoveries about potential future career directions, while all confronted their own strengths and weaknesses as learners and group members in ways that could have an impact on their life and learning choices. In addition, they gained a sense of how their student identity connects with musical life outside the university, so broadening their sense of how and where community music activity flourishes. These connections from self to group to community can sometimes be lacking in higher education, and while they might not have a place in every module, their stronger presence in university music departments could be beneficial for staff, students and community partners alike.

The module design and aims engaged us in creative processes as lecturers, both in designing the module to include genuine risk and exploration of real-world challenges and in embracing ideas of reflective and collaborative learning. It is reassuring to find in the research literature that we are not the first to note the increase in staff time and commitment needed to run a module of this kind (for example, Lea, Stephenson and Troy, 2003). Reviewing his module on 'history in the community', Winstanley (1992: 62) observes that 'demands made by students are less predictable in terms of their timing and nature, as well as being more emotionally and intellectually challenging'. The students' learning experiences in our module were much more visible to us than in a traditional lecture format, as we engaged with them in discussions of the progress of the group work and responded to their weekly reflections on their learning, reading and thinking. Our uncertainties and in-the-moment responses will have been more visible to them too, requiring a mutual rethinking of the academic's role that could usefully have been explored more deeply or overtly. Such an approach offers one form of resistance to the notion of 'student as consumer' (Molesworth, Nixon and Scullion, 2009) by positioning knowledge as a form of co-production between learners, teachers and community partners, and highlighting the different needs and doubts that each party brings to the process of education.

Each partner has so far been involved for one project each, with the first year's two partners acting primarily as traditional consultant employers setting a brief and receiving the results. Heeley Development Trust, however, has expressed a desire to have a future cohort revisit the organisation and monitor the impact of the changes applied from our students' recent recommendations. This suggests an ongoing relationship between the partner and the university beyond that particular student group, following a pattern close to an 'action research' cycle, whereby hypotheses are applied and evaluated in practice, adapted and reapplied (Coghlan and Brannick, 2010). By setting briefs, supporting research and implementing findings, our partners are interacting with our students to produce new knowledge about their organisations and ways of working. This blurs the boundaries between the established academic institution and the field, placing the partners as collaborators in the process – co-teachers, co-researchers and co-producers of knowledge (Lassiter and Campbell, 2010).

So what next for 'Music in the Community'? In future versions of the module, we will need to think further about the clarity of our objectives, finding the balance between learning about community music and learning how to learn. We have also noted the students' appetite for practical training in community music delivery, currently addressed through extracurricular activities such as our student-led Music in the City volunteering programme. We have seen the potential for students to make links between different aspects of their learning and, more significantly, between their degree and their future career plans. The students' practical engagement in the community offered opportunities to see themselves as creative practitioners in the wider world, building connections between their current experiences and those of the partners and visiting lecturers. Longer-term engagement with the partners could help see some of these projects realised in practice, so offering scope for another cycle of creative and reflective learning, with potential benefits for students and community groups alike. In this exploratory attempt to place creativity and community at the heart of students' learning in this module, we have exposed some of the conflicts and challenges that underpin these approaches, but also highlighted the potential for building communities of practice that include us, our students and the wider musical world.

Note

1 See 'Belbin® Team Roles': http://www.belbin.com/ (retrieved 24 February 2015).

References

Absalom, M. and De Saint Léger, D. (2011). 'Reflecting on Reflection: Learner Perceptions of Diaries and Blogs in Tertiary Language Studies'. *Arts and Humanities in Higher Education*, 10(2), 189–211.

Bennett, D., Reid, A. and Petocz, P. (2015). 'On the Other Side of the Divide: Making Sense of Student Stories of Creativities in Music'. In: P. Burnard and E. Haddon (eds), *Activating Diverse Musical Creativities: Teaching and Learning in Higher Music Education* (pp. 21–35). London: Bloomsbury.

Burdett, J. (2003). 'Making Groups Work: University Students' Perceptions'. *International Education Journal*, 4(3), 177–91.

Burnard, P. and Haddon, E. (eds) (2015). *Activating Diverse Musical Creativities: Teaching and Learning in Higher Music Education*. London: Bloomsbury.

Coghlan, D. and Brannick, T. (2010). *Doing Action Research in Your Own Organization*. 3rd edn. London: Sage.

Cole, B. (2011). 'Community Music and Higher Education: A Marriage of Convenience'. *International Journal of Community Music*, 4(2), 79–89.

Conway, C., Christensen, S., Garlock, M., Hansen, E., Reese, J. and Zerman, T. (2012). 'Experienced Music Teachers' Views on the Role of Journal Writing in the First Year of Teaching'. *Research Studies in Music Education*, 34(1), 45–60.

Craft, A., Cremin, T. and Burnard, P. (eds) (2008). *Creative Learning 3–11 and How We Document It*. Stoke-on-Trent: Trentham Books.

Csikszentmihalyi, M. (1999). 'Implications of a Systems Perspective for the Study of Creativity'. In: R.J. Sternberg (ed.), *Handbook of Creativity* (pp. 313–35). Cambridge: Cambridge University Press.

Department of Education and Training (2007). *A 'Critical' Reflection Framework: Information Sheet*. Victoria State Government, Australia. Retrieved 24 February 2015 from http://www.education.vic.gov.au/Documents/childhood/professionals/support/reffram.pdf.

Deuchar, R. (2004). 'Changing Paradigms: The Potential of Enterprise Education as an Adequate Vehicle for Promoting and Enhancing Education for Active and Responsible Citizenship: Illustrations from a Scottish Perspective'. *Oxford Review of Education*, 30(2), 223–39.

Gaunt, H. and Westerlund, H. (eds) (2013). *Collaborative Learning in Higher Music Education*. Farnham: Ashgate.

Goodman, P.S. and Dabbish, L.A. (2011). 'Methodological Issues in Measuring Group Learning'. *Small Group Research*, 42(4), 379–404.

Hart, A. and Wolff, D. (2006). 'Developing Local "Communities of Practice" Through Local Community–university Partnerships'. *Planning, Practice and Research*, 21(1), 121–38.

Higgins, L. (2012). *Community Music: In Theory and in Practice*. New York: Oxford University Press.

Hillyard, C., Gillespie, D. and Littig, P. (2010). 'University Students' Attitudes about Learning in Small Groups After Frequent Participation'. *Active Learning in Higher Education*, 11(1), 9–20.

Kolb, D.A. (1984). *Experiential Learning: Experience as the Source of Learning and Development*. Englewood Cliffs, NJ: Prentice-Hall.

Lassiter, L.E. and Campbell, E. (2010). 'From Collaborative Ethnography to Collaborative Pedagogy: Reflections on the Other Side of Middletown Project and Community–university Research Partnerships'. *Anthropology and Education Quarterly*, 41(4), 370–85.

Lea, S.J., Stephenson, D. and Troy, J. (2003). 'Higher Education Students' Attitudes to Student-centred Learning: Beyond "Educational Bulimia"?' *Studies in Higher Education*, 28(3), 321–34.

McLaughlin, P. and Simpson, N. (2004). 'Peer Assessment in First Year University: How the Students Feel'. *Studies in Educational Evaluation*, 30(2), 135–49.

Mellor, L, (2011). 'What is "Known" in Community Music in Higher Education? Engagement, Emotional Learning and an Ecology of Ideas from the Student Perspective'. *International Journal of Community Music*, 4(3), 257–75.

Molesworth, M., Nixon, E. and Scullion, R. (2009). 'Having, Being and Higher Education: The Marketisation of the University and the Transformation of the Student into Consumer'. *Teaching in Higher Education*, 14(3), 277–87.

Moran, N. and Loening, G. (2011). 'Community Music Knowledge Exchange Research in Scottish Higher Education'. *International Journal of Community Music*, 4(2), 133–46.

Pitts, S.E. (2003). 'What Do Students Learn When We Teach Music? An Investigation of the "Hidden" Curriculum in a University Music Department'. *Arts and Humanities in Higher Education*, 2(3), 281–92.

Rees, C.A. (2007). 'The "Non-assessment" Assessment Project'. *Journal of Legal Education*, 57(4), 521–29.

Rogers, R.R. (2001). 'Reflection in Higher Education: A Concept Analysis'. *Innovative Higher Education*, 26(1), 37–57.

Spendlove, D. and Wyse, D. (2008). 'Creative Learning: Definitions and Barriers'. In: A. Craft, T. Cremin and P. Burnard (eds), *Creative Learning 3–11 and How We Document It* (pp. 11–18). Stoke-on-Trent: Trentham Books.

Williamson, J., Cloonan, M. and Frith, S. (2011). 'Having an Impact? Academics, the Music Industries and the Problem of Knowledge'. *International Journal of Cultural Policy*, 17(5), 459–74.

Winstanley, M.J. (1992). 'Group Work in the Humanities: History in the Community, a Case Study'. *Studies in Higher Education*, 17(1), 55–65.

17 Fostering effective group creativity

Ambrose Field

Introduction

The purpose of this chapter is to analyse the creative processes which enable groups to make new music in educational settings. While the discussion focuses on how this aim might be delivered in higher education, this chapter highlights important links between higher education and professional work. For the purposes of this study, a group[1] is defined as a collection of three or more students, and *individual creativity* is defined as the act of composition where only one person has the full responsibility for generating and refining the musical material – the traditional and iconic model of the composer working as a lone artist. While this concept is certainly still viable, this historical model is not necessarily always appropriate in the twenty-first century as it can actively hinder the realisation of ambitious, large-scale projects within the timescales expected by today's growing media industry. New skills are required for contemporary situations, and it is therefore proposed that group composition in education should not be conceived of as a larger-scale substitute for individual work. Today, group creativity is a professional activity in its own right, with its own set of specific challenges, opportunities and workflows. This chapter discusses these aspects, with a view to identifying opportunities for new practice.

Regarding group creativity as a substitute for individual creativity (perhaps due to time and resources pressure militating against individual tuition) can send powerful signals to students that they must work in a group due to inadequate educational provision. Yet in reality, our culture needs group creative processes. The speed of development of new art forms, musical techniques and ideas has been magnified through global media awareness and the free distribution of individual content on media sharing platforms. To help remain distinctive within an oversaturated sea of artistic content and to meet deadlines, professional creative projects such as compositions for film, public artwork development and popular music production are frequently accomplished in close-knit, bespoke teams whose members may be distributed across a wide variety of geographic locations. Music education has been slow to react to this situation, failing to adopt what is now a normal method of operation in the visual arts and design, where teamwork is valued as highly as individual creative output. Importantly, the balance between 'creativity' (as in creating something which might be new to the individual concerned) and 'innovation' (when that creative act has its own impact on the wider community) is important. If composition is to be a research-led activity, and not simply a new realisation (or outcome) of an existing practice or methodology, new ways of approaching materials, forms, structures and performance contexts must be investigated.

Problematically, finding these for their own sake isn't necessarily what music is about: music doesn't have to be innovative to be highly effective. Furthermore, every composer will have differing views on this issue, due to their own situation. For me, music is not technology or engineering: adding new features to a piece doesn't always make it any better or more appropriate to its context than a previous version. Yet I simultaneously enjoy building on existing work and refining techniques, and finding new approaches to existing musical situations. While innovation in science carries a chronological implication, today's new music may not necessarily be any more innovative than yesterday's new music. Style, genre and cultural relationships are factors in defining this complex situation. Innovation occurs observably and frequently in composition: in the kinds of material people choose to create, through the means with which they communicate it (including the reception processes of the audience) and in their unique approaches to solving creative problems. As a result, this chapter urges students to discover the new and develop innovative thinking through their own creative practice by asking focused *creative questions*, which I am defining as a practice-based equivalent of a research question (albeit one without specific procedural overtones).

Creative questions, such as the 'what if' scenarios outlined later in this chapter, absolve practitioners from having to invent radical new departures for music, and focus their enquiry on an aspect of their work which might require development. Creative questions can drive enquiry and help bridge the gap between what might be new to a student and what might be considered innovative work within a broader context, as to answer them, an appropriate contextual knowledge together with rigorous application and practical experimentation is required. Examples of this process, and the resulting relationship to group work-devising strategies, are highlighted later in this chapter. A new set of skills is required to produce musically competitive work for today's listeners, and it is argued that to achieve a sense of balance between personal development and impactful innovation, these skills are located in the management and organisation of creative collaborators as much as they are in traditional musicianship.

Today, creativity is also a popular recreational activity found within audiences for music. Increasing numbers of listeners are able to restructure, remix and re-create the music they consume. We owe it to our contemporary audiences to create new music which can provide enough substance to integrate with, withstand and, as required, transcend these processes. The next generation of professional composers will also need to provide musical material within tightly defined timescales, explore new forms of expression that are not direct hybrids of the old, and offer new insights into contemporary culture. Notably, these approaches may require a level of innovation larger than that which can be supplied by one individual working alone. Thus, the individual composer has never looked so alone in today's society – so why do university curricula exclusively prioritise the training of individual composers?

While individual attainment is a cornerstone of higher education, and there is a societal need for new and unique music, individual composition could be seen as a social artefact which has arisen from eighteenth- and nineteenth-century models of cultural information transmission. Here, the music simply flows down a one-way street from the individual composer to the consuming public. Today, there is no single reference point for culture, no special need for the romanticised mass adoption of unilateral iconic ideas, and no one-way information flow from producers to consumers. The unfolding argument presented here in support of group work should not be interpreted as a detraction from the craft of individual composition – instead, the intended purpose is to set out a stronger case for team-work today. Thus, group creativity has nothing to do with lessening the impact of originality and need not worry individuals who draw their 'line of empire' (Sterling, Wild and Lunenfeld, 2005: 10) around their individual branding and artistic processes. Group creativity does not threaten individuality, or produce results which are necessarily any worse than those made by individuals. Instead, it has considerable productivity and social benefits, many of which are compatible with contemporary culture and economics.

As would be expected, this situation is not new in industrial applications of composition. The popular music industry has already demonstrated the value of teamwork since the 1940s, as do film, television and media composition today. Notably, large-scale professional projects have long since outgrown the creative reach of one individual – there are few blockbuster movies made by just one person. Appropriate creative workflow strategies can be applied to group work to help the outcomes reflect individuality and innovation. To this end, we will look at the nature of *devising*, a process by which groups make new artistic works, to help reinvigorate group creativity in music education. Research into *distributed creativity*[2] (Sawyer and DeZutter, 2009) maps onto this domain, but there are some important differences. In the pedagogical approach set out here, my aim is to seek out models which enable creative individuals to focus their activity into well-designed group processes, rather than solely being an observed result of emergent behaviour.

I first need to deal with a persistent myth that group work can lead to the lowest common denominator of creativity. Taggar (2002) argues that in business situa-tions, appropriate domain-relevant skills are the key to avoiding this problem. Of course, group work can easily fail due to the wholesale transference of individ-ual working practices to group situations, and through a lack of analysis of the methodology by which ideas are created, reviewed and implemented. Without an understanding of how to negotiate a multi-person creative argument successfully, design by committee might result. This situation can be avoided by assessing the methods through which creative decisions are made, and evaluating the inter-action of those methods with learning and creative objectives. Today's media-dominated culture has new values for authorship and participation, which in turn have changed the concept of the musical work itself (Goehr, 1992). As the musical work as an iconic artefact now rarely exists, should our educational processes now need to adapt correspondingly?

Individual artistic work may not attract the economic currency it once did, whereas being able to manage it, apply it or aggregate it into new forms is big business. Group composition, through teamwork, can be highly adaptable and application-focused within the time available. As public musical products become aggregated into larger distribution networks, it is even more important that the artistic content they articulate is distinctive. There is now no room for musical composition that is observably similar to existing work – it will disappear in the information shadow created by today's methods of articulating consumer choice (information systems, commenting, blogs or social media). For example, the prevalence of technologies which enable creativity without cost have meant that even generic television 'library music' is rarely heard today. There is a problem, however: in professional music and in education, composers need to harness the work-power of a team while retaining something of the artistic distinctiveness and identity of an individual. These factors are also essential in enabling our graduate students for work-readiness and employability (Bennett and Burnard, 2016).

Facilitating creative teamwork starts with people management. It is worth noting that a *functional* group is more than just a collection of individuals. Katzenbach and Smith (2005) indicate that there is a large difference in effectiveness between groups of individuals gathered around a task and teams where individuals have their own responsibilities within more generally managed workflows. For creative group members to work productively, there needs to be agreement on how the workflow within a task is defined. Three distinctive situations can be proposed which foster team creativity:

1. stimulus–response creativity;
2. process-based devising;
3. frameworks-based workflows.

All three types of devising method have different combinations of input and output conditions, which in turn inform the way creative information is managed during the composition process.

About 'devising' processes

All devising processes represent a type of learning which is inherently non-linear, even though both the task itself and the outcome may be clear. For an individual student, there is no single pre-defined path to achievement nor prescribed sequence of actions that can be performed to bring about a successful creative outcome. To follow a prescribed path entirely would be to create replicas or clones of existing ideas. Instead, devising requires students to share their knowledge and modify their learning process as new situations unfold. Devising itself is a useful training activity for both research and professional work. It is not a straightforward process, and there are a number of barriers to achievement which need to be negotiated before successful group creativity can take place. The first barrier which needs to be dissolved is the idea that creativity cannot be taught (Torrance, 1972, addresses this through a substantial body of work undertaken in school education) and that group creativity only problematises this situation further. The right conditions for creativity need to be set up, and that is part of the job of the educator. Inspiring creativity can be a fragile process: university students may already have been used to particular creative methods from their school education, and each student will have different experiences and extramusical contexts to bring to the task. Given this, how can we bring a shared sense of musical purpose to this diversity?

The first approach, which I call *stimulus–response creativity*, is a well-known open-ended devising strategy employed in contexts ranging from primary schools to professional music ensembles. Stimulus–response creativity takes the form of an open-ended group response to fixed input conditions, with a stimulus drawn from the musical or extramusical world. Such a stimulus could be a line of poetry, a painting, a piece of interactive art, or as little as a single note on a stave. While creativity itself might not be able to be taught, it can certainly be encouraged, shaped and challenged by education, and it is important that educators *teach* those processes. Having a diverse set of unique, completely individual solutions to a problem is a situation which is largely confined to group composition in music. In physics, for example, Kim and Pak (2002) show that by the time students enter university, they have a reasonably common procedural approach to problem-solving which is not enhanced simply by solving more problems of the same types. Fortunately, this isn't the case in composition, and the educational challenge lies in creating a workflow which enables the diversity of initial response to be reviewed and evaluated from the early stages of a project, while maintaining the ongoing co-operation of the participants. Composers who work on their own rarely leverage the diversity of social and knowledge backgrounds that group creativity can bring to challenge the design stage of their works. This cultural strength should not be 'engineered out' of a work through increasing idea selectivity, as it is a unique asset of teamwork. It would also be tempting, in open-ended situations, to follow a well-worn creative cycle of create–review–reject–create. However, if this individual workflow is transported into a whole group situation, 'reject' can easily become personal and unproductive. The goal of idea selection processes in group work could instead be to come to a position on the task where each member of the group has had the potential to offer some individuality to the design process, rather than homing in on an individual response to a problem that is deemed suitable by the group (as this will disenfranchise the creativity of most members). So how can this be achieved? The answer lies partly in the typical and historical applications of stimulus–response creativity.

Stimulus–response devising

Used frequently in educational situations, after being developed significantly by John Paynter (in Paynter and Aston, 1970, and subsequently in Paynter, 1992), stimulus–response creativity helped liberate the compositional thinking of generations of schoolchildren. Paynter was able to inspire creativity without children becoming sidetracked into technical issues, due to the purposeful interaction of *defined input conditions* and *undefined creative outcomes* on a task.

In stimulus–response creativity, the final artistic goal is often deliberately not specified fully at the start of the creative process; instead, individual participants must find
forms of expression which arise in response to the original provocation. Personal
resources and mechanical dexterity can also lead to the creation of new material.
Starting from a defined stimulus, Paynter argued, is better than not starting at all.

The stimulus–response models proposed by Paynter have subsequently been
widely adopted in educational composition settings over the last twenty years.
While stimulus–response methods can certainly be inspirational in nurturing creativity, problems in their application can arise. For instance, if regularly reinforced through repeated application, stimulus–response models can also generate
similarly conditioned creative results. Just as Pavlov's experimental subjects
eventually had only one type of action response to a variety of different stimuli,
behavioural patterns can emerge in class situations in response to extramusical
provocations. Even open-ended stimuli can become metaphors for well-worn processes and ideas. An additional problem embedded within this model comes from
the *boundaries* of the scope of the original stimulus. It might perhaps be tempting
to work towards artistic responses that directly mirror the original materials or
reside within the aesthetic boundaries of the original idea. Importantly, the process of devising is not one of translating one idea to another – instead, it relies on
helping people to develop their own original materials and structures.

However, a lack of appropriate technical ability can be a factor holding students back from meeting the creative demands of the task. Technical ability here
is taken to mean not just instrumental ability, but a knowledge of forms and structures which can be used to express musical ideas. As that technical ability is not
codified in a stimulus–response task itself (that is, it is not part of the workflow
as it is described to the students), stimulus–response tasks, despite being open-
ended, can end in the creation of familiar forms and structures for this reason.

Thus far we have established that the success of stimulus–response models
depends on the depth of the individual context which students bring to the creative
task. The nature of this context, though, is changing. Today's Internet technology and on-demand access create the potential for students to experience a wider
cross-section of music than at any time in the past. At this point, it is also worth
noting that Internet-driven music aggregation systems currently aim to expose
listeners to increasingly larger amounts of music which might be new to them,
but that music may also ultimately be related to what they have listened to before.
As educators, we need to break this cycle and also introduce music that might be
totally alien in order to increase the variety of contexts in which students might
evaluate their own creative work. Meanwhile, the gap between what is heard in
games and social communications media and what can be *created* (not just heard,
or encountered), widens still further. This experiential divide, first analysed by
Lamont et al. (2003) in relation to music listening is reinforced today in creative
activities, as students regularly encounter commercial musical output which is
frequently the work of more than one individual.

For university students, stimulus–response creativity can present an unusually
challenging proposition. For them, stimulus–response creativity can sit uneasily

between fully professional uses of the model and personal memories of school-based composition tasks. Previous applications of stimulus–response workflows without the appropriate instrumental technical ability or the appropriate compositional discovery processes may result in a situation where students feel that they have already exceeded the expressive range of these open-ended models by default. The value created within professional stimulus–response compositions is, however, directly linked to the extent to which previous individual and collective knowledge can be leveraged in forming the artistic response. In a professional context, flexible compositional provocations which require personal interpretation can offer economic advantages to performers in a climate where individual distinctiveness is important.

Process-based devising

What I call *processed-based approaches* offer an alternative to the free creativity of the stimulus–response workflow previously discussed. Process-based devising features *undefined input conditions* and *undefined output conditions*, but instead possesses a *defined method of realisation*. Instead of a stimulus, students are given a process: instructions on how they might go about the mechanics of realising a piece. Such instructions can be as open-ended or tightly defined, as necessary. Importantly, they can also be extended to account for the mechanisms by which group members interact, or co-create. An example of a contemporary group-composed process-based work is *freq_out* (von Hausswolff, 2014). Here, performers with laptop computers are allocated an individual portion of the frequency spectrum in which they can freely explore, but within which all their output must reside. Participants can use any starting materials they like, and form any output materials to contribute to the group piece. The net effect of this simple procedure is to create textural interest and structural order at the same time.

More elaborate schemes for process-based devising situations are of course possible, and may include text scores, instruction-based works and open forms. Despite surface similarities in name, this form of devising is not necessarily comparable to the process-driven minimal music of the 1960s, where starting materials form a relatively closed system of interaction with the process. This is the case in Reich's *Violin Phase*, for example. Without Reich's starting materials, the process would be globally applicable to any 'input music', but is only identifiable as Reich's original due to the additional specification of the starting materials themselves. Process-based approaches are stricter in their definition of workflow than the frameworks-based approaches described later in this chapter.

As an educational strategy, process-based composition has many advantages. First, students can be coached in the specific means by which materials can be realised. This creates an educational situation where teaching time can be focused on creative techniques and appropriate methods of performance. Process-based devising strategies permit the shaping of the final product in ways which are straightforwardly definable in musical terms, rather than requiring translation from the extramusical. This in turn enables precise *musical feedback* to be given to students on their performance within the task. Source materials in process-based devising are, importantly, not always stimuli. They provide the seeds of musical development upon which process-based workflows may concentrate their activity. Second, process-based approaches can result in a higher level of musical consistency within the final outcome, as there are fewer possible divergent interpretations of what is required to reach a goal. Therefore, process-based devising has advantages in assisting the rapid development of a work. The balance between adequate specification of the realisation processes and the preservation of enough freedom to enable students to bring new interest to the task is critical: too much description of realisation methods can stifle creativity, too little will result in a lack of creative focus. Process-based tasks are well suited to devising methods involving technology, where the means of realisation and manipulating audio and score (if used) can be codified before any interactions between performers and technologies take place.

A process in this context is a sequence of actions, expressed through instructions. The instructions can be written, visual (diagrammatic or artistic), or can be delivered through other media, such as technology. Processes can be prescriptive algorithms with every step codified, or alternatively, they can be simple, loose or fuzzy descriptions of a workflow. Students will need skills in evaluating the applicability of different types of process, and it will often be necessary to intervene in the results of procedural composition at some point. Where that point occurs can be placed on a continuum which stretches from testing the boundaries and outputs of a process to the other extreme – the simple acceptance of the results of a process as 'text' while making sure that the output is modified as little as possible. While the latter case sounds undesirable, it is worth noting that composers who have dedicated their work to eradicating gestural archetypes from their music, or composers who have sought new expressive languages, have often adopted highly specific procedural approaches. Composers in this situation typically hold their views not out of reticence to the audience ('you'll accept the outcome of my system, like it or not') but because they believe it frees creativity from the baggage of human experience which might intervene in identifying new forms of expression. A particular case in point is the 'happy accident': even the most well-specified devising processes can produce unexpected results.

Processes that are flawed, or that have problematic realisations, can produce interesting results if there is no further attempt to make them systemically perfect. Knowing when to keep a non-operational process that produces good results, or when to perfect a non-functioning process that has potential for producing good results, rests on musical taste, judgement and interpretation. It is these review skills which educators must help develop in tandem with musical techniques and creative experiences. Composers freely reject, modify or reinterpret materials which result from systemic compositional methods. Critically, human interpretation and modification of procedurally generated material is the defining factor in bringing individuality to the music which results. We live in an era of *hybrid remixability* (Manovich, 2013: 119), and there is nothing wrong with combining what might be perceived as oppositional processes in composition. Imagine a new piece where the background structure is driven by traditional tonality, yet layers closer to the surface are more related to radical new note selection processes.

Processes themselves can be candidates for being mixed together or remixed, and they display organisational hierarchies that can be accessed in achieving specific types of creative educational experiences. These hierarchies range from highly specific generative processes on one level to more overarching, generalised structural controls on another. In an educational situation, highly generalised processes can lead to extremely interesting results. For example, processes which organise structures rather than notes could be used to test what happens, for example, if George Ives's[3] experimental techniques of simultaneous musics (Lambert, 1991) are applied to Pérotin. Such meta-level processes are incredibly useful, as they help educators to ask some interesting, experimental 'what if' questions. What if there were ways to edit Liszt? What happens to our understanding of Purcell if we employ creative methodologies from the 1980s, instead of the 1680s, in realising his music? Process-based devising can explore such *creative questions*, which would be impossible to achieve with more open-ended stimulus–response models.

Frameworks-based devising

Frameworks-based devising is a combination of process-based and stimulus–response-based methods. It is characterised by devising strategies that have at their core a set of defined processes by which material can be explored, together with an open-ended approach to shaping content, which can arise from an initial stimulus. In forming this combination, the weighting of these activities is an important defining factor. For example, a strong initial stimulus can be supplied together with a more broadly defined realisation process. Alternatively, a highly specific realisation process can be linked to a loose, but pre-defined, stimulus. In frameworks-based devising, there is a reciprocal relationship in how tightly content provision and realisation methods can be specified. Without space in the workflow for individual input, the devising process will cease. Likewise, without a structured approach to forming content, participants tend towards taking on the roles of realisers or performers. Today, students possess highly developed skills in organising, commenting on and offering on-the-spot critical judgements. In a culture underpinned by social media, it is also likely that they will know the systems by which success is measured or commented upon in greater detail than the means by which they can control their own artistic content. In the world outside the institution, creative responses to art are not metric-compliant – if they were, our arts would reflect an increased standardisation of content. This is a self-defeating situation for an arts economy that rests on the business of aggregating widespread diversity. The skills students employ within their interactions on social media can thus be directly useful in the evaluation of group-produced creative work. Contemporary approaches to 'tagging' or organising information can be employed to make sense of the diversity of individual contributions without disenfranchising the group. Furthermore, these methods do not need to be applied using technological platforms. If information is categorised, labelled and made personal to the whole group rather than to an individual, the person who provided that information stands a greater chance of increasing their share of collective ownership throughout the design process.

The assessment of devised work

The assessment of group work presents known difficulties to educators. Balancing individual contributions, sustained effort, group outcomes and originality all require differing assessment strategies. Assessment in group composition can also be a very practical tool to help keep all members of the group informed on creative progress. Group work and continuous assessment therefore appear to be ideal educational partners.

While student output throughout the creative process could indeed be measured with formative procedures, it is possible that continual assessment strategies brought to bear on devised work may not yield an accurate representation of educational progress towards a shared group objective. Also, devising processes do not always represent a linear path over time towards a solution. Creative discussion may be negative or extremely critical, and result in as much backtracking as it does 'positive' progress. In this situation, a backwards step can still produce vital work. While there is no easy fix to the emotional impact that non-productive work may have, if it is acknowledged that composition will not always be a productive experience at the outset, student expectations can be managed in nuanced ways. In addition, regular academic formative assessment of group work can be a complicated task, as the creative roles of individual members may vary throughout the production. Fairness and equality are key parameters in most educational assessment specifications. Problematically, generating a functional artwork involving many different contributors cannot always be a 'fair' process on a detailed level, especially in the short term. A piece where all musical ideas were represented equally, at all formative stages of the compositional process, with no rejections of material, would not make for a very interesting listening experience.

Academic assessment, then – as opposed to peer review – needs to operate at a level above the day-to-day decision-making internal to the group. Avoiding asking students to produce diaries demonstrating their attendance can help free up space in their thinking that is better used for more useful critical and evaluative purposes, such as reflecting on the insight and research they themselves have brought to the creative process. Furthermore, if the point within the creative process at which assessment is implemented is not carefully timed, it can hamper creative decision-making.

Approaches to teaching and assessment therefore need to strike a balance between offering effective early-stage formative feedback while not restricting the nature of creative choices due to that feedback being untimely. This has implications beyond university assessment, as this particular intervention has the possibility to shape the future of the music which those individuals might create. In business, it is well known that over-assessment or badly timed assessment can lead to constrained decision-making, inaction, and ultimately failure. This is called *analysis paralysis*.[4] Likewise, in composition, it is important to realise that early sketch material may not always be an indicator of the final piece. Sketch material may be rough, or contain errors of judgement, execution and concept. However, composition can be the journey of discovering or exploiting these aspects – it is not simply about 'improvement' or mapping out a single track of progress into the future. Unusual, unexpected or just plain 'wrong' material (as viewed through a traditional assessment context) can make for some of the most exciting musical outcomes if appropriately developed. The educational panacea of early-stage evaluation therefore requires considerable care in creative tasks. To understand this further, we need to assess the broader role of feedback within group work. Therefore, it is vital that evaluation forms a large part of constructing successful group work, but this should perhaps be best conducted by the group itself using its own material as a reference point. Expectations that qualitative evaluation is an activity for every member of the group can be embedded into the devising strategies detailed earlier in this chapter. It is argued here that while continuous educational input and encouragement are of course of value, formative *assessment* (as opposed to comment, feedback or peer review) is less so.

As the point of group devising is to help students experience methods of com-position beyond individual creativity, and deliver their results to other humans, the presentation of this work should have as many attributes of a real-world out-come as possible. The ideal assessment context for devised group work is for it to take place within a professional setting, perhaps involving the public as paying clients. From my experience of employing this structure, the idea that the public will need to pay to hear student-devised work, in a recognised venue, helps raise the bar on what can be created.

Recognising the total contribution of the group within a university assessment strategy is not facilitated by assessment methods which foreground individual achievement. It is well understood that assessing group work is fraught with prob-lems. For example, Davies (2009: 567) identifies issues that result from having 'free riders' who achieve little and depend on the work of others, highlighting the problems caused by interpersonal difficulties. However, in professional projects, none of these factors magically disappear. Professionals have artistic differences, and professional teamwork may not necessarily be allocated in equal shares. It is important, though, that there is a contingency should group work not go to plan, due to illness or other external circumstances – in education, unlike professional group work, it isn't always possible (or desirable) to fire the person concerned and appoint a replacement! Appropriate individual development must be put in place, and team dynamics require continuous self-moderation by all members of the group. Students also need to know where they stand should one member become unavailable. An academic contingency, to give one example, might be that teams are asked to make material that is flexible enough to be repurposed across any reasonable ensemble that would remain after the departure of one member.

Individual assessment, if required, can be assigned at a structural level; for example, an agreed student could take ultimate responsibility for the onstage presentation of a section of the work, or for providing services to other groups (for example, as a vocal coach). It is proposed that summative assessment is a useful tool in this context. The subject of the assessment does not necessarily all need to be based on the practical work either, and, if it is not, the creativity of the students can be further demonstrated through summative extension assign-ments, including: developing a short piece of writing evaluating the creative context and strategies used in the work; video documentation of the work in progress, highlighting the individual's contributions, and the submission of scores, instructions or early-stage sketch materials. The assessment of early-stage materials is sometimes problematic, as these can be too fine-grained or speculative in nature. Without the benefit of an encapsulating structure supplied by the whole group, the ultimate musical worth of contributory individual materials might be hard to evaluate. A final additional summative assessment possibility exists through evaluating new follow-on creative responses to the original concept. The idea of a creative 'response' to existing work provides an opportunity for educators to examine the knowledge gained from a group creative process within an individual context.

Any truly creative work involves risk. At one end of the spectrum, a lack of risk results in emulation and sticking to safe, well-worn musical territory. Experimental music, however, can be placed at the other end of the continuum, as it expressly involves unmitigated risk. In between these poles lies a spectrum of activity, depending on how risks are managed. Yet why is risk so rarely a factor in assessment? Perhaps the concept of musical style inherently provides a level of compositional risk management. Risk management strategies for groups may additionally be as simple as making more material than required, progressing alternative plans in parallel, or agreeing on broad stylistic constraints. The nature of risk in group projects changes according to the size of the group. Sometimes, there is safety in numbers in trying new concepts. However, if all members of the group are encouraged to think about risk (both taking risks and finding suitable strategies for their mitigation), the outcome has the potential to demonstrate higher levels of focused creativity. Risk mitigation strategies in composition do not make artistic decisions any less risky, but instead ensure that the risks with the most potential for interesting results are taken, while maintaining an acceptable level of productivity within the team if the idea doesn't work out.

Conclusion

Successfully combining different creative workflows requires recognising the hybridity of contemporary culture. It is essential to respect individual differences, methods of presentation and belief systems. Hybrid cultures combine these units into a larger-scale diversity which obtains cohesion by virtue of existing in the same space. Hybrid approaches to musical composition can enable juxtapositions between musical ideas, while not attempting to formulate crossovers. Cultural value, added through creating different task responses which exist in the same space, is an advantage of group work. By embracing this process, creators can position their work outside the domain of the original stimulus and create a musical end product that may be more contemporary, or culturally relevant, as a result.

Pooling ideas is often the first task to be accomplished within a group composition. An ideas pool must be seen, by all participants, as a space of shared ownership requiring creators to release their own individual authority. Importantly, this does not equate to a simplistic resolution to use all ideas equally – no design process of creative material operates in this way. The preservation of individual ownership may also not always be expected by students, who have grown up in a society where file-sharing and the free creation of meta-content through highly visible commenting and modification (remix) processes on existing media are commonplace. Pooling ideas must not be about ownership. However, individuals do need to own and take responsibility for parts of the creative workflow which interpret and develop these ideas. This critical difference between management processes and musical material can only happen through *ownership release*. In deciding how to implement an idea, groups will need a robust process of selection, evaluation and rejection and subsequent peer review. For a successful set of personal interactions to emerge, it is essential that rejection is considered as a creative positive, and that a rejected idea is not the signal for an individual to disengage with the ongoing developmental process. The extent of ownership release is thus critical to the success of the task. Two polar scenarios emerge, as shown in Table 17.1.

In situations where creative ownership has been released, a leader is still required – but not necessarily needing to function as the arbiter of selecting or designing the material itself. Category II in Table 17.1 provides greater opportunities for educational gain as it enables students to experience a more diverse interaction with a wider variety of roles.

This chapter has demonstrated that experimental practice and contemporary creative imperatives have converged in ways which were unimaginable only a short time ago. I have outlined strategies for devising work which can help group creativity have a valuable position in this new environment, rather than existing as a simplistic substitute for individual practice. The importance of group-based workflow decisions has been highlighted, and it has been stressed that group creativity need not result in work that is predictable, nor be the result of 'lowest common denominator' decision-making. This approach also has much in common with contemporary models of how businesses develop new work within a shifting economic climate.[5] As such, a repositioning of group work within university composition syllabi is called for, reflecting the importance of teamwork in today's changing compositional landscape.

Table 17.1 Ownership scenarios

Category I	Category II
One student takes ownership, the rest perform.	All students offer creative opinions, and relinquish individual ownership.
Ideas need to be finalised before they can be shared. This process is managed by an individual.	Idea-sharing is implicit with the work process. The group must manage their own collective progress.
The majority of group members use their skills only within performance.	It makes good use of all members' skills in composition and performance.

Notes

1 The terms *group work* and *teamwork* are used interchangeably in this chapter to represent the creative work accomplished by groups.
2 Distributed creativity is a topic which includes research that seeks to assess how emergent behaviours in group creativity define artistic outcomes.
3 History shows that Charles Ives's father George was ultimately responsible for this idea.
4 See Grenning (2002). Note that it is not suggested here that we don't analyse. It is a question of when analysis occurs, and how it is framed.
5 For example, 'lean' start-ups, agile software development and corporate turnaround processes.

References

Bennett, D. and Burnard, P. (2016). 'The Development and Impact of Creative Human Capital on Higher Education Graduates'. In: R. Comunian and A. Gilmore (eds), *Higher Education and the Creative Economy: Beyond the Campus*. London: Routledge.

Davies, W.M. (2009). 'Groupwork as a Form of Assessment: Common Problems and Recommended Solutions'. *Higher Education*, 58(4), 563–84.

Goehr, L. (1992). *The Imaginary Museum of Musical Works*. Oxford: Oxford University Press.

Grenning, J. (2002). *Planning Poker or How to Avoid Analysis Paralysis While Release Planning*. Hawthorn Woods, IL: Renaissance Software Consulting.

Katzenbach, J.R. and Smith, D.K. (2005). 'The Discipline of Teams'. *Harvard Business Review*, 83(7–8), 162–71.

Kim, E. and Pak, S.-J. (2002). 'Students Do Not Overcome Conceptual Difficulties After Solving 1000 Traditional Problems'. *American Journal of Physics*, 70(7), 759–65.

Lambert, J.P. (1991). 'Ives and Counterpoint'. *American Music*, 9(2), 119–48.

Lamont, A., Hargreaves, D.J., Marshall, N.A. and Tarrant, M. (2003). 'Young People's Music in and out of School'. *British Journal of Music Education*, 20(3), 229–41.

Manovich, L. (2013). *Software Takes Command: Extending the Language of New Media*. London: Bloomsbury.

Paynter, J. (1992). *Sound and Structure*. Cambridge: Cambridge University Press.

——— and Aston, P. (1970). *Sound and Silence: Classroom Projects in Creative Music*. Cambridge: Cambridge University Press.

Sawyer, R.K. and DeZutter, S. (2009). 'Distributed Creativity: How Collective Creations Emerge from Collaboration'. *Psychology of Aesthetics, Creativity, and the Arts*, 3(2), 81–92.

Sterling, B., Wild, L. and Lunenfeld, P. (2005). *Shaping Things*. Cambridge, MA: MIT Press.

Taggar, S. (2002). 'Individual Creativity and Group Ability to Utilize Individual Creative Resources: A Multilevel Model'. *Academy of Management Journal*, 45(2), 315–30.

Torrance, E.P. (1972). 'Can We Teach Children to Think Creatively?' *Journal of Creative Behavior*, 6(2), 114–43.

von Hausswolff, C.M. (2014). *freq_out*. Retrieved 6 June 2014 from http://www.freq-out.org/.

Index